EVEREST

Stephen Venables made the 206th recorded ascent of Everest and is probably the eighth Briton to reach the summit. He is certainly the first to do so entirely without the aid of bottled oxygen.

Born in 1954, he has climbed extensively in Europe, the Himalayas and Karakoram, as well as in Africa and South America. His first book *Painted Mountains*, which described two expeditions to Kashmir, won the Boardman Tasker Prize for the best mountaineering book of 1986.

EVEREST
Kangshung Face

Stephen Venables

PAN BOOKS
London, Sydney and Auckland

First published in Great Britain 1989 by Hodder and Stoughton
This edition published 1991 by Pan Books Ltd
Cavaye Place, London SW10 9PG
1 3 5 7 9 8 6 4 2
© Stephen Venables 1989
ISBN 0 330 31559 5

Photoset by Parker Typesetting Service, Leicester
Printed in England by Clays Ltd, St Ives plc

TO MY PARENTS
WHO FIRST TOOK ME
TO THE MOUNTAINS

Acknowledgements

The many sponsors and helpers who made Everest-88 possible are acknowledged in Appendix I, but I would like here to thank all the people who gave so much invaluable help in the preparation of this book:

Lord Hunt for giving me the chance to go to Everest and writing a foreword to the book. Ed, Paul, Robert, Joe, Mimi, Pasang, Kasang and all the members of the expedition support team, for being such good companions and making this book possible.

Robert Anderson, Wendy Davis, Rosie Grieves-Cook, Elisabeth Hawley, Charles Houston, Annabel Huxley, Peter Lloyd, Vivienne Schuster, Ann Venables, Cangy Venables, and Isobel Walder for all their encouragement and valuable criticism of the manuscript.

Margaret Body, my editor, for giving me so much encouragement, keeping me to deadlines and adding the finishing touches with her customary skill. Alec Spark for drawing the maps and diagrams; Lawrence Back and Trevor Spooner for designing the book; Sylvia Mitchell for black and white prints. Joseph Blackburn and Ed Webster for allowing me to use some of their superb expedition photographs. Mike Jones for the black and white photograph on the dust jacket, and Sam Farr for a promotional photograph. All photography in the book is courtesy of Eastman Kodak and Duggal Color Projects. All uncredited photographs were taken by the author.

SV

Foreword

BY LORD HUNT OF
LLANFAIR WATERDINE

On an evening in October 1987, I received a telephone call from New York. A persuasive feminine voice informed me that an expedition was being organized in the United States to celebrate the thirty-fifth anniversary of the first ascent of Everest: Everest-88. Ed Hillary and Tenzing Norgay's sons, Peter and Norbu, had agreed to join the party; the caller, Wendy Davis, invited me, on behalf of the organizers, to accept the title of Honorary Expedition Leader.

I confess to having felt chuffed by this accolade. The title was new in my experience. For all its symbolic, and possible public relations, connotation, it sounded less senile than that of Patron, to which I was all too well accustomed. Anyway, it would have been churlish to refuse. But our expedition in 1953 had been organized in Britain; its members were mainly British mountaineers. I felt that at least one of these latter-day challengers of Everest should be a true Briton, and I said as much to the disembodied voice at the end of the transatlantic line.

A week or two later I met Robert Anderson, the Expedition Leader, during his stop-over in London on his way between his work in New Zealand and his home in the States. I suggested that he should invite a leading British climber to join his party so as to give substance to the notional connection between the expeditions of 1953 and 1988. I suggested the name of Stephen Venables and Robert agreed to write to him. Little did I realize what would ensue from that part of our conversation.

Robert also told me something of his plan to force a new route up the Kangshung Face of the mountain, further to the left of the bold line which had marked the first ascent of that face, achieved four years earlier by another American expedition. He showed me a very indifferent photograph, adding a throw-away comment: 'I think we can use this buttress, which will take us directly to the South Col.' As his strictly honorary associate I expressed admiration, but suppressed my astonishment. For an old-stager like myself, it was indeed difficult to credit the audacity of such a hypothetical venture, which purported to follow a line to all intents and purposes as yet unseen, with a team of no more than four or five companions and without oxygen.

My mind flew back to 25 May 1953, when I had looked down the Kangshung Face during a stroll, at 26,000 feet, across the South Col. Charles Evans, Tom Bourdillon and I were on our way up the mountain, which at that time had never been climbed. As I peered down the steep snow slopes plunging towards the brink of a tremendous precipice, until my eyes came to rest on the Kangshung Glacier 7,000 feet below me, I remember very clearly saying to myself: 'This will never be climbed.' Such were the perceptions of what was impossible to mountaineers of my generation at that time; beyond which, even in our dreams, we did not dare to venture.

The ascent of Everest is nowadays a commonplace event. But Everest-88 is a story which will be told with a sense of wonder for years to come. It is remarkable for the skill required to scale the rampart of rock and ice which defends access to those long steep slopes leading upwards to the South Col, down which my eyes had travelled all those years ago. It is a story of courage and commitment by four climbers, with no reserves to call on in case of accident or illness, who, without resort to oxygen, overcame the combined problems of vertical rock and ice, handicapped by the effects of high altitude.

Even among such exceptional men, the performance of Stephen Venables was outstanding. From the South Col to the summit and, until he rejoined his companions after surviving a night out at over 27,000 feet on the South-East Ridge, he was on his own; his stamina and his willpower somehow kept him going, despite his state of exhaustion after the long days of strain which the climbers had already endured in reaching the Col. I know of no finer example in mountaineering, of mind triumphing over matter.

But for me, the most gripping part of the story lies in the escape from the mountain. Extraordinary tales abound of human survival against the odds set by nature or circumstance; this ranks with the most remarkable among the ordeals from which men or women have returned alive. With some personal experiences of difficult retreats from high mountains, I can appreciate the anxiety, the tension, the exhaustion and near despair which those men experienced, as they fought their way down the Kangshung Face, severely frostbitten, dehydrated and without food, their tents and sleeping bags abandoned, losing trace of their fixed ropes, losing touch with one another. Climbers are proverbially prone to understatement, but Stephen Venables has done his readers a good service by writing himself into this story; by laying bare his feelings as he made his desperate way up and down Everest.

But this is not the whole story. For many readers, much of the pleasure in reading Stephen's personal account of Everest-88 will be found in his perceptiveness of his surroundings; in his responses and reactions to his climbing companions and the Tibetans and Chinese who helped them on their way. The author is a sensitive and sympathetic observer and his awareness of his environment and of fellow human beings provides welcome relief from the descriptions of the technical problems and the supremely strenuous task to which the party set their hand.

And through it all shines the spirit of these men. People who, in this age of ease and plenty, pause to reflect upon the reason why some prefer to do things the hard way, could hardly do better than read this book.

John Hunt
1 February 1989

Maps and Drawings

Contents

The Height of Everest

Everest climbers returning home are usually subjected to predictable questioning, with frequent quips such as, 'Did you see the Yeti?' or 'Did you eat Kendal Mint Cake on the summit?' A recent addition to these old favourites is the jest: 'But haven't they just decided that K2 is higher than Everest?'

My natural response should be to say, 'Does it really matter?' However, I have to admit to a certain childish satisfaction at having reached the highest point on earth and perhaps I should point out that 'they' have now decided that Everest is once and for all the highest mountain in the world.

In 1987 the distinguished Italian scientist and explorer, Ardito Desio, organized an expedition to remeasure the world's two highest peaks from the north. The 1988 *American Alpine Journal* recently reported his findings. Desio's team used a highly accurate electronic diastimeter theodolite, in conjunction with two Global Positioning System receivers, linked to USA Navstar satellites. The height of K2, after computer corrections to allow for the earth's curvature and atmospheric refraction, came out at 8,616 metres, plus or minus seven metres. The height obtained by Colonel Montgomerie of the Survey of India, using rather less sophisticated equipment in 1858, was 8,611 metres.

The traditional height of Everest is 8,848 metres or 29,029 feet – considerably higher than K2. The latest triangulation confirms this supremacy and gives Everest a greater promotion, raising the summit twenty-four metres to 8,872 metres (plus or minus twenty). In other words, it could be over 29,100 feet above sea level. However, the new National Geographic 1:50,000 map of the Everest region, a work of astonishing beauty and accuracy, retains the traditional summit height, upon which all other heights in the area are based. I, too, have stuck to the traditional height, and for the purposes of this book the summit of Everest is 8,848 metres above sea level.

SV

1

After the Storm

THE EXPEDITION was over and we were on our way home, climbing up to the first of the high passes we had to cross on the long drive to Lhasa. Once again the wheels spun, flinging mud up against the banks of the road. On each side the snow was piled up high but from the raised seats of our landcruiser we could look out over the white land. It was 4 November 1987. Two and a half weeks had now passed since Tibet had been swept by the worst storm in living memory, but the wide spaces of the plateau, normally brown and dry, still lay deep under snow.

At the top of the pass we waited for the other vehicle to catch up. Everyone got out to look back for the last time to Shisha Pangma, the mountain which had dominated our lives for the last two months.

There it all was: the great jumble of the icefall and, above it, the ramp, curving round to Camp 2 and the headwall, which we had laboured so hard to fix before the big storm swept through the length of the Greater Himalaya, reaching Tibet on 17 October. The devastation had been appalling but afterwards we had just managed to salvage enough food and gear from the wrecked tents to make another attempt on the mountain, breaking trail through deep drifts and laboriously re-excavating the ropes up to Camp 2. From there, Luke Hughes and I had continued for another two days up the long South Ridge. Now from a distance we could really gauge the true scale of that immense ridge, the great sweep up to the 7,486-metre summit of Pungpa Ri, the descent on the far side and then more ridge, rising in great steps to the 8,046-metre summit of Shisha Pangma itself. We could see the exact point where Luke and I had stopped to dig an emergency snowcave at 7,700 metres and huddle through the night, sheltering from the vicious jet-stream wind. The temperature had been −35°C and, with the wind unabated, in the morning we had been forced to turn back, less than 400 metres from the top.

Now winter had arrived, our time was up and we were leaving empty handed. The surly Chinese drivers told us to hurry up with our photographs and we left, driving away down the far side of the pass.

The end of an expedition is nearly always a time for ambivalent feelings. I was excited to be going home after four months in Asia, but also clinging nostalgically to many happy memories of those months. First there had been the long trek across the Karakoram in Pakistan – days spent with Duncan and Phil on Snow Lake, the wild descent down an unknown glacier to Shimshal, the journey up the Hispar with Razzetti, camping in flower-filled meadows, the return to Snow Lake and my solo first ascent of a beautiful granite tower. Then there had been the long journey south to Rawalpindi and on by train through the Punjab and the Sind desert, right down to Karachi where I joined the Shisha Pangma expedition transferring for the flight to Kathmandu. We had trekked through the monsoon-soaked forests of Nepal to Tibet. Then, under brilliant blue skies, we had worked at the new route on Shisha Pangma. It had been a huge expedition with too many people for my taste; but it had been fun, and even during the three days of the storm, digging constantly to save tents and lives from the crushing snowdrifts, the radio calls between camps had been alive with humour and friendship. There was now just this nagging regret about not reaching the summit. So many people had put so much effort into the long improbable route, and despite the storm we had come so close to success, that I found it more difficult than usual to be philosophical about being forced to turn back so near the top.

Dusk was falling as we entered the wide valley of the Phung

Chu. It was a magical evening with a full moon riding the darkening sky. Ruined towers and battlements, relics of Tibet's destroyed past, were silhouetted against the luminous hills, with dark figures of Tibetan people, on foot and on horseback, making their way homeward across the plain. We rounded a corner of the low hills and suddenly we were heading back south towards the great Himalayan chain and there, unmistakable on the horizon, was Everest.

The driver insisted we drive on to the official photo spot before stopping and it was almost dark when we pulled up beside a frozen stream. We were just in time. For a few precious moments the swirling clouds were pink and orange, the green ice at our feet was suffused with warm pastel tints and in front of us the rocky pyramid of Everest glowed deep blood red. It was now several weeks since the day on Shisha Pangma when I had enjoyed the sudden thrill of recognition, seeing Everest for the very first time. For weeks it had dominated our view east from the high camps but now we were seeing it from much closer. Some of my Shisha Pangma companions would be returning in less than four months with the British Services Expedition to attempt this northern side of the mountain; and as I stared up at the North-East Ridge, the Great Couloir, Changtse, the Yellow Band, the West Ridge – all those features so redolent of mountaineering history and legend – I could not help feeling a twinge of envy.

The colour faded quickly and we drove on into the darkness. The only sound in our vehicle was the drone of the engine and everyone seemed lost in his own thoughts. The poignant magic of that beautiful evening, and now the silver moonlight on the hills, seemed to intensify my own bittersweet nostalgia. Unlike my friends who were to attempt Everest, I still had no definite plans for the following year; but the last four months in the Himalaya had brought such a wealth of experience and fulfilment, happiness and regrets, success and disappointment, new mountains, new friends and new possibilities, that I would have to return, as I had been returning for the last ten years.

*

A week later I was back in London. I still felt tired and
wasted from our exertions on Shisha Pangma and the long
days of travelling across Tibet and China. For the time being
mountains could wait and any future expeditions were far
from my mind that Thursday evening, when I phoned my
parents. My mother knew that I needed cheering up after the
disappointment on Shisha Pangma and was obviously very
excited when she passed on the message to telephone someone called Anderson: 'I should ring him soon. It's an invitation – a very nice invitation.'

I knew immediately that it must be Everest.

My mother had few details. Robert Anderson was an
American who apparently wanted me to join his Everest
expedition the following year. He had not said how many
people were going, what route they were trying or why he
wanted me; but if I was interested I should telephone him in
New Zealand. I failed to get through to him that weekend,
and my first Everest invitation was still a mystery the following Monday when I travelled up to Manchester for a meeting
of the British Mountaineering Council international committee. Unlike some committees, this one has concrete business
to do – the distribution of Sports Council grants to British
expeditions. We had disposed of a few hundred pounds when
the chairman asked: 'What about this one – American-New
Zealand Everest?'

'No, we don't give them anything,' explained Andy, the
secretary, 'but they are eligible for an MEF grant.'

'Oh, yes. A New Zealander . . .'

'Yes, Peter Hillary's on the list.'

I didn't have a copy of the form and tried to conceal my
excitement as I asked my neighbour to pass over his. The
others had moved on to the next application as I examined
the Everest details: Spring 1988. Leader's name Robert
Anderson, American, thirty, reached 28,200 feet on the West
Ridge in 1985 . . . then five more names. I only recognized
the American Ed Webster – recollections of fine photographs
– and of course Peter Hillary, a well-known Himalayan
climber, lumbered with the additional fame of being Sir

Edmund's son. Because he was a New Zealander he enabled the expedition to qualify for a grant, or at least official recognition, from the British Mount Everest Foundation. This Anderson, whoever he was, had only filled in the barest details, but under 'objective' he had put enough to give me a little stab of fear: 'Everest, East Face.'

As the meeting progressed and we discussed the relative merits of Ecuadoran volcanoes, unknown lumps in Pakistan and famous 8,000-metre giants, I kept on glancing back surreptitiously at the Everest form. My name was not on the list, but this was clearly the expedition on which I was supposed to have been invited.

My mind was racing on the late train back to London and when I eventually got to bed at about 4 a.m. I could not sleep. Soon the dawn birds were starting their racket in the street outside as I turned restlessly in bed, frightened and excited about the great East Face – the Kangshung Face of Everest.

I soon gave up the idea of sleeping, had some breakfast and started the day's work of wading through four months' mail. That evening I finally got through to Robert Anderson. For some reason I expected the American twelve thousand miles away to be all gushing, welcoming bonhomie, so I was a little put out by his cool response.

'Well, it's not definite. I'm just asking around to see who's interested.'

'And you're really trying the East Face?'

'Yes, it's the only side I could get a permit for this soon. I want to try a new route, or maybe a lightweight ascent of the 1983 route.' He went on to explain about money. 'It's looking pretty good. We've already got promises from American Express and Rolex. I'm aiming for about $300,000. We should raise most of it but everyone might have to put in about $10,000 of their own.'

This was all sounding rather grandiose and I protested, 'I don't have any money!'

'Don't worry, I'm sure we can work something out. But look, don't go and cancel something if you have other plans, because this isn't definite.'

He was playing it very cool, but he did ask me at least to send him a résumé of my climbing career. He also explained why he had contacted me in the first place. The expedition was being billed as the '35th Anniversary Assault', to commemorate the 1953 first ascent. Peter Hillary had been invited on the climbing team and Tenzing Norgay's son, Norbu, had been asked to join the support team. Lord Hunt, leader of the 1953 climb, had agreed to be honorary leader of the expedition and, when Robert asked him about possible British climbers, he had kindly suggested my name.

On Wednesday I made a cheaper phone call, to John Hunt in Henley, to find out a bit more about the expedition. He was very keen that the team, which was after all commemorating a British expedition, should include at least one British climber. 'Of course it's entirely up to you,' he continued, 'but I'd be delighted if you can go.' It was flattering to be recommended and I had always said that I would find it very hard to turn down an Everest invitation, but at this stage the invitation was by no means definite and I had my doubts about the Kangshung Face, the massive eastern wall of the mountain, which had only been climbed once and which was reputed to be extremely difficult and dangerous. Our patron was also well aware of the face's reputation and summarized Robert's plans with a fine display of euphemistic understatement: 'Well as far as I can gather they're going to try a very *sporting* new line up to the South Col.'

The whole project might be suicidal, but it sounded exciting and it was worth at least keeping a foot in the door until I knew more about it. I sent off my résumé to Robert and a few days later a courier arrived in Islington with a huge bundle of information from New Zealand. I had to rush off to the other side of London, so I took the bundle with me, found a free seat on the underground train and settled down to read through all the papers.

Robert had done an impressive job, sending details of all the climbers, press cuttings, gear and address lists. As creative director of a successful advertising agency he had little time for fund-raising and was employing Wendy Davis, in

New York, to handle public relations. She had been instructed to sell the expedition as: 'The first alpine-style ascent of
Everest's East Face without oxygen.' Everything seemed to
be competently organized and it was reassuring to see that
four of the people on the team had already climbed high on
Everest. I was also reassured to read Robert's scrawled foot-
notes, which were much more friendly than the telephone
conversation. He had even enclosed a wrist measurement
form for my Rolex watch, which suggested that I would
probably be going, though the actual invitation was not yet
confirmed, and I still had to decide about the risks of the
climb. But the lure of a new route on the world's highest
mountain was overwhelming. For a while I pushed fears and
doubts aside and leapt up the left-hand lane of the escalator
two steps at a time, dreaming wild exuberant dreams of
Everest.

Life rushed on. While Robert was making up his mind, I
had articles to write, a book to plan and lectures to give. I
was rarely at home and my delightful chaotic landlords in
Islington, Maggie and Victor, were pestered constantly with
telephone messages, which they left on little slips of paper
amidst the massed debris of the kitchen. One night at the end
of November I arrived back late to find a terse message from
New Zealand on one of the slips: 'Robert Anderson wants
you for Kangshung Face.'

The next morning I was abseiling down a block of flats in
West Kensington. An old climbing friend, Dick Renshaw,
had offered me a week's building repair work. All the work
was done from ropes; the client was saved the horrendous
cost of scaffolding but was still able to pay us each £100 a
day. I had no lectures that week, I was badly in debt and it
was too good a chance to miss. Dick has never been noted for
his loquaciousness and we talked little while we were working, but at lunch I told him about the Everest invitation –
unknown team of Americans, Kangshung Face, no oxygen.

'No oxygen. The trouble is, now you know all the things
that can go wrong, don't you!'

In 1982 Dick had suffered a stroke at 8,000 metres whilst

attempting Everest's North-East Ridge without oxygen; two weeks later his friends, Peter Boardman and Joe Tasker, had died during another attempt on the ridge. More recently, in 1986, the risks of climbing high without oxygen or back-up teams had been highlighted in a ghastly series of disasters on K2. In one summer thirteen people had died on the world's second highest mountain.

Dick also reinforced my doubts about climbing with an unknown team. 'You've got to be really careful climbing with people you don't know . . . and Americans . . . I mean they *are* different.' He laughed at his own uncharacteristic intolerance but when I mentioned the name Ed Webster he reassured me. 'Oh, Ed's all right – a very nice bloke – he's not a *real* American.' He laughed again at his racist slip.

Cho, our foreman, chipped in: 'Yes, I climbed with Ed too.'

A couple of days later our ebullient boss, ex-Marines mountaineer, entrepreneur and entertainer John Barry, leaned over the parapet and gossiped with me as I dangled on my rope repairing a window lintel seventy feet above the ground. 'Everest, eh. Bloody miserable business, isn't it, high-altitude climbing . . . Ed Webster? Yes, I know him. He came to Wales. He's a good bloke. Didn't know he did big stuff, though. I always think of him as a photographer – beautiful pictures – and a rock jock. Does all those hard things in Colorado.'

In fact Ed, as well as being a very talented rock climber, was a very competent all-round mountaineer and had already been twice to Everest. In 1985 he had reached 7,300 metres on the West Ridge Direct. That was when he had met Robert, who had spearheaded the attempt, surviving over a week above 8,000 metres and nearly reaching the summit on a notoriously long and difficult route. Jay Smith, who had led some of the hardest pitches in 1985, was also to be on the 1988 attempt. Peter Hillary had now said that he probably couldn't come; but Jay's friend Paul Teare was definitely booked. Paul was a Canadian living in California. He had never been as high as the others but the previous autumn, with Jay, he had put up an extremely difficult new route on a famous Nepalese peak, Kantega (6,779 metres).

The group certainly looked good on paper. Admittedly, they were not international stars, but nor was I. Ed, by all accounts, was a nice person and a brilliant technician, as well as being competent on big mountains. Robert was obviously very strong at altitude and was sounding increasingly friendly. I could probably afford to take a gamble on the others.

In mid-December I accepted Robert's invitation. This time when I spoke to him on the phone all the reserve had vanished. He was effusive about my 'huge amount of Himalayan experience', brushed aside financial problems, assured me that someone would pay to fly me over to New York for a January meeting and said how glad he was that I was coming to Everest.

Suddenly my life had changed. Half-formulated plans for the next summer had to be dropped and I had to warn Maggie Body, my editor, that the projected book would be late. I had only been back for a month and in another two months I would be leaving again for Tibet. As usual, the fortnight leading up to Christmas was a frenzy of jobs to finish, deadlines to meet and rushed attempts to fit in some sort of social life. I began to wonder if I could really cope and for the first time in my life I experienced insomnia.

Everest was going to be a bigger challenge than anything I had attempted before. I was used to danger and I had learned to live with the possibility of a lonely unnatural death; but now the threat seemed more real and during those dark lonely hours before dawn I lay awake worrying. I had performed well on Shisha Pangma and although we did not make the summit I had reached a new personal altitude record of 7,700 metres. At the end of a full day's climbing I had managed to share the strenuous task of digging an emergency snowcave, and twelve hours later, after a cold night without a sleeping bag, I had still felt capable of continuing; but I knew that climbing to the 8,848-metre summit of Everest without oxygen would be far more committing,

stretching myself to the very limit of human survival, forcing
the body to do things for which it was not designed. As Dick
had said, I knew all the things that could go wrong, and I
imagined all too clearly the consequences of thrombosis,
third degree frostbite, cerebral oedema or hypothermia. I
also feared the loose rock, the massed tiers of tottering ice
cliffs and the huge open snowslopes – the battery of defences
which would send avalanches roaring incessantly down the
Kangshung Face.

George Mallory and Guy Bullock were the first Westerners
to see the Kangshung Face of Everest. It was 1921 and the
British Reconnaissance Expedition was exploring all the
available approaches to the mountain. The southern side lay
behind the closed borders of Nepal, but the other two sides
of the pyramid lay in Tibet, a country which had in 1904
been bullied into a form of alliance with the British Empire.
Now for the first time the Dalai Lama had permitted a
foreign expedition to attempt Everest. For several weeks
Mallory and Bullock, the youngest, fittest members of the
party, had been exploring the Central and West Rongbuk
Glaciers, examining the West Ridge and coming quite close
to the North Ridge; but they had failed so far to find a
feasible route up the mountain. Mallory was determined to
make a thorough reconnaissance, so now they had travelled
round to the village of Kharta and hired local yak herders to
escort them to the eastern side of the mountain.

Mallory and Bullock were led over the high Langma La
and down into the rhododendron forests of the Kama Chu.
This lovely valley was a welcome contrast to the bleak, stony
wastes of the Rongbuk, and at this time of year, August, the
meadows beside the Kangshung Glacier were brimming with
flowers; but any hopes of finding a route up Everest from this
side were quickly squashed when the clouds lifted one morning to reveal at the head of the valley an immense wall over
3,000 metres high. Unlike the windswept rocks to the north
side, this wall was encrusted with the snow and ice of a giant
hanging glacier. With the right snow conditions the upper

slopes might just be climbable, but to approach them from the two-mile-wide base of the wall would involve either climbing up the deep gashes of avalanche-swept gullies or negotiating vertical and overhanging rock buttresses, menaced by a great fringe of tottering ice towers. Mallory later summed up his impressions in the expedition book, concluding with the immortal words: 'other men, less wise, might attempt this way if they would, but, emphatically, it was not for us.'

The team crossed a pass eastward to the upper Kharta valley, discovered another pass back over to the northern side of the mountain and found themselves on the flat snowfields of the elusive East Rongbuk Glacier; and there, right in front of them, was a possible route to the saddle on the North Ridge which they called the North Col.

That year Mallory confirmed that the North Col route was the most feasible option from Tibet, and from 1922–38 no fewer than six British expeditions attempted it, approaching from the Rongbuk valley. The story of those attempts has been told many times and the disappearance of Mallory and Irvine close to the summit, during their brave attempt in 1924, has become as much a part of the British consciousness as the poignant story of Scott's death in Antarctica. Cynics might be tempted to accuse the British of incompetence: why did they persist in trying to climb Everest dressed in woollen jumpers and tweed jackets? Why was every expedition hampered by the political bungling of the Everest Committee in London? And why did they never work out a rational policy on supplementary oxygen?

There *were* mistakes and disasters, but far more impressive than the mistakes were the successes. Given the primitive nature of their heavy, cumbersome equipment, those pre-war climbers achieved astonishing feats. None of the giant 8,000-metre peaks was climbed before the Second World War and while the British were failing on Everest, the Germans were failing on Kangchenjunga and Nanga Parbat, the French on Gasherbrum I (Hidden Peak) and the Americans on K2. The British just failed a bit higher.

Mallory and Irvine used oxygen on their final attempt in 1924 and it is conceivable that one or both of them actually reached the summit. We are unlikely ever to know. A few days before their attempt, Colonel Norton had traversed right across the North Face into the Great Couloir and had climbed out the far side to a new altitude record of about 8,600 metres – only about 250 metres below the summit. He was not using the awkward, heavy oxygen equipment and was surviving only on the tiny amount of oxygen available in the thin air. It was a desperate struggle, but he was still just managing to breathe and afterwards insisted that oxygen was not the limiting factor when he turned back. It was the steeply shelving, snow-smothered rocks on the far side of the couloir which deterred him. He probably could have just climbed them and reached the summit; but, trying to descend late in the day, utterly spent, he would have been unlikely to get back down alive.

Nine years after Norton's brave attempt Percy Wyn-Harris, Lawrence Wager and Frank Smythe all reached the same point without using oxygen. Subsequent expeditions in 1935, 1936 and 1938 were plagued by bad weather and failed to get so high – 8,600 metres remained man's known altitude record. During those attempts of the 1920s and 1930s, battle lines were drawn up over the use of oxygen. Despite the brilliant achievements of Norton and others, many felt that only artificial oxygen could give the speed and strength to surmount those last gasping 250 metres with any margin of safety. George Finch, in 1922, and Peter Lloyd, in 1938, demonstrated that artificial oxygen could enable a much faster rate of progress at altitude. However, the anti-oxygen camp was quick to point out the appalling weight of the sets, their tendency to leak, the icing up of supply tubes and the infuriating misting up of goggles caused by the masks, problems which have still not been solved entirely, even with the technology available in the 1980s.

By the time post-war climbers began to consider new attempts on Everest, Tibet had been invaded by China and closed to all other foreigners. However, Nepal now opened

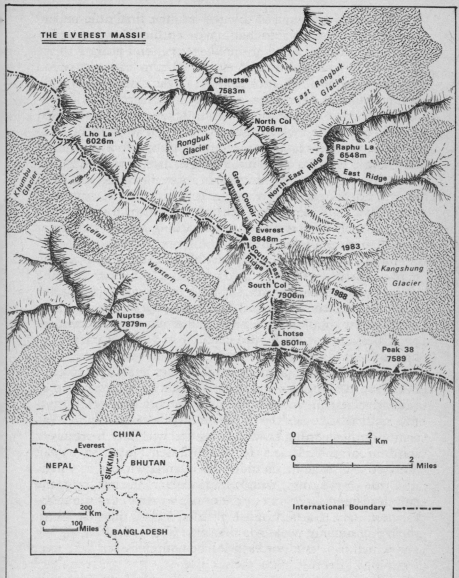

THE EVEREST MASSIF

Changtse
7583m

East Rongbuk
Glacier

North Col
7066m

Lho La
6026m

Rongbuk
Glacier

Raphu La
6548m

East Ridge

Khumbu
Glacier

Great Couloir

North-East Ridge

Icefall

Everest
8848m

1983

South-East Ridge

Kangshung
Glacier

Western Cwm

South Col
7906m

1988

Nuptse
7879m

Lhotse
8501m

Peak 38
7589

CHINA

Everest

NEPAL   SIKKIM   BHUTAN

0   200
Km
0   100
Miles

BANGLADESH

0   2 Km

0   2 Miles

International Boundary   ▬·▬·▬·▬·

the southern approach to Everest for the first time and in
1951 Eric Shipton's reconnaissance expedition found a way
up to the enclosed bowl of the Western Cwm, leading to the
South Col. When John Hunt was called in to lead a concerted
British attempt on this route in 1953, there was very strong
pressure for the expedition to succeed on what would probably be the last chance for Britain to achieve the coveted first
ascent. So Hunt, whose previous experience had been of
small, intimate, low-budget expeditions, found himself
directing a massive quasi-military operation. Oxygen equipment, for all its faults, had now improved significantly and
Hunt and his team were convinced that it was crucial to
success. When Hillary and Tenzing made their historic summit climb on 29 May they were breathing bottled oxygen at
the rate of three litres a minute.

Hillary and Tenzing's wonderful achievement was only
made possible by the dedicated work of a large team building
up a chain of camps and supplies and finally getting the
summit climbers' heavy oxygen equipment to the top camp
on the South-East Ridge. This style of climbing, dependent
on selfless teamwork by the majority and highly competent
directing of logistics by the leader, was to remain the norm
on the very highest peaks for over twenty years. On Everest
everyone used oxygen and the extraordinary achievements of
those pre-war pioneers seemed almost to have been forgotten, until 1978, when the Italian mountaineer, Reinhold Messner, announced that he was going to challenge the received
wisdom of the Himalayan establishment, risk permanent
damage to his brain cells and climb Everest without oxygen.

Three years earlier, with Peter Habeler, Messner had made
an astonishing three-day ascent of the world's eleventh highest mountain, Gasherbrum I (Hidden Peak), the first ascent
of an 8,000-metre peak by a two-man team, climbing alpine-
style, with no fixed ropes or cached supplies on the route.
However, Everest, 800 metres higher, was a far greater
physiological challenge. It was also booked up for years
ahead, so the pair attached themselves to a large conventional
German expedition which had the 1978 spring booking for

what was now the 'normal' South Col route. Messner and Habeler had the support of a large, oxygen-assisted expedition as far as the South Col, but they used no oxygen themselves and on the final 850-metre climb to the summit they had to break their own trail.

They reached the summit, descended safely with brains intact, and finally vindicated Norton's belief that the world's highest mountain could be climbed without artificial oxygen. It was a crucial event in Everest's history, but there was also exciting news from the other side of the mountain. China was about to open Tibet to foreign expeditions. In 1975 a Chinese expedition had reached the summit by the historic 'Mallory Route'. Now the Tibetan side of the mountain was open to outsiders for the first time in over forty years.

From 1979 onwards, undeterred by the colossal charges demanded by the Chinese, foreign climbers flocked in increasing numbers to the northern side of the mountain, but hardly anyone thought about the other Tibetan side of the pyramid, the Kangshung Face. Mallory had dismissed it as lethal, but the only photograph in Howard-Bury's 1921 Everest Reconnaissance book showed little detail to corroborate this judgement. An adventurous American lawyer, Andrew Harvard, was inspired at least to have a look at the great unclimbed face of Everest. In 1980 he received permission to mount a small reconnaissance. The face did indeed look formidable, but climbing techniques had come a long way since 1921. If he could climb the massive rock buttress at the centre of the face he could avoid the biggest, most lethal avalanches which crashed every day down the great gullies either side.

The following year a large American team succeeded in climbing the 1,300-metre high buttress; but they failed to continue up the huge snow spur above, deterred by dangerous avalanche conditions. They returned in the autumn of 1983. Like the South-West Face in 1975, the East Face was to be beaten into submission by a no-holds-barred, no-expense-spared expedition. Thirteen climbers spent four weeks re-fixing ropes up the spectacular buttress and used a rocket

launcher to rig an aerial ropeway for load-hauling. This time
the upper spur was in safer condition. Camps were established and stocked with food, fuel and oxygen and six climbers, assisted by artificial oxygen, reached the summit.

The mighty Kangshung Face had finally been climbed by
what was probably the most difficult route on Everest.
However, success had been achieved by a traditional heavy
siege and it was on the popular northern side of the mountain
that the most revolutionary climbs were being staged. In
1980 Messner set up camp on the East Rongbuk Glacier. His
1978 ascent from Nepal had benefited from the support of a
large team, but this time when he left his advance base at
6,500 metres, below the North Col, he was completely alone
and carried everything he needed to survive in one rucksack.
Three days later, again without oxygen, he completed the
route which had eluded Norton fifty-six years earlier and
reached the summit.

The solo ascent of Everest was probably the single most
outstanding event in the career of a man who revolutionized
Himalayan climbing. His methods were quickly emulated
and by 1988 another eighteen people had climbed Everest
without oxygen; the Nepalese Sherpa Ang Rita had done it
four times. However, Ang Rita's climbs have always been
achieved on the back of traditional heavyweight expeditions.
Far more remarkable was the achievement in 1986 of two
Swiss climbers, Jean Troillet and Erhard Loretan, who sur-
passed Messner's cunning and flair with an extraordinary
rapid ascent of the North Face. They left their Advance Base
at 10 p.m. on 28 August, dispensing with the weight of tents
and sleeping bags, climbing fast through the night and resting during the comparative warmth of the next day. They
continued on the second night and reached the summit on 30
August. After a leisurely rest on top, they made an astonishing four-and-a-half-hour descent, sliding most of the way in
perfect snow conditions, and were safely back down, 3,000
metres below at Advance Base, less than two days after
setting out. It was a brilliant performance by acknowledged
international stars.

But more encouraging to ordinary mortals was the Australian ascent in 1984. Tim McCartney-Snape's small team was obviously very competent and experienced, but few people had heard of these Australians who had never before tackled an 8,000-metre peak. The five-man team put a new route up the Great Couloir on the North Face, without oxygen. Three climbers made the final bid for the summit. One of them had to stop fifty metres short, but his two companions reached the summit. It was clear from their accounts that they were not physiological freaks – just moderately fit mountaineers – and I was particularly encouraged to discover that McCartney-Snape had almost as skinny and flimsy a body as mine. It was his tremendous drive and determination, not an Olympian physique, that had got him to the top: that and the support of a small highly motivated team of friends, working hard together.

Lying awake during those troubled nights at the end of 1987, I tried to remind myself that I too had the motivation and determination to succeed. I also hoped that I would have the wisdom and experience and luck to survive, for on Everest few had yet applied the new methods to anything as difficult and potentially dangerous as the Kangshung Face, the secret side of Everest that had not been touched for nearly five years. I was still not sure about the team, but I had an instinctive feeling that we were going to work well together. By Christmas I was worrying less and my growing confidence was boosted on Christmas Day when Robert phoned from America, full of cheerful optimism. In ten days' time I would meet him in New York and learn more about my companions and our climb.

Robert met me at John F. Kennedy airport. He was tall with dark hair and blue eyes, and as we went out to find a taxi he bounced along with the long, springy strides of someone who seems not to spend much time in an office. In the taxi I commented that his casual clothes didn't look quite right for the co-director of a successful advertising agency. He corrected me.

'In New Zealand this *is* my suit. I just put on a new pair of jeans when I go to pitch for an account. And the client loves it – go in there, tell them what's wrong with their advertising, explain our brilliant campaign, get the account . . . and we all make hy-ooge amounts of money.'

He laughed at the boisterous self-caricature and continued to tell me about the expedition in the same cheerful vein, discussing money, down clothing, a new kind of sleeping pill, high-altitude tents and so on. Jay Smith had dropped out and it now looked as though we were down to a skeletal team of four. Robert had spent a boozy New Year in Colorado with Ed Webster and Paul Teare. They were unable to come to New York, but I would meet some of the non-climbing support team.

By now we were in Manhattan and as it grew dark we drove through Central Park. It was incredibly beautiful, with snow draped on the trees and the lights coming on in the surreal towers and spires around the park. I loved my four days in New York. Exactly a year earlier I had been guiding on Mount Kenya and now again I was lucky enough to escape the dank murk of an English January. It was all new and exciting – the fantastic glass towers, shining brilliantly, far above one's head in the cold blue sky, supersonic elevators, restaurants with menus thirty pages long, the Museum of Modern Art with whole rooms stuffed full of Matisses, making the Tate seem so provincial, and the bar where we drank cocktails the first evening, looking out from some immense height over a fairyland of glittering lights.

'See that one like a castle on the other side of the park? Diana Ross lives there. She owns the *whole* of that top bit!' Wendy David, our press officer, bubbled with enthusiasm, talking and laughing continually, undaunted by the endless search for money and insisting that Everest-88 was the best thing that had ever happened to her. So far she had enlisted the financial support of American Express, Rolex, Kodak and Lindblad Travel, and she was working flat out to attract more sponsors. She kept us busy, with a ceremony for receiving our Rolex watches, sessions at the studio of our

photographer, Joseph Blackburn, more photo sessions at the
Explorers' Club and the Rockefeller Center, visits to Associ-
ated Press to see our pictures being fed into satellite com-
puters, an appearance for Robert and Norbu Tenzing on
breakfast television . . .

Norbu handled the interview with great poise and, at only
twenty-four, seemed very mature. He had been educated in
America, now worked for Lindblad Travel and lived a life
utterly different from that of his father, who as a young man
had earned a meagre income as a high-altitude porter for the
sahibs on Himalayan expeditions. Norbu was looking forward to our journey to Tibet, the land his family originally
came from. Joe also was excited about the trip and its enormous photographic possibilities. He was forty-two, but the
oldest person on the support team was Miklos Pinther, a
delightful Hungarian émigré who is chief cartographer at the
United Nations. I also met our doctor, Mimi Zieman,
looking slightly incongruous amongst the sartorial Rolex
dignitaries in her earthy-crunchy shaggy jersey and wild long
hair, but her beautiful big eyes and irresistible smile charmed
them all.

I was glad to find myself with such a likeable group of
people. I was also reassured, when I finally got Robert to sit
down for two hours and discuss things in detail, to see that he
had everything well organized and that we were agreed on all
the essential food and equipment. The following week he and
Ed would pack it all in Colorado, ready for freighting to
China. Robert and the support team would fly to China and
on to Tibet at the end of February. Meanwhile I would meet
Paul and Ed in Nepal and we would travel up by road to
meet the others in Tibet, aiming to reach Base Camp in the
second week of March.

Robert and I also seemed to agree on tactics. With only
four people, everything would have to be kept as simple as
possible. Nevertheless we needed a secure, comfortable Base
Camp with plenty of good, varied food. On our summit bid
we would have to travel very light and oxygen would be out
of the question. But the lower part of the Kangshung Face

was going to test us with some very steep technical climbing,
where we would have to ferry heavy equipment. Ed had
selected enough gear to enable us, if necessary, to fix over
2,000 metres of rope on this lower part. As for Robert's
route, he showed me the photo.

'You see there's a definite buttress there, to the left of the
1983 route. I'm not sure about this approach up here – the
Witches' Cauldron, Paul calls it.'

'I don't like the look of this lot above it, up here.'

'No.'

'But I suppose once we actually get on the buttress we
should be protected. Some steep climbing though!'

'Yes, that's for Ed, the big wall specialist. That's why I
think we've got such a good team. Ed's a really good technical climber; you've got a lot of Himalayan experience;
Paul's also strong on mixed and he's an excellent ice climber;
and me – well, I've got really long legs for all that wading
higher up.'

It sounded promising. Robert was shrewd and had chosen
a route which really might be feasible for our small team:
hardest climbing low down, safeguarded with fixed ropes,
easier climbing above, travelling light to the South Col, then
the original 1953 route from there to the summit. Of course I
still had my doubts, particularly about the monstrous ice
cliffs on the flanking wall of Lhotse – would our buttress be
engulfed in the inevitable avalanches or would their force be
contained in that depression on the left? The only way to find
out was to go and have a look. The whole trip could be a
total fiasco, but I had an instinctive feeling, reinforced by my
four days in New York, that somehow we were going to
find a safe route and climb it successfully.

I arrived back in London on 9 January. On 12 February I
was due to leave for Bombay to give four lectures at the
Himalayan Club Diamond Jubilee and I would be going
straight on to Everest. So now I had just one month to get
ready. There was little time for sleep during that month. I
had to prepare personal equipment, have injections, get visas,
book flights, do a lecture tour in Ireland, do more lectures in

England, organize a London press conference for Everest, write my monthly magazine column, write stalling letters to despairing bank managers, accountants and tax inspectors, and visit doctors to be reassured that the nagging pain in my chest was quite insignificant and largely a figment of my hypersensitive imagination.

Somehow I had to make time to go and say goodbye to my parents in Bath, meet my newly born nephew in Oxford, say goodbye to other brothers and sisters and enjoy a little precious time with my friend Rosie, whom I had seen so rarely during my brief three months back in England.

The day of departure came. It was a morning flight and we had to get up horribly early. Rosie drove me through the dark empty streets of London and out to the airport. I was fully committed to the expedition and looking forward to a great adventure; but at this stage I also felt tired, unfit and aware that this climb was potentially more dangerous than any I had attempted before.

We checked in the baggage and all too soon it was time for me to go through passport control. I left with a hurried kiss and a lump in my throat. Before disappearing through the barrier I turned round to smile bravely and wave cheerfully, wondering if I would be coming back.

2

From Ocean to Plateau

BOMBAY was the perfect rest cure. The weather was warm and a gentle breeze from the Indian Ocean rustled the palm trees. There was time to sleep and read and enjoy relaxed meals with my hosts, Harish and Geeta Kapadia.

In 1985, Harish had led our Indo–British expedition to the Rimo massif in the Eastern Karakoram. It was good now to revive the friendship formed three years earlier. One morning I was dragged along to one of his beloved cricket matches. I spent a hot afternoon sailing in the harbour by Queen Alexandra Gate. Another day we escaped the smoggy haze of Bombay and drove out to a nature reserve to climb on some rocks near a Hindu shrine. It was a Shiva festival day and the forest below us was filled with the happy burbling of pilgrims' holiday voices.

There was a feeling in that forest of ancient timelessness and continuity. Perhaps I was just succumbing to the Westerner's usual romantic reaction to India; but a sense of love and goodwill and renewal seemed also to pervade the Himalayan Club celebrations. Nearly all the talks emphasized the ancient trade routes, the people who have inhabited the remote valleys from time immemorial and the reverence they feel for their holy mountains. My own talks were less spiritual and were not exclusively about the Himalaya but I was conscious of enormous goodwill and was flattered at the opening ceremony to be welcomed with flowers, presented by Parul and Gigi, two attractive girls I remembered well from 1985 and about whom Geeta teased me mercilessly.

With four lectures to give, I was able to indulge in a huge choice of subjects and reminisce happily about many recent adventures – our trip to Rimo in 1985, winter climbs in Scotland, the Shisha Pangma expedition, the North Face of the Eiger . . .

Everest was hardly mentioned and I felt slightly envious of my Bombay friends planning a long trek through the little known mountains of Kumaon. There had been talk of another joint expedition this year, but I had succumbed to ambition and the lure of Everest.

Geeta teased me: 'Now when you climb Everest and are famous you won't come and see us any more.'

Harish laughed at my choice of team mates. 'Why are you climbing with these Americans? They talk with a funny accent and they drive on the wrong side of the road . . . and they don't play *cricket.*'

After ten days in Bombay, I was sad to leave, but I now felt much calmer and stronger. Geeta lit a candle for me in the family shrine and her two sons, Nawang and Sonam, each gave me a small packet of dried flower petals. The flowers came from an ashram in Pondicherri, which they visited each winter, and were to protect me. If possible I should leave them on the summit. Geeta had tears in her eyes when she said, 'Goodbye. Come back.'

That evening I flew north to Delhi. I was not flying on to Kathmandu till the next morning, so I was able to attend the Diamond Jubilee dinner given by the Delhi section of the Himalayan Club. The guest of honour was Sir Edmund Hillary. He was surrounded by clamouring admirers and I never got to meet him, but I did talk with another very distinguished guest, Charles Houston. As well as being a fine mountaineer he is a highly respected high-altitude physiologist and he had recently published quite critical comments on the risks taken by modern climbers on the highest peaks. I felt very cut down to size when he heard about our Everest plans and said: 'Kangshung Face! Four people! You're mad! Go and climb a smaller mountain!'

During dinner he became gentler, and I quickly realized

that his sharp retort had been out of character. In fact it was his very warmth and compassion that made him so concerned about the risks taken by lightweight expeditions. His fears had recently been vindicated by the disastrous summer on K2 in 1986. He felt that ambition had driven climbers far beyond the traditional margins of safety and that some of them had perhaps shown callous selfishness and disregard for others' lives. He had set his own high standards in 1953 when he and his companions were caught in a similar killer storm on K2. After fighting for their lives for seven days at the top camp they had to descend. One of them, Art Gilkey, was unable to walk due to thrombosis and was only semi-conscious, but the others risked their own lives attempting the almost impossible feat of lowering their friend down thousands of metres of steep dangerous ground. During the descent Gilkey was swept away in an avalanche.

'We were lucky really,' said Houston. 'That saved our lives.'

'So you couldn't have got him all the way down?'

'No, we still had a hell of a long way to descend and it was desperately slow in that storm. We were all on our last legs and that ridge is very hard. If Art hadn't gone we all would have died.'

'But did you ever consider leaving him behind?'

'Never. You don't leave someone who's still alive.'

I wondered whether I would have been as brave and selfless. I wondered what we would do if someone got badly injured on Everest. With only four of us we would be in a desperate position.

After dinner there were speeches. Inevitably, much of the talk was on Everest and Sir Edmund told some amusing stories about 1953. Major Alluwahlia, who made the first Indian ascent in 1965, was also there and Houston looked at them both when he said: 'We know that the people who climb Everest, even the ones who have now climbed it without oxygen, are not supermen. They don't have unique bodies. Physiologically, they're just the same as all the rest of us. No, it's here' – and he put his hand up to his chest '– they have *heart*. It's their spirit and determination and courage that got them to the top.'

It was moving stuff and particularly apposite for me. I had always believed that I did have that inner fire. Occasionally, during sixteen years of mountaineering, I had been given the chance to draw on it; but I had never felt fully stretched to the limit and perhaps in a few weeks' time I might find out what that limit was.

Soon it was time to return to the airport and find a bit of floor to sleep on. When I said goodbye to Charles Houston, he wished us good luck and parted with the words: 'Whatever you do, have a good time, that's the important thing.'

At eleven o'clock the next morning the aeroplane was circling above the Kathmandu valley. Nepal looked so different from the last time I had flown in, a few months earlier, during the Monsoon. Most of the terraced fields still wore their red and brown winter colours and only a few showed the first green of spring. The winters are normally dry but this year there had been rain. The mountains to the north were swathed in dark cloud and the foothills were sprinkled grey with new snow. The weather in the Himalaya had been bad since the beginning of February and showed no sign of improving. There was going to be a lot of snow on the high passes.

Kathmandu is one of the smallest capital cities in the world, but as no one had given me an address it took a while to find Ed and Paul. After an abortive search for Atlas Trekking, the office of our agent Harihar, I decided to visit the British Services Everest Expedition and see if they had met my companions. They hadn't, but they invited me to stay for some beer and lunch at their grand hotel. It was good to meet Dougie Keelan, the leader, who had grown up in the same village as me, in Surrey. He was amused about our expedition.

'Kangshung Face – you must have thought long and hard before accepting that one!'

I also had a good gossip with my Shisha Pangma climbing partner, Luke Hughes, who was enjoying the efficiency of the military machine but a little apprehensive about the long weeks ahead with such a huge team.

'We've got *fifty-two* people. I think I'm beginning to envy you with your team of four.'

'I still haven't met two of them. You haven't seen two lost American climbers?'

He hadn't seen them, but by chance the money-changer he took me to that afternoon was in a courtyard right next to the Atlas Trekking office. After getting some rupees, I went up to the office. Harihar welcomed me with a big smile and instructed his boy to escort me to the hotel where Ed and Paul were staying. The boy took me through the narrow streets of Thamel, the tourist quarter, past innumerable shops full of jewellery, brass Buddhas, Everest posters and second-hand climbing gear. We had almost reached our destination when I found myself staring at a man coming towards us on the other side of the street. He walked with a restless gait, arms held slightly out from his side with open hands. The face looked familiar – dark curly hair, thick eyebrows, longish nose, and the shape of the mouth looked right. But it was the baseball cap that did it. He had to be American.

'Paul?'

'Hallo. You're Stephen?'

'Yes. I recognized you from that photo.'

'Hey, where've you been? We didn't know where you were. I was *gripped*. How are you? Yes – I was *gripped* – where is Stephen?! Ed's gone to get propane cylinders. Hey, it's good to see you. We were twittering. How was Bombay?'

'I had a good time – did a lot of spouting.'

'Spouting? What's that?'

'Talking – lectures,' I translated. Although Paul was born of British parents in Canada, he had spent most of his life in California and was thoroughly Americanized. But he enjoyed my Anglicisms.

'Spouting – I like it. You Brits are awesome.'

I discovered quickly that 'awesome', pronounced

'arsome', could be used indiscriminately as a term of respect, amusement, endearment, fear or loathing for almost anything or anyone under the sun.

The barrage of Paulspeak continued inside the Tibetan Guest House as we unpacked a giant duffel bag full of equipment.

'All this gear – isn't it awesome? It's Christmas time for Stephen. Here's your down bibs, this is your parka, gloves, more gloves – no, have them, they *gave* them to us – trekking boots, nice colours, huh? We wore them in the subway in New York. The black kids kept saying "Hey, man, where'd you get those shoes?"'

There was all manner of ice climbing gear from Stubai, including fluorescent pink crampons. The down gear, as well as jacket and 'bibs' (American for dungarees or salopettes), included a luxurious sleeping bag which, for oncc, was actually wide enough and long enough to take six foot three of climber dressed in bulky clothes. My Christmas package also included the statutory powder blue fleece jacket with the Everest-88 logo. It was to be the uniform of the expedition and earn us the nickname of 'powder blue poofter kids'.

Paul moved restlessly round the room, talking all the while. Accustomed to the wary reserve and studied understatement of British mountaineers, I was slightly alarmed by Paul's effusiveness. Within half an hour of meeting, he was telling me about an ice climb he had done recently in Yosemite.

'Really steep, I mean, vertical – overhanging on one bit – I soloed it.'

I almost felt like saying, 'Shut up Paul – you don't have to try and impress me.' I wondered if perhaps he was very insecure and was going to be a pain in the neck on the mountain, but of course my first impressions were quite wrong and I soon came to realize that these outpourings had just been the manifestation of an open, impulsive, generous nature; as the expedition progressed I found myself increasingly enjoying Paul's company, even though our backgrounds, tastes and personalities were so different.

When Ed arrived I also recognized his face from a photograph – the slightly spiky, thick, dark hair, the beard and
above all the eyes. They had looked striking in the black and
white photo but I hadn't expected them to be blue – the
piercing blue eyes of the romantic dreamer who was always
in love. This year it was a beautiful girl called Randa, far too
good and young for an ageing thirty-two-year-old climber
like Ed. He was clearly devoted to her, talked about her
constantly and always kept her photo with him, even when
we started climbing the mountain.

Ed's romanticism also embraced climbing. Like me, he
wrote a regular column for a climbing magazine and he had
with him his latest offering. It was a resounding attack on the
modern rock climber's competitive obsession with technical
difficulty at the expense of risk, which has led to routes being
pre-inspected, pre-rehearsed and pre-bolted to make them
totally bland and safe. After this dismissal of the modern
Philistines, Ed indulged in some unashamedly purple prose,
recalling his own childhood adventures and then his development into an all-round mountaineer, equally skilful on the
hot canyon walls of Colorado or a Himalayan icefall, inspired
by imagination, a spirit of adventure and respect for the great
pioneers. Although his skill and experience as a technical
rock climber were far greater than mine, both of us, and
Paul, shared a similar outlook on climbing.

That night we went to the American Embassy club and did
American things like eating hamburgers and drinking cold
fizzy beer from tin cans and watching television, while Paul
with unerring instinct homed in on a girl with long golden
hair called Arlene.

In the morning I met our Sherpa cook, Pasang. In 1986 he
had been the cook for Roger Marshall's solo attempt on the
North Face of Everest. Ed had been the expedition's official
photographer and during the long spells of watching and
waiting at Base Camp, he had got to know Pasang well, had
enjoyed his excellent cooking and had told Robert this year
that he was not returning to Everest unless Pasang came. I
never would have guessed that he was forty-nine. His face

did wrinkle slightly when he broke into one of his huge smiles but it was hardly middle-aged and he still had a full head of thick black hair. Even by Sherpa standards he was very short, with stumpy legs and a barrel chest. He had first been to Everest in 1962, as cookboy to the first Indian expedition, with the legendary Angtharkay as sirdar. In 1969 he had worked as a porter for the Japanese and had been to the South Col. Nowadays he worked part time for Harihar's new agency, leading the occasional trek or cooking for expeditions.

When Pasang was born, no Westerner had ever been allowed into his native high mountains of Nepal. In 1949 the first foreign expedition was allowed in. Now about three hundred and fifty thousand tourists visit Nepal every year and tens of thousands invade the Sherpas' homeland, Sola Khumbu, the area of high valleys immediately south of Everest. The Sherpas with their innate enterprise and efficiency have made the most of tourism. Pasang runs a successful lodge and restaurant at Namche Bazar, the main centre of Sola Khumbu, and one of his daughters runs another one in Lukla. He is a successful business man. Nevertheless, Nepal remains one of the poorest countries in the world and by Western standards Pasang lives very modestly. The remarkable thing about his Sherpa people is that, in spite of constantly witnessing the incomparably greater wealth of foreign tourists, most of them have managed to retain their legendary dignity, humour, efficiency and generosity.

Pasang took on most of the work in Kathmandu, buying pots and pans, pressure cookers, a big gas stove and thirteen large cylinders, tarpaulins and, to supplement the supplies freighted through China, fresh potatoes, onions, garlic, ginger, carrots, cabbages and five hundred eggs to see us through to May. We even bought a folding table and chairs for Base Camp. Harihar organized transport to the Tibetan border and Chinese visas. Then he received a telex from the Chinese Mountaineering Association to say that the Tibetan transport would be late due to snow-blocked roads, so we had a full week to enjoy ourselves in Kathmandu.

The unseasonable rainstorms mainly struck at night, leaving the days bright and washed clear of dust. Bicycles can be hired very cheaply in Kathmandu and we spent hours exploring the city and surrounding countryside. One day I got up early to bicycle out to Swoyambunath, the Monkey Temple. The town was still in shade but I could see the two minarets and central golden spire shimmering on the hill beyond the river. I crossed the bridge, left my bike at the bottom of the hill and started the long climb up endless steps, past prostrating old ladies, stone effigies and chortens, all preparing for the magical moment when one climbs out into brilliant light and sees for the first time the whole of the giant chorten – a radiant white dome, culminating in a square pedestal with two great Buddha eyes gazing out inscrutably from each side, this topped by the dazzling gold spire seen from the valley. I spent an hour up there, enjoying the silver morning light and the wonderful blend of the sublime and the profane: monks chanted, a tiny boy played with a puppy, old men mumbled and schoolgirls laughed as they circled the chorten, spinning the prayer wheels, a man refilled oil lamps, women fed their babies and prepared breakfast, the pigeons sat cooing amongst intricate gold leaf pagodas and the playful monkeys scampered up the white dome, to slither back down again, grabbing at prayer flags as they went.

I returned to the hotel for breakfast; then Ed, Paul and I bicycled twelve miles out to the ancient royal city of Bakhtepur. Spring was in the air as we raced through fields of yellow rape and fresh green leeks and the first pale haze of cherry blossom. It was an exhilarating ride and I was pleased to manage the steep hill up to the town without dismounting. All the time we were surreptitiously preparing ourselves for the great effort on Everest.

At Bakhtepur we indulged in an orgy of photography. Durbar Square was magnificent: the elegant pagodas, the brilliant inventiveness of the wood carving, the golden Vishnu, sitting so serenely on top of a slender column, like the lion of Venice atop his column in St Mark's Square, the great stone elephants, rhinos and lions flanking the steps up to another pagoda, the imaginative athleticism of the coupling figures, carved so brazenly on wooden roof struts...

I was a busy day. After bicycling back to Kathmandu we were taken by Pasang to the immense temple at Bodrinath. A lama at the nearby monastery, who was a ringpoche – a reincarnate – from Sola Khumbu, had agreed to bless us, and I for one was glad of any protection on offer. We were taken up to a murky room where a very old man in his saffron robe was slumped on a bed, surrounded by a dusty clutter of books, oil lamps, half-eaten food, dead flowers and mouldy bananas. Just as medieval laymen in Europe paid alms to their monasteries, we each dutifully handed the lama a hundred-rupee note, wrapped discreetly in a prayer shawl. Then we bravely sipped foul, salty tea, while the lama mumbled and blew on red strings. Then we took it in turn to kneel in front of him, have a string placed round our neck and receive a pat on the head.

After our blessing we stopped for a moment at the rich colourful mysterious temple downstairs. A few Westerners, all with the inevitable plaits or shaven heads, busily searching for themselves and derided by Paul as 'the social misfits of the West', sat cross-legged at the back. Try as hard as they could, they just didn't seem to fit, and they lacked the dignity of the robed monks. The ceremony took the form of chanting with instrumental interludes. The monks would do a spell of basso profundo mumbling, then the huge room would reverberate with the discordant cacophony of wheezing shawms and plangent horns, accompanied by cymbals and drums. To my untrained ear it did not compare favourably with Palestrina.

Our week's holiday passed all too quickly. Inevitably one is affected in Kathmandu by the rich mixture of Hinduism and Buddhism which pervades life there so completely, but I have to confess that I was also relishing my last few hedon-istic days of good restaurants, plentiful alcohol and hot baths. (Ed and Paul, like all good healthy Americans, preferred to 'take a shower', as if it was some kind of medicine, and laughed for weeks to come about my propensity for 'having a bath' – pronounced with a full rounded Southern English 'a'.)

Again, as in Bombay, I was conscious of enormous good-will from everyone – the charming Tibetan staff at the hotel, the equipment shop owner, Tsering, whose beauty is renow-ned amongst mountaineers throughout the world, the American friends who took us climbing on the local crag, Dorje McTavish, the Sherpa who picked up a Scottish sur-name in the Cairngorms, Arlene of the flaxen hair who succumbed so joyously to Paul's charms, Tom and Susan from Colorado and Vicky, the English girl we met at the Marco Polo restaurant on our last evening in Nepal.

Early the next morning, 1 March, Harihar saw us off and we were away, driving up the Friendship Highway, built by China to promote trade with Nepal and probably to aggrav-ate Nepal's southern big brother, India.

It was a lovely morning of mists and dewy glittering fields, so different from the dark, wet day in September when we had driven this way to Shisha Pangma. Soon after passing Bakhtepur the road heads north and crosses the first pass to the deep green gorge of the Sun Kosi. A few miles before the town of Bharabise, we had to get out and walk, as the road had been destroyed by the river. From here up to and beyond the Tibetan border the road is threatened by landslides, several sections are frequently swept away and porters trans-port baggage across the gaps. This is the major trade route for Chinese imports, so the traffic is busy, and one gets the feeling of travelling through a border no man's land where everything is directed solely towards the moving of goods backwards and forwards. Everywhere there are porters hanging around, headstraps at the ready. From Bharabise we hired a truck for the luggage and a taxi to drive Ed, Paul, Pasang and me up to the border. I felt a flash of nostalgia as we passed a precipitous side valley, for six months earlier we had thrashed our way down that valley, through bamboo jungle, at the end of our acclimatization trek. And now we were coming up to the little town of Tatopani, with the wonderful hot springs, and on to the border post of Kodari.

After going through Nepalese customs, we had to walk the final steep destroyed road up the far side of the river to complete the seventy-six-mile journey from Kathmandu to the Chinese border post of Zangmu. Pasang supervised the hire of porters, while I walked across Friendship Bridge to show the necessary documents to the Chinese guards who looked as incongruously young and innocent as ever in their bright green uniforms. I had no trouble but when Paul arrived they gave him a hard time, instilling in him an instant dislike of Chinese officialdom. They also nearly sent Pasang back to Kathmandu. The previous year he had been through with his wife and mother-in-law on a holiday to Lhasa. To return to his home in Sola Khumbu, rather than come all the way round by road, he had taken the obvious, direct route home − over the Nangpa La, a glacier pass which has been used by Tibetans and Sherpas since time immemorial. He liked to joke about how he had dragged his sixty-five-year-old mother-in-law across the snows of the 5,800-metre pass, in defiance of the communists who now forbid unauthorized crossings of the Tibetan border. Now the bored young guards at Friendship Bridge scrutinized his passport and noticed that he had no exit stamp on the previous year's visa, but luckily they succumbed to his apologetic smile and let him through.

We spent two nights in Zangmu waiting for onward transport. The impermanent no man's land atmosphere here is even stronger. The highway climbs up in long zig-zags, lined by ramshackle houses, built out on stilts and clinging precariously to the slope, 500 metres above the crashing grey torrent of the Bhut Kosi. The northern end of the town was recently obliterated, along with over two hundred lives, when the entire mountainside above peeled away, to crash thousands of metres into the river. A dangerous new track has been bulldozed through the debris, but each year the Monsoon rains bring down more rock and earth to sweep it away. Often vehicles cannot pass, for weeks at a time, and goods have to be carried across the quagmire by porters − either the Sherpa, Gurkha and Tamang Nepalese who are always crossing the border, or the young Tibetans, who lounge around in the filthy street like the disaffected youth of some deprived inner city, staring scornfully at the dapper Chinese officials.

In the evening Ed and I walked up to the old village. It was good to get some exercise and the steep climb focused our thoughts on the challenge we would soon have to face. Ed asked me what I thought about not using oxygen.

'I hope I'm up to it, but I don't really know whether I'm strong enough.'

'No, nor do I.'

'You were very fast on Changtse.' (In 1986 he had soloed a new route on Changtse, the 7,583-metre North Peak of Everest.) 'If you can manage that sort of speed at 7,000 metres, you'll probably do well at 8,000 metres.

'Maybe.'

'I *think* I can do it. On Shishers we reached about 7,700 metres and I was still going OK . . . well, you know, totally knackered but still managing ten steps at a time. The main thing is not to hang around. If the weather breaks we just have to go straight back down.'

We had all learned enough from the successes and disasters of recent years to know exactly what we should do. But knowing the theory was one thing; it was quite another to put it into practice. When we were high on the mountain, driven by ambition, would our oxygen-starved brains be capable of remembering the lessons? Would we notice the warnings of the high-altitude killer, cerebral oedema? If the weather broke, would we really force ourselves back down before it was too late? One thing was certain, the slow approach through India, Nepal and now Tibet was the best possible preparation, a simultaneous unwinding from the frenetic rush of London and a building up of strength for the climb. Tomorrow we would see Everest, but tonight that seemed hard to believe. We were only 2,800 metres above sea level and a warm breeze rustled the leaves of the forest as we walked back down through the gloaming to rejoin Paul and Pasang.

That night we had supper with Tibetan friends of Pasang. They gave us rice, lentils, curried potatoes and deep-fried yak meat. The main room where we ate was typical of Tibetan and Sherpa houses. A brightly painted chest supported the family altar, which had a colour poster of the Buddha, an oil lamp of gleaming silver, seven brass bowls full of water, which are replenished every day, and an eclectic mixture of offerings – rice, flour, butter, sweets, old bread, plastic flowers, peacock feathers, coins and a Chinese banknote of surprisingly large denomination.

After supper we sat in the kitchen with the family of our host, Tashi, and some of their friends. Five of the men danced, self-consciously at first, then with gusto, rough boots stamping a complex rhythm in unison, as the arm-linked line swayed backwards and forwards to the strummed music of a small instrument like a mandolin. Sitting quietly by the stove, Tashi's wife looked quite serene, her mouth occasionally widening into the natural, effortless smile so characteristic of the Tibetan people.

Then Tashi put on a cassette tape made in Dharamsala, the Indian home of the Tibetan government in exile. This music was quite different – a polished recording of a man singing a wistful ballad, accompanied by a guitar. We could not understand the words, but Pasang told us that they spoke of lost freedom and the riots, deaths, and imprisonments in Lhasa the previous October. It felt strange to be sitting in that house, so defiantly Tibetan, listening to that song and knowing that the Chinese garrison was only a few hundred metres down the road. It was only months later we heard that in that same week about eighty more Tibetans in Lhasa were beaten to death.

The next morning we left Zangmu. A small truck took all the baggage, while we travelled luxuriously in a Japanese landcruiser. The spare place was taken by a Japanese climber on his way to join the Asian Friendship Expedition – a massive operation planning live satellite television coverage of a simultaneous traverse of Everest from north and south, by Chinese, Japanese and Nepalese climbers.

The road climbed relentlessly up and through the Himalayan range. Soon broad-leaved forest gave way to pines;
then we were above the trees, driving through the recently
cleared snowdrifts, and Paul was pointing up excitedly at
huge pristine powder bowls and longing for skis. We
stopped briefly at Nyalam, the Tibetan village below Shisha
Pangma, huddled behind grotesque new Chinese buildings,
then drove on, climbing up the bare windswept slopes of the
Lalung La.

Once again we stopped to look back to Shisha Pangma.
There was still a lingering sadness as I pointed out our distant
route of the previous autumn to the others; but by now I had
almost come to terms with my disappointment and this time
I was starting, not ending, an adventure. In four hours we
had driven straight up from Zangmu to 5,050 metres and
none of us had even a headache. I felt slightly breathless but I
was also invigorated by the sharp clear air, the brilliant light
and the huge space of the Tibetan plateau, so utterly different
from the gorge we had left that morning. Now, as we
descended the far side of the pass, we were heading eastward
along the northern side of the Himalayan range. But Himalayan geography is so complex that, although this world was
utterly different from Nepal, the Phung Chu, the river which
we were now following, flows south, like the Bhut Kosi,
cutting right through the Himalayan divide, where it enters
Nepal as the Arun river and continues south, ultimately to
the Bay of Bengal. As in much of the Karakoram range, the
great giants of the Himalaya do not actually form the con-
tinental watershed: that lies on the lower, barren hills further
north.

My first expedition, in 1977, had been to the Hindu Kush
range, in Afghanistan. Our mountains there drained into the
Oxus, that river of fable and legend which flows northward
through the deserts of Russian Asia to the Aral Sea. Since
then I had been working eastward on successive trips,
through the Karakoram and Kashmir Himalaya, where the
melting snows feed the mighty Indus. In 1987 I had finally
visited Nepal and Tibet for the first time, and climbed on the

East Face of Shisha Pangma, whose melting snows drain into the Sun Kosi. Now we were heading a little further east, past another 8,000-metre giant, Cho Oyo, and on towards the mountain whose snows feed the Arun system – Everest.

We rounded the corner and there it was again – the huge, elongated pyramid of the North Face. It was a beautiful clear afternoon, but we could see a mass of cloud sitting heavily over the valleys on the far side of the mountain and higher up, on the summit, there was the usual plume of cloud and wind-blasted spindrift streaming out to the east. Paul was filled with gloom.

'Look at that plume. The wind's blowing all that snow down onto the Kangshung Face, just building up lots of windslab to avalanche us. It's *awesome*. And look at that cloud below – just sitting over our valley!'

'It's the Kangshung micro-climate.'

Ed, the indefatigable photographer, burned off several rolls of Kodachrome, then we continued on the last part of the drive to Shekar, where we would meet the rest of the team.

It was supper time when we reached the Chinese Mountaineering Association compound in Shekar. The echoing dining hall was filled with about a hundred climbers – a great throng of Japanese in red down suits, Nepalese in orange and Chinese in green – and it took a moment to find the delicate powder blue jackets of our small group, tucked away in a corner. I rushed over, kissed Wendy and Mimi and said hallo to Robert; then Ed, Paul and Pasang came in and everyone in our small group was talking at once, trying to outdo the massed hordes of the Asian Friendship Expedition. I already knew Joe, Norbu, Miklos, Wendy and Mimi, and the only new faces on the support team were Robert Dorival, who had organized the food in America, and Sandy Wylie, the expedition accountant. He wore a sort of romper suit in red furry material, a white scarf, and a fur hat above mirror sunglasses and a moustache, and looked, if anything, even more effete than the powder blue poofter kids.

The Chinese Mountaineering Association is not noted for

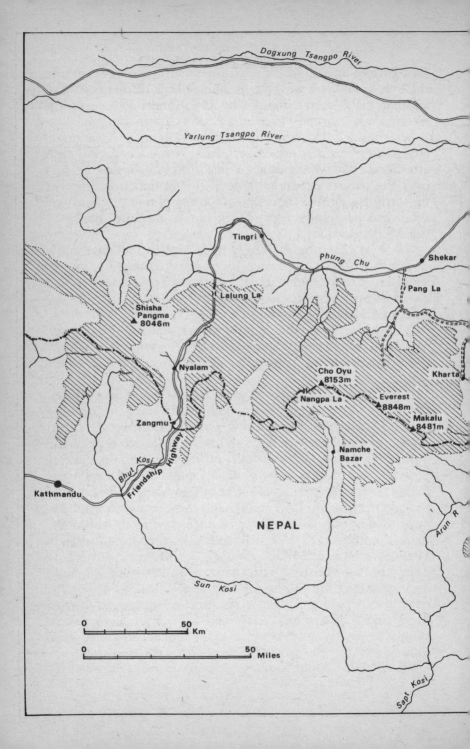

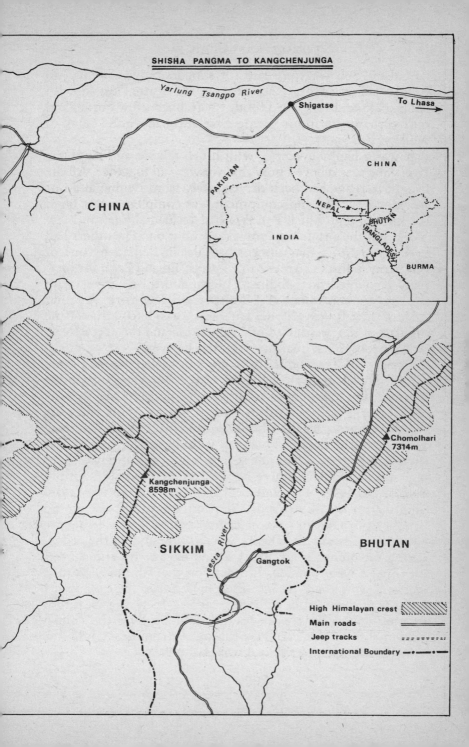

its cuisine and we were late for supper. However they do supply plenty of beer, so, after a half-hearted tussle with chop sticks and congealed food, we grabbed a few bottles and retired to our dormitory, where we also had a good stock of whisky.

It was a happy evening, with much talking and laughter. Everyone was relieved now that we were all together. All the freight baggage had been driven safely from Beijing and our truckload of food and equipment was complete, apart from the kitchen tent which Pan Am had accidentally left in New York; but the airline was going to send it on. The others had been treated to a magnificent banquet in Beijing by one of our main sponsors, American Express. Ed and Paul, for their part, recounted their flight to Nepal and their success with the baggage controllers at JFK airport in New York. A proud flash of their Rolex watches had been enough to convince the officials of the prestige of our expedition and the necessity to wave through vast quantities of extra baggage.

Robert told us about the Chinese officials we had been assigned. Apparently the liaison officer, Mr Yang, was quite pleasant, but everyone was already fed up with Mr Shi, the interpreter. Having failed to arrange our transport from the Nepalese border, he had been sent off that day to Zangmu, where we had already given up waiting and organized our own transport. We had not seen him during the day and no one at Shekar knew where he was, so there would be more delays. However, I was glad of the delay for we were now higher than the summit of the Matterhorn and we would benefit from a day or two of acclimatization. I was feeling the altitude and beer and whisky were compounding the effect, giving me quite a headache. I would have to try and sleep it off. First I went outside. Up here on the Tibetan plateau it was still winter and, if anything, colder than the last night I had spent here, four months earlier. It was a beautiful evening and again there was a full moon over the ruined battlements of the dzong – the once magnificent hill fort which dominates the town. I was glad to be back.

3
The Kharta Valley

AT DAWN we got up to photograph the dzong. Joe, the professional, carried his 10×8 view camera and heavy tripod to the best vantage point and worked for an hour in the biting cold air. Back at the CMA compound, breakfast was the usual damp, anaemic, steamed doughnuts.

Once the sun came up the morning was warm and windless and we all sat outside. The yellow box, Robert's ghetto blaster, was brought out and Miklos, our cartographer, put on some Verdi. Mimi then played us some earthy-crunchy folk music. But Paul was getting restless and irritable, and only looked happy when he finally had his way and blasted the courtyard with suitably metallic rock music. When he disappeared back into our room I turned down the volume.

Since leaving England I had been keeping a diary. That morning in Shekar I wrote:

Friday – March 4th
    I feel slightly that I am a passenger. Paul and Ed have organized the gear, Robert is the leader, Pasang is working his balls off, Norbu fixed all the travel, Wendy raised $150,000, Joe is constantly photographing, Sandy is busy sorting out accounts and Mimi is the doctor. I seem to have had very little work to do and I just keep on receiving freebies – the latest a giant Therma-Rest sleeping mat.

Because this was an American expedition, every possible need was catered for and there was a good deal of surplus equipment. The other three climbers, for instance, seemed to take it for granted that each of them should have two pairs of high-altitude climbing boots, as well as big fur-lined boots for Base Camp and a further choice of boots for the walk-in. Of course a lot of the equipment was donated by sponsors and during the last few frantic weeks in New York Wendy and Joe had done excellent work, getting financial support from a Mr Weaver, who wanted us to try out a parka that converted into an emergency sleeping bag, and from Kiehl Cosmetics, who gave us $10,000 and about ten years' supply of excellent moisturizers, lip salve, sun creams, wind creams and every other conceivable beauty aid, all made from the finest ingredients and normally sold at high prices to the jet-setters of New York.

I did find it strange to be on an expedition for which I had done so little work; but I was content to sit in the sun and write my diary while the experts went about their business. Sandy was busy calculating the extent of our deficit and working out exactly how many more thousands of dollars we would have to pay into the coffers of the CMA to help sustain their growing army of incompetent bureaucrats. Robert was telling Dr Mimi about the advertising campaign he had dreamed up for the new Roche sleeping pills we would be trying out. Later, while I was trying to concentrate on writing my column for *High* magazine, I caught a snatch of self-caricature from our ad-man leader: '. . . I was in the helicopter, riding back from the lecture I gave to BMW . . .'

Our expedition was lavish by English standards and was not quite as simple as the affair I had envisaged in New York; but it paled into insignificance beside the three-nation Asian Friendship Expedition, about to start operating from the Rongbuk and Khumbu Glaciers. For China and Nepal the television spectacular was a marvellous exercise in political propaganda. For Japan, providing the cash and the equipment, it was a commercial opportunity to advertise all the very latest communications technology.

That evening we met Shigeyuki Okajima, head of the Japanese press corps, who showed us the expedition Filofax,

crammed with route maps, satellite link-up diagrams, details
of radio equipment, fax machines and the direct-dialling
telephone exchange, diagrams showing exactly what would
be in each tent, exhaustive food and equipment lists, mind-
boggling oxygen statistics and photographs of all the two
hundred and fifty-two members of the expedition. Each
climber was categorized as either a climbing leader, deputy
climbing leader, climbing member or a lowly associate
climbing member. Mr Okajima had a staff of nine journalists
and photographers on the Rongbuk, with another four on
the Khumbu, on the Nepalese side. And they were not to be
confused with the sixteen television cameramen and their
eleven porters.

It was a brilliant exercise in logistics and communications,
but whether it had anything to do with mountaineering is
another matter. Tashi Jangbu and another famous Sherpa,
Pertemba, were in charge of the Nepalese contingent this
side. Tashi, an extremely competent mountain guide who
trained in Chamonix with the French star Christophe Profit,
saw the expedition as a job, an interesting organizational
challenge. At this stage he was quite enthusiastic, and it was
only afterwards that we heard how once again, the strength,
skill, and expertise of Sherpas had been exploited to further
the ambitions of weaker foreigners, in this case the Chinese
hosts, whose much-vaunted 'friendship' degenerated into
obstinate autocracy.

I met our own Chinese friends the next day. Mr Yang, the
liaison officer, was well into his forties, had a lean face,
which occasionally broke into a hesitant smile, and, in his
old-fashioned Mao suit, he had a certain inscrutable dignity.
The CMA in their wisdom always provide a liaison officer
who speaks not a word of English, so he has to be accompanied by an interpreter, in this case the callow youth, Shi
(pronounced Sher). After his bungled attempt to meet us in
Zangmu he had now found his way back to Shekar. He was
only about twenty, had never been outside Beijing before
and was quite out of his depth travelling through Tibet,
frequently erupting into childish tantrums. The poor youth

was also totally lacking in charm and uncompromisingly ugly.

Robert was in the middle of another wrangle about transport. The plan was for most of the support team to come on the trek to Base Camp, then leave for home (only Mimi and Joe were staying with us during the climb). They would need transport back from the roadhead at Kharta and the CMA were trying their old ploy of insisting that the only vehicles available would be in Lhasa, hundreds of miles away and, surprise, surprise, we would have to pay their exorbitant mileage rate for empty vehicles all the way from Lhasa. Robert insisted that there were vehicles available much closer, here in Shekar.

Robert: But you've just arranged a truck from here for tomorrow.

Shi: Not possible.

Robert: But you've done it – today – you've just proved it *is* possible!

(At this point Shi conferred in Mandarin with his superior, Yang, then returned to the fray.)

Shi: You see – to get truck from Shekar causes problems with local government . . . contradictions . . . if we get truck from here again we will have much arguing.

Robert: But you're meant to be saving us money. If you bring a truck all the way from Lhasa it costs us thousands of yuan. I'd rather have you arguing than us spending lots of extra money.

Sino–American relations never really improved. Unlike Pasang and Norbu, neither of the Chinese officials naturally spoke any Tibetan, so they would be no use for negotiating with yak herders. This limitation, coupled with Shi's manifest incompetence on rough ground, had already convinced Robert that they should not come to Base Camp, and after leaving Kharta we would not see them again till the end of the expedition.

In the afternoon I climbed up a hill opposite Shekar. I needed some exercise and climbing to about 4,850 metres would be good acclimatization. I also wanted to see Everest again. The distant cauldron of the Kangshung basin was still filled with cloud, while the northern side was mainly clear and I could make out the long, almost horizontal, upper part of the North-East Ridge where Mallory and Irvine had disappeared in 1924, on the third expedition to the mountain. Since then there had been another fifteen British expeditions to Everest. Only three of them had put people on the summit.*

The odds on success were not high, and I had to keep reminding myself how much luck there was in this game. We did not even know yet whether we would find a feasible route for our small team. And, even if Robert's plan did work and we climbed successfully to the South Col, our arrival there would have to coincide with reasonable weather if we were to continue to the summit. And even if all those factors were right, we still had to discover whether or not we were capable of that final climb without oxygen. As I had told Ed, I believed that I could do it: to succeed on Everest you have to believe that you are capable of it and you have to want very much to get to the top. But also I had to be prepared for the disappointment of failure through no fault of our own.

At least we had time on our side. It was now 5 March. The next day we would drive to Kharta and, if the yaks were ready for our baggage, we would leave the following day on the five-day walk-in to Base Camp. That would give us over two and a half months to play with before the probable arrival of the Monsoon at the end of May. If we were efficient on the face, we should be ready and acclimatized to start making summit bids from mid-April. Surely between then and the end of May we would get a lucky break?

Mr Shi's problematical truck materialized in the morning and we left for Kharta. We already had one truck full of baggage, now the surplus was piled up in the second, to pad the wooden floor. Even by Himalayan standards it was a

*Ed Hillary and Tenzing Norgay by the South Col on the first ascent in 1953: Doug Scott, Dougal Haston, Peter Boardman, Pertemba and probably Mick Burke, in 1975 by the South-West Face; Bronco Lane and Brummie Stokes by the South Col in 1976. (Chris Bonington climbed Everest with a Norwegian expedition.)

violent frightening drive, with billows of thick dust pouring in through the back, as we careered down from the 5,200-metre Pang La towards another tributary of the Arun. We stopped for lunch at a dusty hamlet, then headed east, encircling Everest, as we bounced precariously along the bank of a spectacular gorge. The driver took the bumps faster all the time, each jolt sending us flying up in the air. He was drinking beer at quite a rate, and every few miles another empty bottle would fly out of the cab. When he stopped for about the fifth time to relieve himself, Paul reprimanded him: 'Stop drinking. Too much pissing. Too dangerous.'

In the afternoon we headed south again, now following the main Phung Chu, or Arun river. The Wild West desert landscape was softened by a scattering of juniper trees, and the villages we passed had plantations of willow. But on the willows and other deciduous trees there was still no hint of leaves. When we reached the government compound at Kharta a bleak wind was blowing up the valley and the hills above were white under glowering black clouds.

The local government official showed us a room to use for the night. We unpacked the kitchen equipment and some food, and Pasang started cooking his first meal for the expedition. He did an excellent job with a limited selection of vegetables and seasoning and the atmosphere in that small candlelit room was altogether more friendly than in the great dining hall at Shekar.

Kharta is not a single village. It is a whole area of hamlets of which Kharta Shika, where we were now staying, is the administrative centre. It was here that the leader of the 1921 reconnaissance, Lt.–Col. C. K. Howard-Bury, had made his base for exploring the eastern side of Everest. The hamlet lies on a shelf above the Arun river. It is a dry spot but only a mile downstream rain frequently creeps up from Nepal to nurture the birch and other trees which cluster thickly round the entrance to the Arun gorge. From Kharta, at 3,650 metres above sea level, the river cuts straight through the Himalayan range, plunging to 2,850 metres in only twenty miles. The gorge is cloaked in dense semi-tropical forest and is almost impenetrable, but our route would take us away from the gorge, to the east, up the tributary Kharta Chu. (*Chu* is the Tibetan for river or river valley.)

We hoped to start our journey up the Kharta Chu early in the morning but, in spite of Norbu and Psang's Tibetan diplomacy, it took most of the day to organize transport.

Monday – March 7th
 Beautiful morning: frosted grass, wispy silhouettes of pollard-ed willows, dark figures against frost, smoke rising from village, horses feeding and white mountains behind.
 Breakfast: Wendy washing up. Paul comments: 'Wendy, you could make a really good wife for some Sherpa.'
 Yaks started to trickle in at eleven. Eventually sixty filled the compound. Sandy, in red suit, mirror glasses and pith helmet, directed distribution of loads, inventory in one hand, pointing pen in the other. Incvitably the CMA's promise of 60kg per yak was wrong, and all the loads had to be reorganized. The last set of yaks left at 3.30 p.m.
 Meanwhile we had an orgy of mutual staring with the entire population of the village.
 Afternoon walk: two flirtatious teenage girls accompanied me and Sandy. Knitting socks as they walked along.

We had been walking for less than an hour when everyone stopped. The yaks munched at the dead winter grass beside the river, while all the men, women and children of the caravan sat in groups making tea and drinking the inevitable chang and rakshi. Chang is a milky coloured strong beer, rakshi is the clear distillation thereof. Tibetans are renowned for their casual attitude to work and there was a gentle holiday atmosphere as they all sat around in the sun, chattering and laughing. The two girls were still giggling and pointing at me and Sandy and putting on their most charming Tibetan smiles for our cameras. The last mountaineering expedition to visit the Kharta valley had been the American one in 1983 and there cannot have been more than two or three foreign trekking groups since then, so we were something of a novelty.

After the obligatory chang stop we continued perhaps one more mile before stopping to camp beside the river. With Pasang's help we managed to organize the rabble into putting all the loads into one neat pile, before they left with their yaks. They had to return to their homes to collect food and equipment for the four-day journey over the Langma La, the high pass we had to cross to reach the Kangshung Face, but they assured us that they would be back the next morning and ready to start at nine sharp.

Tuesday morning was as sunny as Monday. If this weather held we might have no problems getting over the 5,500-metre Langma La. Robert Dorival had started opening some of our blue plastic barrels of imported food and I noted in my diary: 'Breakfast: pancakes, stewed apple, jam and semi-liquid margarine, which like most things from America is squeezed out of a plastic bottle.'

The yaks were late, in the best Tibetan tradition, but I was happy to adopt the Tibetans' indolent way of life. The weather was fine and I enjoyed the leisurely morning, sitting in the sun and watching the yaks being loaded. They are very powerful animals and one of them gave a good demonstration of that power. She was tethered by her nose to two large duffel bags, weighing about a hundredweight in total. For some reason she was feeling restless and started moving backwards. The plaited hair rope stretched and the wooden nose ring pulled tighter and tighter, pulling the yak's nostrils further and further out of shape. Her eyes, normally dark and beautiful showed angry whites, her thick, powerful neck was straining and suddenly, with a final tug, she shot off backwards, yanking the two duffel bags through the air and trampling on more baggage behind.

She was calmed down, re-tethered and eventually her turn came to be loaded. She tossed her head angrily and the two boys had to use all their cunning to avoid her elegant dangerous horns, as they strapped two heavy barrels to the beast's back. Loading is always a tedious business and it took to midday, but once loaded, the yaks seemed content to amble along the chosen route, a picture of benign docility.

Ed and I strolled along beside them, bringing up the rear of our rambling caravan. After an hour we caught up with Norbu, Sandy and Robert Dorival. Norbu was talking urgently with an old man. Perhaps there was an obscure local dialect of Tibetan, because Norbu was having some difficulty understanding, but eventually he understood and explained to us that the old man, Tashi (the third Tashi we had met this week), claimed to be a relative of Norbu's father, the famous Tenzing Norgay or 'Sherpa Tenzing'.

'Norgay' means 'fortunate one'. Tenzing chose the name because his intense ambition to climb Everest – an ambition then not at all characteristic of his mountain people – eventually in 1953 brought him not only lasting satisfaction, but also fame and riches, enabling him later to send all his sons to the famous St Paul's public school in Darjeeling, followed by American universities. When he died in 1986 he knew that Norbu and his other sons and daughters would never have to climb mountains to earn a living.

Ed, Sandy, Robert and I now accompanied Norbu, as the old man Tashi, limping as fast as he could on arthritic legs, led the way through the boulder-strewn fields to a small cluster of stone houses. Word was getting around that Tenzing's son was here, and about thirty men, women and children chattered and stared as Norbu was shown round the hamlet of Mojun. Nearly everyone claimed connections with Sherpa Tenzing and it was very moving for the rest of us to witness Norbu, this sophisticated man of the West, meeting peasants who claimed to be his relatives. Norbu's face has the typical Mongolian features of his people, but his skin is quite pale and smooth, and he is much taller than most Tibetans. So here he was, tall and dignified, cleanly dressed in America's smartest outdoor clothing, talking with men who still wore pigtails and had probably never heard of America.

Ed was furiously recording the meeting on film, to keep a record of this historic moment. The beautiful filthy children in their dark woollen tunics were enchanted by the brilliant red and orange of the discarded Kodak boxes, and there was a mad scramble every time Ed finished a roll of film.

Tashi took us to lunch at his house. Wooden steps led up to a veranda on the first floor, where juniper and cotoneaster firewood was piled up either side of the doorway. Inside it was very dark and the wooden ceiling of the kitchen was shiny black with the smoke of centuries, although most of the smoke from the central cooking fire did escape, illuminated in a shaft of blue light from a hole in the roof. Norbu spoke with Tashi, while Tashi's teenage son fetched bowls, and his second wife, who was suckling a baby, prepared tea. Tibetans have been known to drink over a hundred cups a day. Even when they are travelling, frequent tea stops are *de rigueur* and in 1921 Howard-Bury noted that distances in the Kharta valley were measured in cups of tea. (He estimated that three cups of tea equalled only five miles!) For an Englishman, I am a disappointing imbiber and when it is salty Tibetan tea, with lumps of yak butter floating in it, I find it particularly hard to get enthusiastic. I far preferred the cool astringency of the chang and Tashi kept on refilling my wooden bowl until, by the time we left, I felt pleasantly inebriated.

Tashi accompanied us a short way up the valley, delaying the moment when he had to part with Norbu. When the time came to say goodbye, he clasped Norbu's hands firmly and there were tears in his eyes.

About three miles beyond Mojun, the Kharta valley is almost blocked by two high moraine ridges, remnants of a glacier that once flowed from the left. Our route to the Langma La led up the side valley once carved by this glacier. The yak herders had stuck to their usual leisurely progress that day, and the actual walking only totalled two hours. Nevertheless, after the moving encounter with Norbu's friends we were well disposed towards all things Tibetan, even indolent yak herders, and the campsite, nestled in a meadow between the two old moraines, was so idyllic that no one complained about our chronically slow pace.

Paul was cajoling, shouting, and laughing with the herders, trying to rationalize the loads in readiness for a quicker getaway in the morning. But it was no good, as I recorded in my diary the next day:

Wednesday – March 9th

Yak herders impossible. They waited till *after* it had started to snow to make a move and didn't get away till after 12 a.m. I was ahead with Paul, Joe and Joe's two 'concubines' – the delightful, giggling, singing girls who carry his delicate camera equipment – one girl's load weighing at least 70lb. On into driving snow and snow underfoot. Paul concerned about the girls – once again his warmhearted nature and thoughtfulness for the locals (tinged with a touch of show) emerged as he insisted:

'These locals can die just like that. I don't want these girls getting exposure. In '85, you know [during a big storm in Nepal], we carried down three Sherpas . . . one survived, two just died – *jinjiput.*' With the assured Nepali accent and inimitable motion of brushing away with the hands, '*Gone – jinjiput.*'

He duly found a good shelter. Meanwhile I had given one of the girls a pair of socks and a ski stick. Then a happy group by the boulder, with a little food and a fire and the girls wearing our duvet jackets.

Paul and I played at some climbing problems on the boulder, then walked a little higher up the valley, prospecting the route, but our efforts to establish an initiative were in vain. Miklos appeared with the news that everyone had halted further back, so we escorted the girls down to the spot where their spineless friends had stopped, only an hour above the previous campsite. Pasang and Norbu had spent the whole day interpreting for an increasingly irate Robert, trying to cajole the Tibetans into action. Now, in the evening, as we stood around in the snow drinking tea, the only thing to do was laugh about it. Paul and I made a joke of berating the pathetic men and pointing to the two girls who had actually done some work. Paul shouted, 'Look!' making a huge bicep and pointing to the girls, then to the men and deflating it. The men laughed unashamedly and Paul concluded, 'I guess they don't know about Rambo philosophy.'

We managed three hours on Thursday, arriving hot and headachy in a bowl below a steep rise. We were now at about 4,900 metres (over 16,000 feet) and all the sahibs were feeling the altitude. In 1921 Howard-Bury had complained at the slowness of his men, stopping here on the first day. Mallory's party, travelling a few days ahead, had climbed a little further on their first day. We, in 1988, had taken three days to reach this spot and now the Tibetans announced that they could take their yaks no further. The weather had been beautiful that day, but they had been forced to lead their animals through snow. Beyond the steep rise, they said, there would be much deeper snow lying above boulders – ankle-snapping terrain for their precious beasts; and there was still a long climb to the pass.

Each yak had been carrying two duffels or barrels, and that afternoon we asked the herders to collect all the loads into one pile. (I had already had some clothes stolen and we had to watch the loads carefully to try and limit thefts.) Then Robert announced that as the yaks could go no further there were jobs on offer for any people who wanted to come and help shift one hundred and twenty porter-loads across the Langma La. The herders would camp here that night, then descend with their yaks in the morning and, we hoped, return with one hundred and twenty able-bodied people.

The yaks duly set off the next day, romping back down with their owners in pursuit. We remained at Lhatse – 'the place below the pass'. The sun shone for a while, but by evening it was snowing again. That night, lying in the tent listening to the melancholic strains of Mahler's Ninth Symphony on my headphones, I thought of my chance meeting with Rosie in London, a year and a half earlier. Joe, whose tent I was sharing, was also thinking of home and later, as he offered me a swig from his secret bottle of Cointreau, he talked about his wife, Ellen, and his baby daughter, Claire, ten thousand miles away in Connecticut. Then he reminisced about his days in California when he left the Navy to study photography, inspired by the unsurpassed Yosemite landscapes of his friend and guru, Ansel Adams.

It was still dark when we were woken by women's shouts on Saturday morning. By dawn there were about fifty people gathered by our campsite at Lhatse and as we ate breakfast the crowd swelled. Soon the promised hundred and twenty men, women and children were crowding round, noisily defying our attempts at an ordered distribution of loads. Joe, normally so calm, swore hysterically at them. Norbu, forced into the impossible position of negotiator, looked increasingly gloomy. Inevitably, the re-arranged yak loads were not all equal in weight, so the men gave all the heaviest loads to the women.

It was a grey gloomy morning; nevertheless, Sandy and I set off in the lead, sincerely hoping that the first group of twenty was about to follow. We waited at the top of the steep rise. After an hour it started to snow again and when I looked back down to Lhatse, I saw no one had left the campsite. It looked as though no porters were going to the Langma La today. However, curiosity and boredom compelled us to continue on our own. After an hour of steep slithering on snow-smothered boulders we realized that the pass was a great deal further than any of us had thought. We could see now why the people had refused to take their yaks any farther. We also had to concede that conditions were not safe for human portering, for the Tibetans' primitive tents, meagre blankets and flimsy shoes bore no comparison to our sophisticated equipment.

We descended in vicious, driving snow to Lhatse where we were greeted by loud music and the spectacle of our doctor Mimi dancing with a very drunk Tibetan. Mimi is a talented dancer and the crowd loved it, but we were loving them less every day. On Sunday it was again cloudy, with intermittent snow. The porters were infuriating everyone by crowding round our breakfast and Paul was gesticulating with shouts of 'Go! Go away!', eventually throwing up his arms in mock despair and shouting, 'I give up, I can't direct this crowd. CUT!' Things improved after he enclosed our area with a rope, muttering promises to bring an electric porter fence next time.

It started to snow again. The porters were running out of food, firewood and chang, and showed no sign of starting for the pass, so Robert instructed Mimi's dancing partner, Jirmi the shop steward, to take everyone back home and return when the weather improved. Gloom pervaded our camp. It was particularly hard on the support team, for they had put so much into the expedition yet their promised trek had got virtually nowhere and now they were almost due to leave for home. They had not even seen the Kangshung Face.

Snow fell all night and it was still falling in the morning when I was woken by the sound of shovelling outside the tent and Robert's obstinately cheerful voice: 'Day Two of the "light spring storm". I'm glad I grew up in Colorado. My parents used to send me out to play in this sort of stuff. It's not a "nightmare situation" – it's a "winter wonderland".'

Breakfast was a miserable business, standing in shin-deep snow, with more coming from above, huge soggy flakes falling onto our pancakes and maple syrup.

It was time for the support party to leave. We had a poignant parting ceremony in the falling snow. Wendy directed and Joe recorded everything on Kodachrome, as Miklos presented the United Nations flag destined for the summit and Norbu handed over the Explorers' Club flag and replicas of the trinkets his father had left on the summit thirty-five years earlier.

We helped the others down with all their heavy luggage as far as the previous campsite, breaking trail through knee-deep snow. Luckily the pre-arranged porters appeared to escort the support team the rest of the way down to the first village. The weather, with its usual finely timed sense of irony, staged a dramatic clearing. The sun broke gloriously through shifting clouds, bringing light and colour and form to the snowscape, and we parted on an afternoon of rare beauty. The others disappeared over the snowy horizon, as if re-enacting a scene from *Dr Zhivago* and, as we climbed back up to Lhatse in the deepening twilight, we knew that it would probably be another three months before we saw them again.

4
Langma La

SPRING was slow coming. Since the beginning of February storm after storm had been dumping new snow on the Himalaya and that pattern was to continue right through March. In the end we had to wait fifteen days at Lhatse before we could take porters across the Langma La.

The delays were frustrating because we had deliberately come early to have the maximum time possible at Base Camp before the Monsoon arrived. While we were stuck at Lhatse, my friends on the British Services Expedition had driven up the Chinese road to the Rongbuk Base Camp. They and the Asian climbers would already be getting to work on the northern side of the mountain. On the Nepalese side, with no 5,500-metre pass to cross, the other part of the Asian expedition and the Australian Bi-centennial Expedition would be pushing a route up the Khumbu Icefall.

It was annoying, but afterwards we realized that in fact two weeks of hanging around at nearly 5,000 metres, with occasional forays to slightly higher altitudes, had been a perfect opportunity to acclimatize while the Kangshung Face waiting for us was still out of condition. It was also a time to get to know each other better. I was enjoying my time with the Americans and my only real grouse was the offensive ghetto blaster. Even I had recently succumbed to the private indulgence of the Walkman, but this was the first time since leaving school that I had been exposed at length to *other people's* choices, and it seemed a travesty to shatter the sublime silence of the mountains with rock music that was either

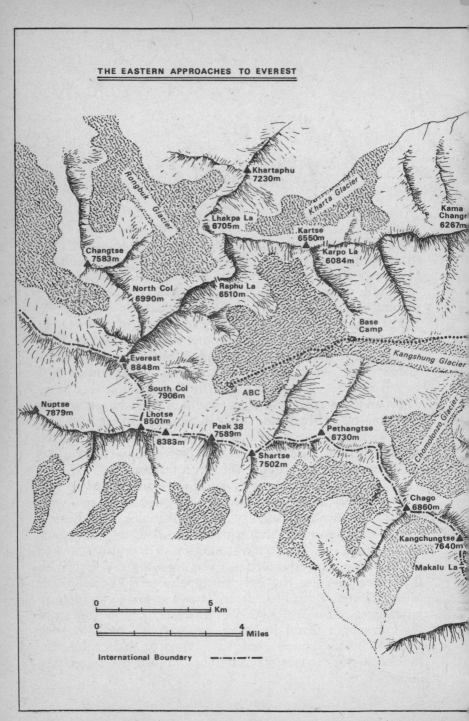

THE EASTERN APPROACHES TO EVEREST

Rongbuk Glacier

Khartaphu
7230m

Kharta Glacier

Lhakpa La
6705m

Kartse
6550m

Kama Changr
6267m

Changtse
7583m

Karpo La
6084m

North Col
6990m

Raphu La
6510m

Base
Camp

Everest
8848m

Kangshung Glacier

South Col
7906m

ABC

Nuptse
7879m

Lhotse
8501m

8383m

Peak 38
7589m

Pethangtse
6730m

Chomolonzo Glacier

Shartse
7502m

Chago
6860m

Kangchungtse
7640m

Makalu La

0   5 Km

0   4 Miles

International Boundary ─ · ─ · ─ · ─

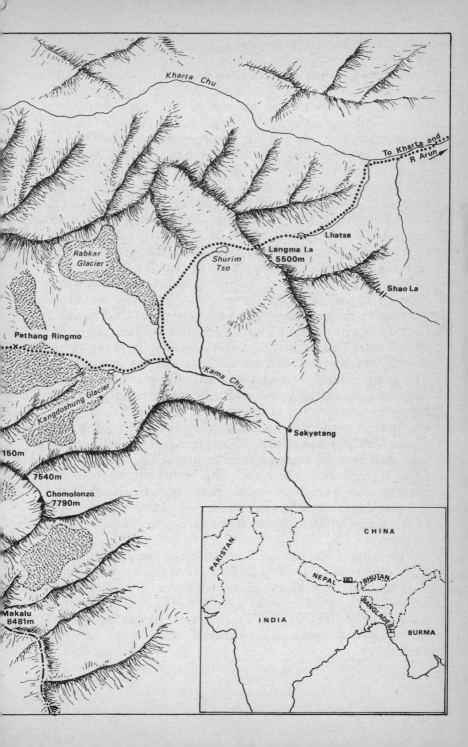

aggressively strident or as bland as a Chinese steamed dough-
nut. However, it was not an issue worth fussing about and I
confined my complaints mainly to the diary, consoling
myself with the thought that this forcible exposure to late-
twentieth-century culture must be very character-building.

The sun shone brightly all that day, consolidating the
snow, so that the following day the six sahibs could at last
climb up to the Langma La. It took about four hours on this
first recce. It was a beautiful day with wonderful views out to
the north-east, to the unknown peaks of the Gyankar range
and, later, a brief glimpse through a cleft to the distant mass
of Kangchenjunga. I realized with satisfaction that I had now
seen all the world's fourteen 8,000-metre peaks.

We took turns to lead, stamping out a really firm trail
through the snow in the hope that the porters would be
coming up the next day. The pass was the most dramatic I
have ever seen. Joe and Mimi were ahead of me, bright red
and powder blue against the snow, heading up to the gap in
the ridge, where prayer flags on canes stood against the sky
like some giant flower arrangement. Only a distant fluted
ridge of Chomolonzo, just visible beyond the gap, hinted at
the revelation to come as one stepped up onto the pass to be
confronted, suddenly, with a vast confusion of peaks,
glaciers, valleys and clouds. Then the visual confusion resol-
ved itself into the massive architecture of Chomolonzo and
Makalu, high above the Kama Chu on the left; on the right,
in front of us, a tangle of smaller peaks and glaciers which the
pre-war expeditions had explored; and, set back at the head
of the Kama valley eighteen miles away, the brooding mass
of Everest.

The summit was hidden in cloud, more cloud boiled about
the base and only the middle portion of the icy Kangshung
Face was visible, with occasional glimpses of the South Col
as the clouds parted between Everest and Lhotse. Even at this
distance we could see that the face of Lhotse, just to the left of
our proposed route, was streaked black from constant
avalanches.

It was a beautiful and awe-inspiring sight which left everyone subdued, particularly Paul. As he explained later, 'I was there for half an hour before you guys, watching it . . .' He paused to remember the vacuous pseudo-philosophers one meets so often in the mountains, and continued with heavy irony: 'It was kind of a personal experience.'

I think we were all quite frightened by our first sight of the Kangshung Face. However, the sense of menace came more from the oppressive afternoon clouds than the mountain itself, and we were pleased to have reached the 5,500-metre pass at last. Unfortunately, although the trail was now pre-pared and the weather was perfect, no porters appeared that evening. The next day the weather remained fine, but there were still no porters, so we treated ourselves to a day of rock climbing on the cliffs above camp. I loved it – the warmth of the sun-baked granite, the luminous yellow and orange lichens, the fun of puzzling out delicate moves . . . it did not get us any closer to Base Camp but it was very enjoyable.

That afternoon the Coleman Sheik kitchen tent arrived – all twenty-seven kilos of it – carried up by Phuti, the elder of Joe's two 'concubines'. The tent had finally reached Kharta from New York and the departing support team had sent it up with the girl. She was an attractive twenty-two-year-old and, despite the slightly waddling gait forced on all the women by their stiff bulky clothes, she seemed to have a dignity and serenity that most of the others lacked and her smile was utterly charming. Now we discovered from Sandy's note that her family also claimed connection with Tenzing Norgay. She was accompanied by her young pig-tailed brother, Pinzo, a strong handsome boy of about thir-teen, who also had more poise than most of the porters. Perhaps we were reading too much into it, but the family really did seem to have special qualities that put them above most of the Kharta rabble.

Phuti told us that the mob would be back up the next day.

Friday – March 18th
Five weeks since leaving England. Weather closing in again, just as everything was ready to go, trail cleared to pass, loads

repacked to even weights, porters trickling back to Lhatse . . .
Heavy snowfall.

Saturday – March 19th
    Would be nice to be having breakfast in my room with Rosie,
listening to *Record Review*. It snowed all night – with wind.
Nepal Radio announced 120 mph winds in Kathmandu. Over
100 people killed in avalanche in Kashmir. Is this a repeat of the
big autumn storm?
    Continued to snow all day. Porters went back down again.

Sunday – March 20th
    After another night of wind and snow, it started to clear a
little. Erected the vast Coleman Sheik tent, so at last we can eat
meals in comfort, sitting upright.
    Afternoon – Robert, Paul and I went back up towards Langma
La, breaking trail through thigh-deep heavy snow to far side of
frozen lake. Back to excellent dinner of pasta with tomato-olive-
bean-mushroom-garlic-sauce and cheesecake.
    A clear night at last.

Monday – March 21st
    Ed's birthday. The cycle repeats itself – back to sunshine and
washing day. Amazed at my idleness, relying on Pasang and
Kasang to do all the work.

    Before Phuti brought up the magnificent Sheik palace we
had acquired in Kharta an ancient bell tent, made in Britain
and probably dating from one of the pre-war expeditions, for
Pasang to use as a kitchen. The rental fee was one dollar a day
and included the hire of a cookboy. We were a bit dubious
about the gangly gormless youth, Kasang, but apparently he
came with the tent. Pasang wanted a helper and agreed to
take the boy on trial. Now Kasang was slowly grasping the
bewildering complexities of Anglo–American eating habits.
He was also learning a few words of English and the morning
tea was always delivered with a cheerful 'Goomornu'.
    That evening we celebrated Ed's birthday with Mexican
food and most of a bottle of Glenlivet. He had a great
package of presents to unwrap, given to him by his girlfriend
Randa before he left. There were tapes, books and a pair of

shorts, presumably for sunbathing at Base Camp; but when Ed peeped inside one wrapping and looked extremely baffled, then turned pink, it was obvious that this must be a very special present – some poignant reminder of a less austere life at home. It was a pale green silk négligé with delicate lace edging. She never said whether she intended him to wear it to the summit.

The cycle was repeating itself. On Tuesday we broke trail yet again to the pass. At least we were getting very fit and my pulse in the morning was a respectable 56. This time we left much earlier and climbed much faster, reaching the pass early enough for a reasonably cloudless view. We examined the Kangshung Face through Robert's × 48 telescope, but most of our difficult lower buttress was still hidden behind an intervening ridge.

The next morning Ed, Joe and I went up again, leaving in the dark, racing up in one and a half hours and arriving on the pass for a biting cold photographic session at sunrise. I was glad to see that, even after racing back down to Lhatse and eating a large breakfast, my pulse was still only 72. Mimi had been doing check-ups on all of us to see that we were maintaining the comparatively low blood pressures and pulses necessary to operate at extreme altitude. Robert Dorival and Ed had done an excellent job in the Colorado supermarket, buying up a balanced and varied diet, appetizing enough to ensure that everyone ate well, and Robert Anderson had supplemented the food with a bewildering array of vitamin pills.

One day a man arrived at Lhatse with a Federal Express package which had been sent safely all the way from New York to the remote village of Kharta. It contained notification of $30,000 sponsorship by Burroughs Wellcome with samples of Actifed, a new anti-congestant drug to test. We expected to suffer from coughs and blocked noses high on the mountain. A blocked nose at night forces one to breathe cold dry air straight through the mouth, irritating the throat, and accounts of Everest expeditions over the last sixty-seven years had been packed with chronic throat complaints. Many a climber had been defeated by a racking cough and anything that reduced wear and tear on the larynx would be useful.

Mimi, our doctor, took quite a puritanical line on drugs whereas Robert, who had written several advertising campaigns for drug companies, was intrigued by their products and eager to try everything going. He was considering using Adalat, a vasodilatory drug which artificially lowers blood pressure. The Swiss climber, Troillet, had used it to try and enhance his performance during the brilliant two-day ascent of Everest in 1986. Robert was, in fact, never to use the drug on the mountain and I think that all of us were quite wary of tampering with the vascular system in this way. Dilating peripheral blood vessels can be dangerous in situations of extreme cold and exhaustion, when one is liable to hypothermia. But apart from safety considerations there was also the ethical question: if Adalat really does enhance one's performance, doesn't it detract from the achievement of climbing without supplementary oxygen? Because mountaineering is, thank God, not an organized Olympic sport, there are no regulations about the use of drugs, so the choice is up to the individual. I did not want to try Adalat and I also had no intention of using the well known acclimatizing drug, Diamox, although I would carry some as an emergency diuretic treatment for pulmonary or cerebral oedema. I have always believed that the only way to climb big mountains is to take things very slowly at first, letting the body do its own acclimatizing. At Lhatse we were being given the perfect opportunity to do just that, undergoing complex chemical changes and gradually building up haemoglobin levels in the blood, so that we could extract the maximum oxygen possible from the low-pressure air drawn into our lungs.

The weather held and that afternoon, for the third time, the porters started to return. On Thursday morning eighty porters assembled. Robert and Paul stayed behind to wait for the stragglers, while the rest of us set out, at last, to cross the Langma La.

*

After we crossed the Langma La our troubles were not over. There were more delays and disputes, caused by another storm and the procrastinations of our porters who, as a group, apparently had no trace of initiative or motivation nor any concept of what constitutes a day's work. However, we had to remember that we were here under the auspices of a foreign colonizing power, a situation not likely to endear us to the Tibetans. There was a strong sense in Kharta of a people who had lost their leadership and sense of direction after the Chinese invasion and ruthless destruction of the monasteries. As if to reinforce this, Angchu, the charming man who had taken over from the drunken Jirmi as shop steward, pointed out to us the site of a destroyed monastery.

It was the second afternoon. The previous day we had crossed the pass and now we were on our way down into the Kama Chu, enjoying one of the most beautiful day's mountain walking I have ever experienced. Ed and I had taken the lead with Pasang and Angchu, breaking trail past the frozen Shurim Tso lake, and on across huge snowfields on a radiant morning, with the summits of Lhotse and Everest clear in the blue sky ahead. After a picnic lunch we had continued across huge meadows of winter-flattened flowers, heading down towards the Rabkar Glacier which gouged its way into the Kama Chu. Now we were resting on a shelf high above the glacier.

Angchu pointed to a distant meadow beyond the glacier, explaining that there had once been a monastery there. It had only been a tiny settlement inhabited by a handful of monks, and had not equalled the splendours of the bigger monasteries of the Kharta valley; nevertheless the Chinese had come right up here, to this remote beautiful valley, to destroy it.

We enjoyed a peaceful cigarette in the sun, then the rabble caught up. It was like a scene from a Western as they appeared, silhouetted on the skyline ninety metres above us. Then with a great shriek all eighty men, women and children, oblivious of their heavy loads, came charging down the hillside. They arrived happy and laughing and expecting to stop for the night, but for once we were determined to get our way, so Ed and I ignored their surprised complaints and carried straight on. It was lovely walking, on springy turf dotted with azalea bushes along the crest of an ancient moraine. Then just above the junction of this valley, the Rabkar Chu, with the Kama Chu, we descended steeply to the river bed.

The porters, thank God, did follow us and everyone camped by the river. It was a lovely spot, nestled in a thicket of bushes. The rhododendrons would not flower for several weeks yet, but there were already the first silky pussy willows of spring. Once again it was a fine evening. Pasang kept the Thermos constantly filled with tea, while Ed and I sat by a fire drying boots. At dusk Mimi and Joe arrived, then Paul and Robert, who had brought the last batch of porters over and had come all the way from Lhatse in one day.

Of course it was all too good to last and in the morning a veil of high cirrus haloed the sun with a mother-of-pearl shimmer of violet, green and bronze. It was beautiful but ominous and the porters knew exactly what was going on. They delayed departure till 11 a.m. and, sure enough, by midday it was snowing, we had only travelled one and a half hours and we were not going to travel any further.

This time it was a miserable campsite and it snowed for over thirty-six hours. We were all longing just to get to Base Camp and settle in. When the snow stopped there was a huge dispute. It was the usual scene: the women preparing quietly to get on with the day's work while the younger boys laughed and watched the older men, drunk from chang and rakshi, shouting and protesting for bad weather money. Robert refused to pay any money to any porter until he reached Base Camp, explaining yet again that if they had not procrastinated so much, they never would have been caught out in bad weather. Pasang shook his head in disbelief: in comparison to his industrious Sherpa people, this lot were pathetic. Robert finally lost his cool and rushed at the men with a blood-curdling shout, thrashing the air with a ski stick. Luckily he is very tall and they were very small so they gave up shouting at Robert and started shouting at each other instead.

I think it was about 1 p.m. when we finally left on the day's one and a half hour march, a delightful stroll with a sudden brilliant view of the Kangshung Face as we rounded a corner. By evening everyone was happy and the porters were an obliging tourist picture of ethnic Tibetan life.

Monday – March 28th
Evening camp. Scent of juniper and yak-dung fires. Tents perched on dry hillocks of grass and figures with firewood bundles silhouetted against lambent mountains. Clouds swirling round crazy pinnacles of Lhotse's summits with Scottish grass-and-snow streaks in valley foreground. Magical moment as sun disappeared – a huge white globe sinking behind South Col, half-obscured by swirling diaphanous clouds.

We were camping at Pethang Ringmo, a meadow where the people of Kharta had brought their yaks to graze every summer for centuries. It was here that Mallory and Bullock had made their base for reconnoitring the East Face in 1921. We were almost there and on Tuesday the face grew steadily closer, like a great wall blocking the head of the valley. We walked a few miles further and arrived in the afternoon at the huge windswept meadow above the glacier that was to be our Base Camp. Robert, Pasang and Angchu sat inside a porter fence, distributing wages to the group leaders and soon most of the rabble had departed for home, leaving just twenty volunteers who wanted to earn a little more carrying loads to Advance Base.

The thirty-mile approach was finally over and we had arrived, twenty-three days after leaving Kharta.

When I was invited to join Everest–88, one of the things that attracted me most was the rare opportunity to visit the Kama valley which had so delighted George Mallory. Now that we had finally arrived I was not disappointed. We had glimpsed

the luxuriant forested gorge curving south-eastward towards
the Arun, as we entered the valley from the Rabkar Chu,
but we had turned right, up and away from the forest,
following the Kama Chu to its source in the Kangshung
Glacier. Now our Base Camp was about ten miles up the
glacier.

Like all the best base camps, ours was in an ablation valley,
the fertile hollow lying between the crest of the glacier moraine and the mountainside. At about 5,100 metres, we were
far higher than Mont Blanc, but at this more southern lati-
tude plants can survive up to about 5,500 metres. The moraine hid the glacier from sight, so that from our kitchen we
looked straight across the grassy meadow to the wall of
mountains on the far side of the glacier.

Starting from the left was Chomolonzo, nearly 8,000
metres high, with three massive granite towers; set back to
the right, we could see the summit of Makalu, fifth highest
mountain in the world, remote in the sky and half obscured
by the nearer, lower summit of Makalu II or Kangchungtse.
The frontier ridge between Tibet and Nepal continues to the
right to Pethangtse. It is only 6,730 metres but from our
viewpoint it looked magnificent, an archetypal Matterhorn
pyramid striped with coloured bands of rock. To the right of
Pethangtse, the ridge curves up to the summits of Shartse and
Peak 38, which still bears its old British survey number, then
continues up in another great sweep to Lhotse, the four-
summited 'South Peak' of Everest, given its Tibetan name by
the 1921 expedition. At this point the frontier ridge curves
round, enclosing the cauldron at the head of the Kangshung
Glacier. The North-East Wall of Lhotse is over 3,000 metres
of rock and ice capped by the summits of Lhotse Shar, the
two Lhotse Middle spikes and Lhotse, the main peak, fourth
highest in the world. From here the ridge drops to the wide
gap of the South Col, before rising 850 metres to the summit
of Everest. This is the South-East Ridge, the 1953 route by
which we hoped to complete our ascent. To the right of the
summit was the immense, sprawling North-East Ridge,
taking three miles to drop 2,500 metres to the Raphu La.

This fantastic cirque of peaks was to be our home for the next two months. Base Camp was about five miles from the foot of Everest and we still could not see the lower part of our proposed route, so on the first morning Robert and Ed set off with Kasang to take a closer look and find a good site for Advance Base, as close to the face as possible.

The rest of us worked hard at Base Camp. Pasang supervised some of the Tibetans building a stone kitchen dresser inside the main chamber of the Sheik tent. The two end chambers served as dining room, medical room and dark room for Joe. Kasang's mother had sold us three lengths of stout timber and Joe and I now used these and tarpaulins to construct a large porch extension to the kitchen. The wind blew almost constantly up the valley and we were determined to have a really secure restful base. Paul press-ganged some more Tibetans into helping with the lavatory. Their brawn coupled with Paul's engineering skill produced a magnificent rock throne with an inspiring view out to Pethangtse.

There were over a hundred loads to unpack and sort: personal clothing to claim, ropes, pitons, tents and snow shovels to be sorted into priority loads for Advance Base, cooking equipment for Advance Base, lightweight stoves for the higher camps and food – sixty barrels of food to be rationalized – cereals, pasta, seasonings, vegetables, dried fruit, biscuit (no – crackers), chocolate (sorry – candy), flour and pancake mix, drinks, dairy products, tinned fish, puddings . . . Then we stacked about thirty empty barrels on their sides in the porch, making cupboards for all the categorized supplies. Another eight barrels of food were packed ready for portering to Advance Base.

Evening clouds, drifting up from the Arun, wreathed spookily around the camp as Paul and I packed these last loads. Pasang was busy cooking supper and dusk was falling when the others returned from the glacier.

Wednesday – March 30th
    Evening. Robert and Ed arrived back from their recce. Great to hear that there is a safe A.Base site, clear of the 'Witches'

THE KANGSHUNG WALL

Lhotse Shar
8383m

Lhotse
8501m

Shartse
7502m

Peak 38
7589m

Sou
Co
7906

1988
Buttress

KANGSHUNG

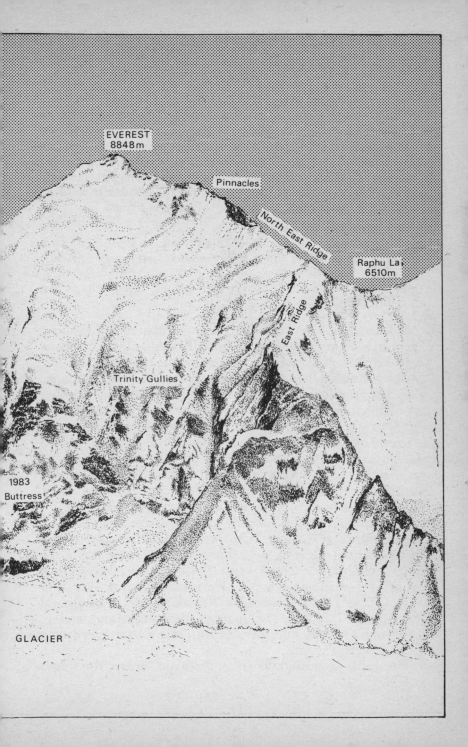

EVEREST
8848m

Pinnacles

North East Ridge

Raphu La
6510m

East Ridge

Trinity Gullies

1983
Buttress

GLACIER

Cauldron' below Lhotse, and a probable route up our buttress. But again, they are so American – 'Yeah, take everything – all the rope, all the screws.' When in doubt, multiply by two, let excess rule the day and always count on the great god of Technology to answer all problems. And they *will* talk about 'specialties': 'I think each person should lead on their specialty.' So Ed shouts, 'That's my pitch!' Paul shouts, 'I'm doing the ice,' as if to say that there is no place on this trip for ordinary mountaineers who just take their turn and lead whatever happens to turn up, whether it be rock, ice, snow, mud, grass or a mixture of all those things.

Thursday – March 31st
  Enough grousing. In spite of cloud and snow I managed to get people out of bed to organize the agreed porter carry to ABC. Wonderful to have twenty loads carried over there for us. None of that eternal humping loads across glacier that is normally such a feature of these trips.

Miklos had given us an aerial photograph of the Kangshung basin and Robert used this to show Paul and me the route to Advance Base. He accompanied us for the first five minutes, walking through the swirling mists to the crest of the moraine. Here Paul and I said goodbye and entered a different world as we plunged down into a barren chaos of boulders and picked our way laboriously over the rubble-strewn ice waves of the glacier. Later that morning I drew ahead of Paul, failed to find the best route and got very cold and tired, struggling up the apparently interminable glacier, crossing hummock after hummock, frequently sinking into soggy snow and twice plunging into hidden pools of icy mush.

I was very relieved eventually to find the marker flag left by Robert and Ed at Advance Base. It was a good enough site on a medial moraine, one of the strips of rubble carried down the centre of the glacier. There was still a lot of winter snow which could be levelled into tent platforms and there was a big pool of meltwater for our cooking and drinking. It was a practical enough site but the surroundings were huge, oppressive, terrifying. For once that abused vogue word was appropriate: it really was awesome.

Damp cloud pressed down on the basin, hiding the ridges

and summits above, and I could see only the bottom thousand metres of the wall encircling the glacier. On the left I could just make out huge detached ice cliffs overhanging the smooth rock walls of Lhotse. On the right was the towering buttress of wildly striated brown, grey and black rock, climbed by the Americans in 1983. Between that improbable route and the Lhotse wall, set back in the corner, was our Buttress. In that grey light the whole cirque looked hostile and menacing and whenever the clouds lifted slightly it was always to reveal more seracs, the great fragmented towers of ice which seemed to hang threateningly over every conceivable line of weakness.

For weeks now we had been building ourselves up for the climb, alternating neurotically between fear and hope, but now I sank gloomily into a new trough of despair, convinced that the whole project really was suicidal. Robert had only told me recently that several leading American climbers had turned down invitations to join the expedition. One of them, John Roskelly, had come out with the 1983 expedition and turned back for home as soon as he saw the face, and he had been equally sceptical about Robert's project.

I was shivering violently by the time Paul arrived. 'I fell in those bloody pools twice,' I told him, 'up to my knees! It looks horrible, doesn't it?'

'"Other men, less wise . . .."' Paul laughed blackly at Mallory's oft-quoted words, then continued, 'I don't know where Robert's route is supposed to go.'

'Well, do you think that's his Scottish Gully up there – the really steep ice runnel, then slanting right. He said we'd slant right above it. It looks lethal to me.'

'Yes, you see the Sickle? You see? That big detached sickle of ice – it's a monster. It'll wipe out the whole gully. All dead! *Jinjiput!*'

The Buttress was about a mile away from us. It was roughly triangular, with the apex crowned by seracs, the fringe of the hanging glacier above. The Sickle was part of this fringe and looked extremely unstable, threatening the gully at the centre of the Buttress. On the right-hand side of

the triangle a further tongue of hanging glacier reached
down, encrusting the crest of a ridge with a series of huge
bulbous ice towers. It too threatened the central face of the
triangle. We had seen it through the telescope from the
Langma La and had christened it the Cauliflower Ridge.

Paul and I were alarmed to discover that the route Robert
and Ed were apparently proposing looked so dangerous. We
stared hard and talked about safer possibilities. Perhaps we
could climb those vertical rock cliffs straight up and onto the
Cauliflower Ridge. Most of the threat seemed to be to the
left, whereas this route would climb straight up. However it
looked extremely hard and, even though Ed had the expertise
to tackle overhanging artificial climbing, it could be desperately slow.

We examined possibilities to the right. Between our Buttress and the 1983 buttress there was a huge depression.
About a thousand metres up it was menaced by a gigantic
band of seracs, which Paul had christened Big Al. Above
that, tier after tier of ice cliffs and unstable snow slopes also
threatened the depression of Big Al Gully. It was the natural
funnel for all avalanches between the two buttresses and any
climber who strayed into it would almost certainly die.
However, it might be possible to sneak up the left-hand wall
of the gully – the right-hand wall of our triangle.

'Yes, I think it might go: zig-zag up those snow terraces on
the toe of the Buttress, then up that rock wall and into the
wide snow gully, right up to those overhangs. Then slanting
up right, right up under the overhangs, it should be high
enough above Big Al Gully to be safe. Also those overhangs
should protect it from anything coming down off the Cauliflower Ridge. Then it looks as though you can climb out left,
coming right up on the top of the Cauliflower Ridge. It
might just be safe.'

The porters arrived and dumped their loads. Now the
clouds were lifting a little, and everything looked slightly less
menacing, reinforcing the new optimism arising from our
rational examination of the face. Nevertheless, we were still
adamant that neither of us had ever been in such an awe-

inspiring place. Now we could see over to the really dangerous area of the face, to the right of the 1983 buttress, and with
perfect timing a huge serac collapsed, sending hundreds of
tons of pulverized ice roaring in a great cloud down to the
Kangshung Glacier. The Tibetans pointed up at the face and
at us and shook their heads disapprovingly, no doubt thinking how presumptuous we were to challenge the incredible
forces of Chomolungma, the Mother Goddess of the Earth.

After my soaking on the way up I was anxious to avoid
hypothermia so set off home at a brisk pace. Back in the Base
Camp dining room everyone talked at once. Paul and I
questioned the sanity of Robert's Scottish Gully until he
understood what we were talking about.

'You mean that really steep ice runnel up the middle?'

'With a funnel slanting out right at the top–'

'God no – that would be suicide – I wouldn't go near that.
No, I mean that gully over on the right –'

'Right on the flank of Big Al Gully?'

'Yes – bottomless, with a rock wall below it.'

'It doesn't look very Scottish to me. But that's great, at
least we're all talking about the same route.'

It was a relief to discover that we had all been thinking
along the same lines and that Robert and Ed were sane after
all.

The remaining twenty porters left for Kharta the next
morning. The previous day they had been very fast across the
glacier, carrying heavy loads and wearing only flimsy
sneakers on their feet. They had been anxious to finish the
job, get their extra money and go home. In a small group,
properly motivated, they could be as efficient as anyone and
by taking twenty loads straight up to Advance Base they had
saved us days of tedious load-carrying, enabling us to profit
from our thorough acclimatization and start immediately on
the far more interesting job of tackling the Buttress.

Angchu, the man who had emerged as the natural leader,
took some messages for Messrs Shi and Yang, our minders,
who were languishing away in Kharta, and promised to
return on 30 April to see how we were getting on. Kasang

stayed. He was still rather confused by our catering arrangements, but Pasang was getting on well with him, needed
some help and would be glad of company while we were all
away at Advance Base. Kasang would also be very useful as a
messenger and porter to keep Advance Base re-supplied.

So now there were just eight of us, isolated in the Kama
Chu. It was a sunny day but still wintry.

Friday – April 1st
    Bitterly cold day at BC. Valley wind blasting up valley from
east. High winds streaming past in opposite direction, with huge
plumes off Makalu, Chomolonzo, Lhotse and Everest. As in the
autumn, Lhotse has the biggest plume, like the smoke from a
giant chimney stack. Last night the Nepal Radio forecast was for
90-knot winds and – 30°C at 9,000 metres. [Everest is 8,848
metres]
    Pujah ceremony in the morning. Pasang built two fine chor-
tens, from which are strung the prayer flags. Yak-dung fire with
juniper added, and rice and Famous Grouse sprinkled.
    Evening. Mimi presided over a Passover ceremony. Shame
that we did not have the usual obligatory four glasses of wine to
kick off with. Talk of Jewish food and customs set me off
reminiscing about Yakum.

Yakum was the kibbutz where I worked in the summer of
1972. Then I hitched up through Turkey, Greece, Bulgaria,
Yugoslavia, Venice, the Alpine passes, and enjoyed my first
alpine climb in the Dauphiné. That was the year of Herrlig-
koffer's attempt on Everest's South-West Face, and the first
Bonington attempt, defeated by screaming winter winds
which actually picked up thirteen stones' worth of Doug
Scott and hurled him across the face. Now we were here in
April and we could see those winds flinging snow up into the
air from the high ridges. Later we heard that the British and
Asian teams, hidden from us on the bleak exposed Rongbuk
side of the mountain, were plagued by malignant cold winds
at this stage.

Base Camp was a wonderful refuge from the realities of
the mountain. Pasang, as well as being an excellent cook, was

becoming a father figure. He had been on many Everest expeditions – to the South Col himself in 1969 – and he knew all about the dangers. The pujah ceremony was a form of blessing for the expedition, which we were all very happy to take part in. Ed reminded us that Roger Marshall, during his solo attempts on the North Face, had been very scornful of Pasang's Buddhist beliefs and had refused to have anything to do with pujahs. Pasang had been at the Rongbuk Base Camp on the second attempt, less than a year ago in 1987, when Marshall fell to his death.

The pujah was our final blessing before starting the climb. The next day all four climbers, Mimi and Joe went up to Advance Base, carrying heavy loads of personal clothing and equipment. Joe would never go anywhere without a vast panoply of gadgets, and he suffered on the long journey over the glacier, weighed down by a monstrous rucksack. However, to be fair to him, on this occasion most of the weight was necessary camera equipment, including the big-view camera and a huge range of lenses for the Nikon, so that he could zoom in on us and record every move we made up the Buttress.

The weather seemed to have set fine and it was a beautiful evening at Advance Base. Lighting makes an incalculable difference to the atmosphere of any place and that evening the Kangshung basin seemed much less frightening. Our reaction was wonder and delight, not hysterical panic, when we witnessed our first Lhotse avalanche – a miraculous white wave falling through the air at the speed of sound, then exploding with awful beauty as it hit the floor of the Witches' Cauldron. By the time the cloud had rolled across the basin to us, most of its force was spent and the ice particles blew harmlessly past. Bigger avalanches were to blast Advance Base with stronger winds, but never strong enough to do any real damage, and we were relieved to see that we had chosen a safe site.

Now for the first time Paul and I could see the whole of our route, very foreshortened, leading to the South Col – 'the highest wind tunnel in the world', over 2,500 metres above us. From our angle the face of Lhotse on the left was less foreshortened, and now we could see its full extent, 3,000 metres of fearsomely steep rock and ice, with the remains of a hanging glacier at two-thirds height, stretching a gigantic barrier right across the face. It made our route on Everest seem quite reasonable.

Robert suggested that he and I should go up first in the morning. We would try to find a way through the icefall guarding the Buttress, then climb the initial snow ramps up the toe of the Buttress, aiming to reach the rock wall – the 'Headwall' barring the way to the Scottish Gully. We would fix ropes for Ed and Paul to follow up, carrying more equipment to be used above. The following day we would swap the lead and so the four of us would work our way up the Buttress, day by day, extending the safety line of rope and abseiling back down to Advance Base each night, until we had fixed a route up to the easier slopes over a thousand metres above. It was a ponderous method, compared to the lightning ascents of Messner or the Swiss duo on the North side, but on our route, starting lower on a completely unknown route, with much harder technical climbing, a pure alpine style ascent was probably out of the question.

I had a busy evening, trying to drink plenty of liquid, change into dry clothes, pitch my tent (levelling a platform well away from the others 'so that I can listen to Mozart in peace'), fit crampons to my boots, fit safety leashes to my ice axes, gobble down some supper and help Paul sort out rope, slings, karabiners and pitons for the first day's climbing. After the sun sank behind the South Col the Kangshung basin became fiercely cold, so that we had to wear all our down clothing. For the first time I put on my down bibs – the wonderful salopettes made by Bolder Designs, which came right up to my chest and had full-length leg zips, so that they could be taken on and off over full climbing gear.

In spite of all our warm clothing, we had to stop frequently to blow on numb fingers while cooking and eating. Before going to bed we left everything ready for a pre-dawn breakfast – the water in the pan would freeze overnight, but it would be sitting on top of the gas cooker, with cereals, coffee, sugar and milk powder laid out ready.

The shadow of evening crept up the russet pillars of Chomolonzo, down the valley, and soon the granite faded to a prosaic grey. But almost immediately, as the main part of the sky grew dark and starry, there was a silver glow on the horizon just to the left of Chomolonzo, brighter and brighter as the moon rose – the full moon, climbing into a perfectly clear sky and illuminating the huge white face above us. I thought how incredibly lucky I was to be here, in this wonderful valley, just as I had felt so lucky the night below Shekar Dzong. Since then we had endured a month of delays and setbacks but the irritations had been minor and my dominant feeling had always been one of wonder at my good fortune in coming on the expedition. Tomorrow, if our luck held, we would become the first people ever to set foot on this new route up the most dramatic face of the world's highest mountain.

5

Neverest Buttress

I DETEST alarm clocks. The four o'clock awakening was the usual brutal disruption of pleasant dreams, calling me out into the cold darkness. I lit a candle and started the tedious business of getting dressed: first, long underwear, then a pile jacket and balaclava, then the contortionist struggle into my one-piece windsuit. Large and ungainly, cowpat-coloured and complete weatherproof, it was called my sewer man's outfit. Next I pulled on down bibs and jacket, to keep me warm until we left for the Buttress. Now that the whole body was protected, I could deal with the feet – two pairs of socks, felt inner boots, plastic outer boots and gaiters.

After about twenty minutes I was ready to unzip the tent door and clamber out into the starry darkness, shouting at the others to get up. I had wanted to leave much earlier but had compromised on a five o'clock breakfast. The stars were already fading, and by the time I handed the first cup of coffee through Robert's tent door it was nearly light. The pink glow of sunrise spread quickly down the East Face, then brightened to white. Suddenly there was a huge roar from the massive complex of gullies and spurs to the right of the 1983 buttress. A huge, beautiful, creamy wave poured down one of the gullies, billowing bigger and bigger, before crashing onto the glacier floor and blasting down the Kangshung valley to our right. A moment later there was another crash to our left, high on the face of Lhotse. A section of the main serac barrier had collapsed. Within seconds the avalanche had become airborne, descending a vertical mile in a few more seconds, then erupting onto a 600-metre high cloud which raced out across the Witches' Cauldron. This was much bigger than the previous evening's demonstration, and it landed much closer to our Buttress. However, it was a relief to see that most of its energy was dissipated before the fallout hit our approach route.

Robert and I finally left at 6.30, walking up the smooth snow crust beside the moraine. It was the first time I had roped up and carried an ice axe since the day we descended from Shisha Pangma, five months earlier. The sun was already on the glacier and we had to stop soon to take off some clothes. The first problem we had to solve was the icefall. Below Big Al Gully the glacier bay was criss-crossed by crevasses, cutting the bulging surface into giant detached blocks. As we neared the Buttress, we picked a route close to the flank of this icefall, trying to keep well clear of the Witches' Cauldron on our left.

About forty-five minutes after leaving Advance Base we reached the foot of the Buttress. Crazy turquoise ice towers hung out against the dark sky, nearly a thousand metres above our heads. These towers and the great flake of the Sickle threatened the lowest central point of the Buttress. We hoped to take a safer route, starting up a system of ledges and ramps, above and to the right of the lowest point, so we were pleased to discover an easy snow gully sneaking up right between the rock wall of the Buttress and the jumble of the icefall. At 5,500 metres one cannot rush, but we did keep moving as fast as our lungs would allow, zig-zagging steadily up the gully.

Soon it was time to step onto the Buttress. I started, leading up to the left, crossing a snowfield and a small rock outcrop, before stopping below another outcrop. I fitted two nuts – alloy wedges on wire loops – into cracks in the rock, tied myself into them, pulled up the slack in the rope and shouted to Robert to come up.

'Where d'you think we should go from here?' he asked when he arrived.

'What about over those rocks on the right?'

'Looks a bit steep.'

'Yes, but it's direct – you'll get the rope in a straight line.'

He decided to ignore me and take the easier line round to the left. Even if it was a bit indirect, the easy ground would be quicker and on a big Himalayan climb speed is paramount. He had already quoted his favourite gem from the 1985 Colorado expedition: 'There are two types of Himalayan climber – the quick and the dead.' Now he was pleased to see that I had the second rope all ready to pay out to him.

'You seem to have the right idea about climbing in the big mountains.'

'Yes – I'm an impatient bastard.'

'That's good. Sometimes you end up with people who are brilliant on their home cliffs and they get in the mountains and try to treat them like some small crag, hanging around at belays, taking hours to get ready . . .'

'Right. Off you go.'

Robert disappeared round the corner. After about fifteen minutes it was my turn to follow. The rope was to be fixed permanently, so rather than tie into the end, I attached myself with jumars – camming devices which you can slide up the anchored rope. The jumars are attached to your waist harness with lengths of tape; when you lean back and put weight on one of the jumars the toothed cam bites on the rope. I followed up over a rock step, back right up more rocks and then straight up a big snowfield.

Robert had led out most of the hundred-metre rope, tying it off to a piton which he had hammered into a crack at the base of another rock outcrop. I led out the rest of that rope to the top of the outcrop. We now had only one rope left and it looked as though we might actually climb the rock headwall that day. So we left the next section for Paul and Ed to fix, using our third rope as a movable safeguard. The route went up another snowfield, through a little rock band then out right across another snowfield towards the huge depression of Big Al Gully.

It was easy, kicking steps across a forty-degree snowfield, but what a position – poised between steep walls above, dripping in the morning sun, and more steep walls, cutting away the buttress below. I traversed right across, as close to Big Al Gully as I dared, before stopping under the Headwall, at the foot of an obvious corner. The rock was clean cut granite; nevertheless, there were some loose blocks, and I spent some time selecting safe cracks to hammer in three pitons and make a really secure anchor.

When I was safely tied in, I shouted to Robert to follow. Standing there, taking in the rope, I felt very content. Everything was going so quickly and smoothly and we were actually gaining height on this extraordinary East Face of Everest. As I faced out from the Buttress I could see right down the Kama valley. On my left, though, my view was blocked by the immense walls of the 1983 buttress, what we had come to call the American Buttress. In the morning heat fragile ice towers and rotten rocks were breaking loose, filling Big Al Gully with the echoing whrrr and boom of falling debris, and round to the right there were frequent great roars from the face of Lhotse. It was very satisfying to stand in the sunshine, in this place where no person had ever stood before, listening to those apocalyptic displays from a safe distance.

Robert arrived: 'This is fantastic. It's only eleven and we've already reached the Headwall. Do you want to lead this next bit?'

'What about Ed? I think he was hoping to lead it.'

'We can't afford to hang around. We've just got to keep pushing these ropes out as fast as we can.'

'Yes, Leader.' Ever the gentleman, I asked, 'Are you sure you don't want to do it?'

'I think you should lead it. I haven't done much proper climbing over the last couple of years.'

'OK. Thanks.'

So I took all the remaining nuts and pitons and set off. After two moves I stopped: 'Hang on, I'm just going to take off my crampons. It's mainly rock above.' I removed the set of spikes from each boot, clipped them into my waist harness, and continued with naked rubber soles on the granite.

There had been talk of complicated artificial climbing, but in fact I was finding beautiful free climbing, following the natural line up an open corner. Every ten metres or so I attached a nut or sling to the rock and clipped the running rope into it with a karabiner. A fall was unlikely, but if I did come off I wanted to be stopped before falling too far and hurting myself.

After about thirty metres the wall above steepened and I followed a line of weakness out to the right. Now I was on a band of quarzite, smooth textured but square cut, with enough horizontal edges and cracks to find holds. It was such fun: a tiptoe move right to a ledge, a pause to stand storklike and re-attach crampons to each foot in turn, then a few moves across a smear of ice, then more stork manoeuvres to remove crampons and step up, rubber soled, on little quartz-ite nicks, reaching up to a deep crack and fitting in a Friend – an ingenious camming device that will sit securely in almost any shaped crack. Once the rope was clipped safely into that, I felt more confident about the next awkward step-up. I was now trailing over sixty metres of heavy 9mm rope behind me; it was starting to drag me down, but I could not bear to stop. I continued, greedily hogging the whole wonderful wall, revelling in the next set of steep moves, reaching up over another bulge, impatient to see over the top of the Headwall.

After forty minutes of exhilarating climbing I pulled over the top, shouted down gleefully, 'I'm in the Scottish Gully,' and continued for a few more metres to another band of granite, where I spent ten minutes hammering in some very firm pitons to tie off the rope. I left some slack, so that Robert had spare rope to make knots and tie off at a couple of points on the way up. On an eighty-metre diagonal pitch intermediate anchors were necessary to avoid dangerous swinging and bouncing on the fixed rope.

'Welcome to the Scottish Gully!'

Robert panted up to the anchor and enthused about the route ahead: 'That's perfect. We'll zoom up that tomorrow.'

From below we had had no idea of the width and depth of

the gully. It really was far grander than anything on Ben Nevis, yet it was just one small feature of our Buttress, which itself was one tiny feature of the Kangshung Face. However, the gully looked easy and Robert was correct that he could climb it quickly the next day. It might be only one small feature of the face, but on a route this big, with a team this small, it was essential to break the route down into realizable objectives. Today we had judged the scale correctly and we had even fixed one rope ahead of schedule. And it had been such fun: my first proper pitch on Everest had been a dream of rock climbing, with even a bit of ice to add interest. What more could one ask for?

We slid down the rope on our figure-of-eight descendeurs then soloed back across the snowfield below the Headwall. This traverse was easy but during the many journeys to come, particularly at the end of much longer, more tiring days, we would be glad of a fixed rope. On the lower snowfield we met Paul and Ed. They had done good work, straightening and rationalizing the ropes, and replacing a loose piton. Ed reprimanded me: 'It just pulled straight out!'

'Sorry. There *was* a back-up peg, but it's still disgraceful, I know. I won't do it again. What's that you've put in there? Ah – a nut – yes, much better.'

He had hammered a wedge-shaped nut deep into the crack. It was typical of his thorough technique, learned pains-takingly on the massive canyon walls of Colorado and the sandstone spires of Utah. He pointed out how much stronger the double anchor now was, and showed me how to link the two anchor points with a sliding sling and karabiner, ensur-ing that the strain was always equalized. The man with the 'huge amount of Himalayan experience' still had plenty to learn.

Robert and I were back in camp in time for afternoon tea. Mimi had done a wonderful job, sorting all the food in the blue barrels which doubled as cupboards and tables. A spare barrel was filled with water from the pool and a large pan was boiling on the gas stove.

Pasang and Kasang had come up with a load of food and

equipment from Base Camp and, after a cup of tea, were about to set off back home. I was very touched when Pasang came specially over to my tent to say goodbye. 'Stephen, we are going now. In two days we come back and bring what you want. Goodbye. Be careful.' The last two words were said with such heartfelt sincerity that I wondered if he was still pondering Roger Marshall's death the previous year.

Joe had been busy that day recording our every move: 'I've got some really good coverage. I started with the 28mm, then the 35, then the 80, then the 300. Then I put on the doubler to get in really close.' However, for the purpose just of watching, Robert's telescope had the best optics and it zoomed in to an intimate ×48. Joe was now using it to scrutinize the Buttress.

'There's a cloud in the way . . . ah, yes, I can see Paul now, really moving. You guys are *fast.*'

'Is he on the snowfield?'

'Yeah, just coming up to the Headwall. He's trailing a yellow rope –'

'That's an eight-mil. That'll be quite strong enough there.'

They returned just in time for supper. Paul was in high spirits, enthusing about the Headwall.

'Good lead, Venables. Really nice pitch.'

'It was good, wasn't it? And not too hard.'

'Awesome letter boxes.'

'What? I can never understand what you Yanks are talking about.'

'I'm Canadian. Letter boxes? Big holds, like this.' He stuck his hands out into an imaginary horizontal slot.

Robert said that he would like to lead the Scottish Gully the next day. Perhaps Paul would like to start on the traverse beyond? Ed and I could come up behind with more rope.

We needed to prepare the rope, so I gave the others a knitting lesson. The 100-metre lengths were supplied on plastic spools, impractical for use on the mountains. I unwound the spools, plaiting each rope to a third of its length, then coiling the plait into a manageable bundle which could be stuffed in a rucksack. The plait had a leading end, secured with a special knot. When the rope came to be used, this knot would be untied and the plaits would unravel as the leader moved up the mountain.

Ed and I left quite late the next morning. The sun was blazing hot and the melting snow clung stickily to my crampons, leadening my feet and making me extremely bad tempered. In my rucksack I was carrying 100 metres of 11mm rope, 100 metres of 8mm and a large rack of ironmongery, as well as personal odds and ends like spare clothing, sunglasses and water bottle. It must have weighed at least twenty kilos and I found the jumar back up the Headwall exhausting.

I caught up with Paul, who was paying out Robert's rope. The higher we climbed up the Scottish Gully, the more spectacular it became. Huge rock walls hung over us on the left and another wall hemmed us in on the other side, protecting us from the menace of the infinitely larger Big Al Gully on the right. When one looked up, the walls seemed to curve in like dark horns, framing the even darker blue sky.

Robert used two full lengths of rope to reach the top of the gully. He spent ages searching for an anchor, out of sight at the top, while Paul and I shivered under a dripping rock, a hundred metres below, shouting up impatiently to ask what the hell was going on. Eventually my turn came to follow, sliding my two jumars up the rope, climbing up a rock band, then following more footsteps up the snow, until I emerged from the gully.

Robert was crouched under a huge overhang of stacked blocks, tied in to several pitons in the banded granite and shale. Across to the right there was a huge slope of steep ice and snow, studded with granite blocks. Paul was kicking and hammering his way across this slope, forging a diagonal line upwards, keeping as close as he could to the overhanging rock walls above. Below him the slope swept down into the avalanche-scoured basin of Big Al Gully. On the far side and above the basin, tier after tier of beautiful bizarre snow flutings and ice towers were stacked up against the sky. I had never been in such spectacular ice scenery.

I unpacked my load of equipment and tied it into the anchor. Then I rested for a few minutes, talking to Robert and waiting for Ed to arrive before setting off down the ropes, revelling in the whizzing slide back down to the glacier. I left my descendeur tied into the bottom rope, picked up my ice axe and ski stick and ran down the gully to the main glacier. Here there was a safe sheltered spot under an overhang, where we always left two short lengths of rope to safeguard the walk back across the glacier.

Ed arrived about thirty minutes later, full of praise for Paul. 'Did you see him on that traverse? Really going for it, a flurry of arms and legs!'

We walked back to Advance Base at a more sedate pace, stopping to photograph and to stare up at the bottom lip of the Cauliflower Ridge, where the horizontal bands of glacier ice had eroded into strange towers, hanging like giant chess pieces high above our heads. From close under the face, wherever you looked up the sky seemed to be filled with ice – hundreds of thousands of tons of ice pressing down on the lower walls of Lhotse and Everest.

I walked on, with Ed following behind, keeping the twenty-metre rope semi-taut between us. He was in good spirits and shouted, 'I don't know about you, but after today I feel much happier about the route. Yesterday I really didn't like it but today I felt very safe in that Scottish Gully.'

'That retaining wall's perfect, isn't it? Really protects us from Big Al. But I think the bottom of the Buttress is quite dangerous. We shouldn't be climbing it after sunrise, with all that stuff above starting to melt. Anyway, it's crazy to wear ourselves out in the heat.'

'Yes – you're insufferable once the sun comes up.'

On Day Three I had my way. By 3 a.m. I was up and fully dressed, preparing hot chocolate and shouting to Ed to get a move on, and by four o'clock we were on our way. The waning moon illuminated the upper part of Everest but our approach was deep in shadow. The temperature must have been well below freezing, but after about ten minutes' exercise we had to stop and remove down jackets, packing them in our rucksacks in case of cold delays later in the day.

This was much better, the peaceful measured walk across the glacier under a starry sky, enabling us to climb up the gully in the cool and start up the ropes before sunrise. Not until the first rope was I able to switch off my headtorch. Far down the valley the eastern horizon was orange and soon the highest rocks on Lhotse, far above us, were glowing pink. I stopped below the Headwall to remove my pile jacket and balaclava, exchange clear glasses for dark ones, and smother every square inch of exposed skin with suncream. Then on up the ropes.

From Advance Base it took four hours to reach Paul's highpoint. I dumped my load, then went back to collect another rope from the top of the Scottish Gully and photographed Ed, jumaring up out of that spectacular funnel which framed the long view down the Kangshung Glacier to the Gyankar range beyond Kharta.

Going back across Paul's traverse, I was infuriated with Ed for insisting on rearranging all the ropes. He was quite right that the tension between the anchors needed altering to ensure quick smooth journeys in future, but I was longing to get on to new ground and make the most of the fabulous weather. It was about ten in the morning before we did. Ed deserved a turn at leading, but the front points had fallen off his crampons on the way up, so I had the fun of being in front.

The route from Paul's highpoint was obvious, diagonally right, up to sheltering rock walls. It was quite difficult, the sort of climbing that one might find on the harder sections of one of the big Alpine or Canadian north faces. The snow was sugary and unstable, the ice thin and hard, and much of the rock was friable shale. I managed to place one dubious Friend for protection and higher up, after a long search, I found a good piton crack in an island of solid granite. Once the rope was clipped into the piton, running through a karabiner, I felt reassured. Nevertheless there was still a long way to go. On this section, with its many abrasive rocks, we were fixing heavy 11mm rope, and it dragged unnervingly on the final moves up a steep wall of sugar. I was a long, long way above that piton and very conscious that I must not fall, as I thrust ice axe shafts into the crumbly bulge and kicked hard to make secure steps.

It was wonderful to pull over the top into the haven which we called the Terrace. It was a snow ledge, only a metre wide, right up below beetling rock overhangs. It must be one of the safest places on the entire mountain and even if the whole of the Cauliflower Ridge above had fallen into Big Gully we would have been safe at the Terrace.

I pulled up the slack, tied it off, apologized to a shivering Ed for the time I had taken and waited for him to jumar up, removing the now superfluous protection points as he came. As soon as he joined me he set about re-organizing the anchor: 'Let's take that peg out . . . and those nuts . . . right, let's have that long blade peg and put it in this constriction here.' He hammered it into the crack in a vein of pale granite. 'See, at that angle it's getting a nice torque. The down pull will twist it tighter into the crack and it's good for a side pull from the next section.'

The next section was an exciting traverse out to the right. I had used about sixty-five metres of the rope and now Ed belayed me as I led on with the remaining thirty-five metres, easing myself round the great bulge of snow. It was delicate airy climbing, on little snow ledges which led across a wall of sharp brittle shale. I had to remove a lot of rubble to find solid placements for a nut, a piton and a Friend. I left the rope running freely through a karabiner on each anchor, but when Ed followed he would tie off the rope at each point, securing a stable handrail for all our future journeys back and forth across this wall.

The rope dragged as I disappeared round the corner, using both my ice axes for handholds as I crossed a sixty-degree icefield. That led me into an evil corner. Smooth grey ice plummeted steeply into the bed of Big Al Gully, now far below. Above me the face steepened into more loose walls, which were clearly the source of dangerous rockfall. Above the rocks I could just make out the huge ice overhang of the

First Cauliflower Tower or Greyhound Bus, as Paul preferred to call it. To add to the atmosphere of hostility, clouds were swirling about the face and a cold wind was blowing. Our route continued diagonally right and I tiptoed that way as far as I could, across rock splinters embedded in iron ice. It was precarious and brutally tiring on calf muscles, so I was glad when the rope came tight and it was time to stop. After an age of poking, prising and hammering, I had a safe anchor organized.

That was enough for one day. We left surplus ironmongery and a couple of ropes hanging at our highpoint, then whizzed back down to Advance Base. Coming home in the evening was great. Robert and Paul had risen late that morning, had seen sun-loosened rocks whirring down the exposed bottom section of the route, and had decided wisely to take a rest day. Now they had gallons of hot drinks waiting for us and supper on the way.

Ed told them about his long wait below the Terrace. 'It was as cold as a winter day's ice climbing on Mount Washington. Man, I was glad I kept my parka with me. I had a long time to look at Big Al and I noticed that he has a loose denture.'

The further we extended our route the more wild the scenery became. The great detached block on Big Al would come down one day, but we had managed to keep our route high on the wall of the gully, well clear of the main avalanche furrow. Today I was a bit disappointed with our paltry hundred metres of progress, but we were still well on schedule.

Wednesday – April 6th
Rest day. At last a full night's sleep. Up late to hot sun, porridge, salami and strong real coffee. Sorry to say goodbye to Mimi and Joe [descending for a spell at Base Camp]. Robert and Paul were starting up the new pitch as we ate breakfast. Wonderful to watch them through the telescope – stick figures climbing up under that great bulging Cauliflower Ridge.

We watched Paul climb up a steep gully, leading right from my highpoint. Then we saw him poking around for ages, fixing up an anchor. When we next looked, Robert was at this anchor, standing on the apex of a snow arête. Paul had disappeared round the corner and for hours Robert did not move, but we could see him, illuminated now in midday light, tilting his yellow helmet to look steeply up at his leader. He was over a mile away and far above us but we could sense the tension as he slowly paid out the rope and watched Paul's every move.

Our job today was to relax, paying serious attention to our eating and drinking. We talked about the Eiger, about Ed's projected book on the legendary K2 pioneer, Fritz Wiessner, and about Ed's American climbs – famous new routes on Long's Peak, Mount Washington, the Black Canyon and the surreal red sandstone towers of Utah. Neither I nor the other two could begin to match his record of big bold rock climbs, nor did we have his technical expertise; nevertheless he still seemed quite awed by our audacious route on Everest and unsure of his ability, should we reach the South Col, to continue without oxygen.

At this stage the South Col was still a distant challenge which we would not have to face for a while. It was a beautiful day and we were relaxing at a mere 5,450 metres above sea level, fit, content and enjoying the free run of all Joe's Nikon lenses to photograph our fantastic cirque. I had a good time with the 300mm lens, recording all the beautiful intricate detail: the turreted ridge of Lhotse, with its untouched Middle peak, surely the most inaccessible summit in the whole world, the immense seracs to the left of the South Col, the daunting cliffs of the American Buttress, the three slender spurs further right, each nearly 2,000 metres high and separated by gullies far more treacherous than Big Al Gully. I called them the Trinity Gullies, after the famous winter climbs on Snowdon, but really there were four gullies here, separated by three spurs. Further right the main part of the Kangshung Face was enclosed by the East Ridge, which we called the Peruvian Ridge because for its entire length it was festooned with elaborate double cornices, reminiscent of the hardest Andean ridges. The difference was that this ridge was longer than anything in the Andes; it started at about 5,500 metres and it finished at nearly 8,000 metres – finished only in the sense that it joined the main North-East Ridge, at the point where that comparatively easy ridge becomes hard, the notorious Pinnacles. I could see the steep pitch on the Pinnacles which Dick Renshaw had led in 1982, when his whole life was suddenly changed by a stroke. He had been forced to return home, but two of his companions had gone back up to and beyond that pitch, where the route looked increasingly hard. Somewhere up there, pushing on without oxygen, amongst those gigantic cornices hanging out over the fragile flutings of the Kangshung Face, Joe Tasker and Peter Boardman had died. Looking up at the daunting length of that upper ridge, a mile and a half of difficult climbing, all above 8,000 metres, I felt glad that we would be attempting the summit by the shorter easier South-East Ridge.

Robert and Paul returned at six in the evening. We had everything ready, a big Thermos of tea, more water on the boil, supper cooked and just waiting to be heated up. They gulped down liquid and Paul raved about the day's climbing. 'It was hard, man – awesome – eighty-degree ice, sometimes vertical. I had to rest on this ice screw, you know, just hanging on, legs screaming. I was gripped. Then I found this letter box – that was great – just stepped into it for a rest – "Kangshung Face! Four people! You're mad!"'

Gradually we pieced together the day's events. During those hours out of sight, Paul had led a fearsome steep pitch. I asked him whether the ice had shattered, causing plating.

'Yeah, there was a bit of plating, but not too bad – lunch plates, not banquet plates. It was wild. And big rocks stuck in the ice, as big as television sets.'

'Did you tell them about the library books?' Robert interrupted. 'We had this belay –'

'Where you were standing all that time?'

'Yes. Well, Paul was leading this hy-oooge ice pitch, two hundred feet – steep – you could see his legs shaking. I was really tense and I had this *belay*. I mean, there were things everywhere, ropes in every direction, half an ice screw, upside down pegs, a couple of nuts and this Friend just shoved in between some blocks, like a pile of library books. Afterwards I decided the Friend was superfluous, so I just lifted the top books off the pile and took it out!'

He went on to explain that, instead of traversing right, as we had planned, they had continued straight up towards a break in the Cauliflower Ridge. 'Tomorrow I think you two should get up onto the ridge. I think you'll come out above the second tower.'

'But why not continue right?'

'It looks really nasty – you'll see – big things hanging over it and rockfall –'

'Big rope-cutters!' Paul interrupted. '*Ptrrrrrr.*'

The beautiful weather held and next morning Ed and I enjoyed an orgy of photography on the fixed ropes in the dazzling early morning light. At the top of the Scottish Gully, Ed recounted a visit many years earlier to the famous editor of *Mountain* magazine, Ken Wilson.

'He looked at my pictures and said –'

'You mean "spat".'

'Yes, that's right – spat it out, really loud. Anyway he shouted: "I can see you're an up and coming photographer. These pictures are all right. Look, this has got the three essentials for a good climbing picture: it's in focus, there's good action and you can see the climber's face."'

For the rest of that day Ed was never left in peace and our journey up the ropes and onto his new pitches was punctuated constantly with shouts of 'Can't see your face . . . Turn round . . . Look up . . . Where's your face? . . . Oi! Head! . . . Why the hell do you wear a white helmet?'

There was a certain perversity in asking Ed to co-operate on photos all the time, because earlier I had been complaining at the delays while he perfected the line of ropes. The previous evening Robert had remonstrated, 'There isn't time, Ed. The only thing that matters is getting to the South Col, and farting around re-arranging anchors doesn't get us any nearer the South Col.' It was the old battle of alpinist versus big wall climber.

I shared Robert's alpinist's approach and this morning I had started to get quite angry, shouting down, 'Ed! Get a move on! This isn't the bloody Black Canyon. We're not in Colorado now; we've got a mountain to climb.'

He was amazingly tolerant of my bad temper, and we continued without argument. It was now a long journey up the ropes to our highpoint beyond the Terrace, then on up a steep gully, breaking out to the snow ridge, where Robert had stood so long the previous day. I pulled up to the ledge he had cut, and suddenly I could see round the corner. To continue right, as we originally intended, would have entailed crossing horrible bands of loose rock embedded in ice, with a huge splintered serac threatening from above. Instead, the rope led almost straight up and I could see Ed jumaring towards an obvious break in the seracs, leading out to the crest of the Cauliflower Ridge.

It was a stupendous pitch to jumar: now I had left the mixed ground behind and I was suspended on a 9mm thread of nylon, dangling in a world of pure ice. The only rocks were occasional boulders half buried in the ice, Paul's 'television sets', waiting for the day they would eventually melt out and crash down into Big Al Gully. Paul's pitch did indeed steepen to eighty degrees and I attached a footloop to the lower jumar, so that I could use one leg to push up, supported on the rope. This gave calf muscles relief from the strain of kicking crampon points into glassy ice. After about seventy metres, the rope was tied off to two ice screws which Paul had hammered into the wall. I found the letter box, a hollow underneath an embedded rock. I stood in it and rested for a minute, then clipped my waistline into the anchor to secure myself while I re-attached my jumars to the rope above the knot. Then I unclipped the safety line and continued, panting hard, over an overhang. A stone broke loose, up to the right, slid, turned on end, starting spinning and bounded past me with a vicious *ptrrrr*. Robert and Paul had been right not to go out that way.

Above the overhang, the rope led up a gentler snow terrace to two more ice screws, below another steep wall. This was the previous day's highpoint, and Ed was waiting at the anchor, eager for his chance at last to do some leading. I hung up my rucksack, adding to the tangle of equipment already hanging there. Then we sorted it all out, hanging up the rock gear, which we would probably not need now, selecting some ice screws and karabiners for the next pitch and preparing a rope for paying out.

Ed had new front points bolted firmly to his crampons, and had apparently forgiven the manufacturers to the point of instructing me to get lots of photos. 'This is a really good pitch to show off the ice gear.' It certainly was photogenic: the fluorescent yellow crampons a few metres above me to the right, with just the two front points on each foot daggered into the marbled blue-green ice, above them the red-clad body, held in balance by an ice axe in each hand, and Ed's smiling face dutifully turned down towards the camera to avoid the illusion of a headless monster.

Crampons and ice axes were the four points holding the figure on an eighty-degree wall of ice. The figure climbed smoothly, moving one point of contact at a time, stopping every few metres to remove a tubular ice screw from his belt, tap it into the ice, screw it home until only the eye protruded, clip in a karabiner, then clip the rope into that. He was heading for the royal blue sky in the gap between two towers. The safest, most direct route was straight up. However, that led over a slightly overhanging bulge; so, for the purposes of leading, Ed took a less strenuous line out to the right, under the splintered menace of the right tower, then back left, following a ramp up into the gap. He disappeared from sight, then moved faster and had dragged out the full hundred metres of rope before a distant shout told me to follow. My job was to jumar up the rope, removing all the ice screws as I came, so that for future journeys the rope would hang straight over the safer direct line. Even Ed's easier line involved some delicate balance work, particularly on the precarious crampon shuffle up the ramp. Above that, easy angled snow, another little ice bulge and a final trudge through knee-deep powder led up and out onto the crest of the Cauliflower Ridge.

'Well done. What an ice pitch! Let's have some lunch.'

We sat in the sun and ate what I call Bombay Mix, but what the earthy-crunchy shop in Colorado labelled Savory Trail Mix. Our drink was a solution of orange juice and Carboplex, a corn-based powder with a very high concentration of carbohydrate which, unlike sugar or glucose, is released slowly in the body.

It felt weird to be on flat ground again. The snow terrace was right on the crest of the Buttress and by standing up we could see down to the glacier. The yellow tents of Advance Base were invisible from this height, but we could see exactly where they must be, so we waved to the audience.

We were pleased to have reached the Cauliflower Ridge but unfortunately one of the cauliflowers blocked the route ahead. It was the third of the four big steps we had seen from as far back as the Langma La, and it proved now to be a vertical and overhanging cliff of ice. After lunch Ed kicked his way up deep snow to the foot of the cliff. I thought that I had seen an easy way round to the left, but when Ed looked round the corner he shouted down, 'Not a chance.'

'Not even if you go *right* round to the left?'

'No way. It looks really dangerous and the cliff overhangs by about thirty degrees.'

'You'll have to go straight up then.'

'Thanks.'

So Ed tackled the barrier head on. At this central point the cliff was only about twenty metres high but, looking up the smooth bands of glacial ice, he could see that the wall steepened from ninety to one hundred degrees. He had never climbed overhanging ice before, but at 6,600 metres on Everest was as good a place as any to learn.

It was a masterly performance. First he took off his rucksack and left it on a ledge, clipped for safety into the rope. Now, without the weight of a sack, he could at least stay in balance for the first moves up a little ramp which leaned rightwards into the cliff. He moved confidently up this, placed an ice screw, climbed higher, then placed another ice screw, clipped in a footloop and used this to surmount an overhanging bulge. Then he moved back left, like some spidery crab spreadeagled on four clawed legs. The most impressive part was the speed and skill with which he placed protecting ice screws, whilst hanging so precariously from one ice hammer. He climbed diagonally left for about ten metres, then moved straight up.

The wall was obviously starting to overhang again, for now Ed was taking his weight directly on ice screws, and standing in footloops to move up. After two moves he shouted down: 'I've run out of ice screws!' He was still about five metres short of the top and needed more equipment to make progress by artificial 'aid climbing'.

I suggested, 'Can't you aid off one of your ice hammers?'

'I suppose so, but I'll have to remove the lower screw as well.'

He lowered himself, reached down, almost upside down, unscrewed the previous anchor, and then used that higher up, to lever himself up the wall. Above that he whacked in the pick of one of his ice hammers and hung on that to remove the screw a second time. This leapfrogging continued for three or four moves, until he was almost at the top of the wall. He was now hanging in stirrups from one ice screw and one ice hammer, with the other hammer held in his left hand flailing around, desperately seeking some purchase on the lip of the overhang. Loose snow and chunks of rotten ice poured down and Ed continued flailing to no avail, until he shouted gleefully: 'Of course – the snow pickets!' We had both forgotten about the two long snow stakes hanging from his waist harness. He reached down to unclip one, then held it up and outwards to hammer it deep into the sugary snow above his head. He clipped in a tape sling, pulled up, stood in it and was able to reach right over the lip of the overhang to place the second stake. In a moment he had disappeared over the top of the wall with a great shriek of delight.

Ed reappeared to lift out the two snow stakes, then walked back up the invisible terrace above, to anchor the rope well back from the cliff edge.

When all was ready I followed on jumars. Once again my job was to clean the pitch, removing all the ice screws, so that when I had finished the rope would hang down in a straight line. Anyone experienced in artificial big-wall climbing would have made quick work of it. I dithered and whimpered, terrified unnecessarily of the potential sideways swing into space after removing each screw on the diagonal section. Then came the final overhanging section up to the crumbling lip of the wall, where my inelegant struggle was a travesty of Ed's methodical professionalism. After much puffing and panting I was thrilled to pull over the top and join Ed on the next terrace.

We were almost there. Only the Fourth Cauliflower Tower lay between us and the easier snow slopes at the top of the Buttress. The tower was bigger but clearly easier than the wall Ed had just climbed, and I was tempted to continue. However, it was now quite late in the afternoon, cloudy and cold, and time to go home. It was nearly dark when we plodded wearily into Advance Base at 6 p.m.

The others had watched it all through the telescope and Paul greeted us with shouts of 'Webster! You're mad – you're crazy. What a pitch. We called it Randa's Shroom!'

'What the hell's a shroom?' I asked, and Paul explained it was mushroom – apparently the vegetable terminology for the ice ridge had changed. 'Yes – Randa's Shroom – he must have been inspired by her . . . You did it all for Randa, didn't you, Ed?'

While we took off crampons, put on warm clothes, and gulped down drink after drink, Paul told us how Kasang had been up that afternoon to take a look through the telescope. 'He couldn't believe it. He was twittering and pointing and shaking his head, kept on jabbering at Pasang in Tibetan, then having another look.'

There was a wonderful warmth of team spirit that evening. Paul put on a tape of Pink Floyd in deference to my

antiquated and limited taste in rock music. Optimism ran
high and we discussed the naming of our route. 'International Buttress' was suggested but we decided that, after
these days of intensive work, 'Neverest Buttress' was more
appropriate.

Robert was delighted with our progress and predicted an
early summit success. 'Soon we'll be at the top of the Buttress – in a day or two, I think. Then all we have to do is
wallow. I'm really good at wallowing. I brought out you
guys to lead all the hard stuff, but I'm a real expert wallower.
I'll wallow for 5,000 feet and you guys can wallow behind on
a 3mm rope, and we'll wallow all the way to the South Col.
Then we just clip into the Japanese television wires–'

'Hey – these television wires don't fit my jumar!' Paul
yelled, reducing everyone to hysterical laughter.

It was now dark, I had been up for seventeen hours, I was
yawning my head off and my whole body was aching with
weariness, but I was determined to go back up the Neverest
Buttress with Paul and Robert the next day. They had selected a big payload of rope and the first supplies for Camp 1 – a
tent, stoves, gas cylinders and food. I wanted to help get the
load up there and I wanted greedily to claim my lead of the
Fourth Cauliflower Tower.

I rushed through the evening routine of preparing the next
day's water bottle, sorting out film, changing socks, packing
my rucksack ready for the morning and settling down as
soon as I could, to snatch some sleep.

Friday – April 8th
  Day Six on Buttress. Up very wearily at 2.30 a.m., determined to help Paul and Robert carry and to lead the next ice
pitch up Fourth Cauliflower Tower.
  Very slow. Pain under ribs. Cough. Sore throat. Legs like
lead. Weight of 100–metre rope, gas stoves and food. Counting
ropes – now twelve of them in place, mostly 100–metres – so
over 1000 metres to climb back up. Again it was a fourteen-hour
day – like doing a major alpine route two days running, with
only five or six hours' sleep in between. And at a much higher
altitude.

It was hard work and I was due for a rest, but I would not have missed it for anything. Each afternoon high cirrus cloud had been streaking the sky, warning of an impending break in the weather. This might be our last day's climbing for a while and, now that Ed had so skilfully opened the way, I wanted to be there when we broke out onto the top of the Buttress.

We stopped for lunch at the same spot, then tackled the stupendous jumar up Webster's Wall, dangling dizzily, nearly a thousand metres above the Kangshung Glacier. We dumped all the Camp 1 supplies at Ed's highpoint, then Robert and Paul generously let me continue up the Fourth Cauliflower Tower.

Over on the left was the giant detached splinter of the Sickle, which Paul and I had stared at so nervously on our first visit to Advance Base. Now we were almost level with it, having avoided its threat by our devious route up the right-hand side of the Buttress. The Sickle hung in an extremely dangerous fractured wall but further right, directly above us, the ice looked solid. I tied onto the end of an 8mm rope and set off, stomping up the snow terrace to the foot of the cliff.

All my paranoia about being confined to 'specialties' had proved groundless: in this first week I had led on rock, mixed ground and now pure ice. And what an ice pitch! It was a good sixty-five metres straight up a smooth runnel, poised right on the Cauliflower Ridge, as if on the crest of a gigantic wave about to crash down into the Kangshung basin. All my tiredness vanished and I raced on adrenalin, stabbing my way manically upwards as the clouds closed in, swirling grey round the Kangshung cirque. My calf muscles were screaming for a rest on the final vertical moves at the top and I had to hang, exhausted, on a hastily placed ice screw before escaping to easy snow where I hammered in two stakes and tied off the rope.

Paul jumared up with another rope for me to lead the next pitch. It was getting late and the cloud was darkening, but we had to see over the top. I kicked furiously up left, heading for a gap between smaller towers. I was now anxious for there seemed to be some sort of gap through there. Please not – please not a crevasse! There must be a way through.

I climbed up towards a huge gargoyle, hoping to look through its Cyclops eye. But it was too high to reach and the gargoyle seemed to be tottering precariously, waiting to crash down. I left well alone, but I did manage to look through a slit below it. I peered through the deep turquoise gash to see a huge chasm beyond. And we had thought that the difficulties were over! Surely there was a way round? I went down to the left, stopped to place an ice screw for protection, then edged my way round a bulge of crumbling snow and stepped up into another steep runnel. For a moment I looked down fearfully into the swirling depths of the Kangshung basin, then I moved up, watching crampon points carefully on seventy-degree brittle ice. I climbed seven metres up the runnel until I could reach up and wrap both arms round the top lip of the wall, pull myself up and look over.

Suddenly all the excited optimism of the last six days was knocked out of me. I was staring down into a huge crevasse, thirty metres deep and fifteen metres wide. It was the chasm I had glimpsed through the slit a few minutes earlier. The far wall was smooth and overhanging. I stared down to the right and saw that the chasm extended right into Big Al Gully. On the left the walls also continued, sliced clean to reveal the horizontal layers of glacial accumulation. An immense oblong block had fractured and stood leaning against one wall, like some tilted skyscraper; but it gave no chance of a crossing and the crevasse clearly continued round the corner to the left, far too wide to offer any hope of a snowbridge. Just fifteen metres in front of me, I could see the smooth snow slopes leading out onto the upper spur – our route to the South Col. But between me and those slopes the crevasse spanned the entire width of the Buttress.

6
The Crevasse

PAUL was getting impatient, shouting, 'What are you doing? What's going on? What's it like?' I was far too preoccupied to answer and just yelled 'Wait!' I was in a precarious position, clinging with my arms to the lip of the crevasse, trying to take some of the strain off my calf muscles. I had one ice screw left and with great difficulty, balanced precariously on teetering crampon points. I managed to get it half-way into the wall to my right, wrap a sling round it and tie in.

Now I was safe. I could see Robert appearing out of the cloud to join Paul and I shouted down to both of them, 'Do you know anything about Tyrolean traverses?'

'What!?'

'We can't go on. There's a huge crevasse. We'll have to fix a rope across it.'

'There must be a way round!'

'There isn't. I'm coming down. Can you give me some slack? I'll have to abseil down this bit. I'll bring the rope back for the moment.' I pulled up some slack, so that I could double the rope and abseil back down the runnel, leaving the ice screw anchor behind. Once I was down to easier ground I untied from the rope, pulled the doubled end through, retied and continued back across to Paul, with him belaying me.

Robert and Paul looked gloomy, for we had hoped so much to complete the Buttress today. Robert thought there might be a way round to the right so I climbed up to have a look, kicking furiously up deep snow and over a jumble of ice blocks, spurred on by Paul's shouts of, 'You're awesome, Venables, like a machine.' But, as I had thought, the Crevasse extended right into Big Al Gully. It would be possible from here to descend back onto the flank of the gully and climb past the mouth of the Crevasse, but at this stage the last thing we wanted was to lose height and this option would mean a long traverse under overhanging seracs, with God knows what problems hidden round the corner.

We could do nothing more that day. The weather seemed to be breaking, we all desperately needed a spell of rest and the problem of the Crevasse would have to wait. We left spare rope and gear tied to the anchor, piled up snow on top to ensure against any melting out of the stakes, and abseiled back down the Fourth Cauliflower Tower. It was starting to snow at the terrace below as we packed all the Camp 1 supplies into a sack and tied it to the rope, marking the spot with a bamboo wand. Then we took it in turns to walk down the rope, lower ourselves over the lip of Webster's Wall, kick off and whoosh through the air. One and a half hours later we were down and walking back across the glacier. I was still in high spirits, pulling hard on the rope, dragging the other two behind me as I stumbled and wallowed homewards in the afternoon slush.

Paul grew tired of this and instructed me in pure Californian: 'Slow down: we've got to finesse it.'

'To hell with finesse — I want my tea!' I shouted, and kept dragging them forward as fast as I could. As we neared camp the light was fading and a vast thunder cloud flickered somewhere over the Arun valley.

That night I enjoyed eleven hours' unbroken sleep. The weather, amazingly, was fine again in the morning. Robert was hovering over the kitchen area like some long-legged tropical bird, brilliant in scarlet hat, powder blue jacket, with a rim of bright red vest showing below, bright green long johns and silver inner boots. He made a huge pot of coffee, boiled water for the freeze-dried maple syrup and tossed his own specially-created brand of high-fibre pancakes.

By midday it was snowing and in the evening three of us

lay in our tents while Our Leader delivered supper-in-bed. It snowed all night and in the morning the drop in atmospheric pressure induced in all of us a crippling lethargy. The time had come for proper recuperation at Base Camp.

After eight days' absence it was wonderful to climb back over the crest of the moraine, leave the wastes of the glacier behind and walk across the soft springy turf of the ablation valley where Mimi and Joe were coming up to meet us. Pasang had a huge kettle of tea ready in the kitchen and we sat down to eat and drink, finish off the remains of a bottle of whisky, enjoy a well-earned cigarette and gabble manically about the events of the last few days.

It had stopped snowing now and Joe was setting up the view camera outside, adjusting the bellows and disappearing every few moments under his black hood to compose his view across the Kama valley to Chomolonzo. He was ecstatic about the ethereal light on those distant granite pillars, and then the ghostly revelation of Makalu, even higher in the sky behind, as the clouds drifted apart to reveal more delicate pink snow and sculpted rock. As Mallory had observed all those years ago, although Everest is the higher mountain, 'Makalu is incomparable for its spectacular and rugged grandeur.' For at least half an hour we were entranced by the constantly changing shapes and colours as the clouds shifted backwards and forwards and the light grew ever more intense, finally touching just the summit of Makalu with brilliant red before it was suddenly extinguished.

We had two full days' holiday at Base Camp. It was wonderful to be pampered by Pasang and his assistant. Kasang was now transformed into a model of efficiency, busy in the kitchen doing all Pasang's donkey work and attending to our every need at the breakfast table. Pasang had even persuaded him to forsake Tibetan tradition and have a proper wash. His clothes were clean, his smooth brown skin was gleaming and he had combed out, washed and re-plaited his waist-length hair. One of his jobs now was to boil up a giant cauldron of water for us. Most British climbers seem to share the Tibetan's reluctance to wash; but this American bunch, despite their many oddities, did not equate filth with manly ruggedness or Buddhist serenity or any other advanced state of being, and were happy to wash regularly. They had even bought a torn old tent in Kathmandu to serve as a bathroom (I use the word in its English sense). This may sound effete and prudish, but even on a fine day the slightest breeze at 5,100 metres could reduce a wet body to instant hypothermia, so we were all glad of shelter for our ablutions.

I made a huge salad for lunch. Robert Dorival had supplied us with a wonderful range of food, including excellent freeze-dried vegetables, so that I could add to the tabouli (precooked dried wheat) French beans, mushrooms, sweet corn, parsley, chives and sunflower seeds, and marinade the whole lot in a rich dressing made from tahini, sour cream, olive oil, lemon juice and Dijon mustard. The freeze-dried cream was horrendously expensive and, as they pushed their giant trolley round the Boulder hypermarket, Ed had persuaded Gourmet Dorival not to buy twenty bags but settle for two. Obviously on the mountain itself our diet would be much simpler but at Base Camp, and to a lesser extent Advance Base, we enjoyed an excellent varied diet.

We had all read Bill Tilman's account of the 1938 Everest expedition, where he directs his inimitable wit at the gastronomic excesses of his predecessors and prescribes a 'no frills' diet which he deems quite adequate for climbing Everest. The fact is that there were frequent complaints from some of his fellow climbers, who suggested that not only was the food dull and insufficiently nourishing, but also that there was not enough of it. The grumbles were probably justified, and staunch admirer as I am of the unsurpassed explorations of Tilman and his famous partner Eric Shipton, I think that when it came to food they were both utter Philistines.

No one was going to make us suffer. We realized that variety was important to ensure that we continued to *want* to eat. We knew how one starts to crave for strong flavours, hence all the mustard and mayonnaise. We knew that at altitude a vegetarian diet induces better health: protein is

absorbed more efficiently from flour, pulses, milk powder
and cheese than from meat. I had brought along some Neg-
roni salami and Parma ham, but on the whole I was happy to
stick to a vegetarian diet. In 1984 Jim Duff, the doctor to the
Australian expedition, had contributed enormously to the
climbers' success by prescribing a vegetarian diet, supplemented by vast quantities of vitamin pills. Perhaps it is all
psychological; if that is the case, it is very good psychology
for we, and the Australians in 1984, maintained excellent
health, suffering nothing worse than slight altitude coughs
and occasional indigestion.

Tuesday – April 12th
   Precious sound of songbirds in the morning, making me think
of spring at home. But here it is still a long way off. Another rest
day. Now impatient to get back to work and push on to the
South Col.

That afternoon I wrote a long letter to Rosie and another
long one to my family, enthusing about our beautiful valley
and our fantastic first week of climbing on Everest. I had
started to convince Robert that a Tyrolean traverse – a bridge
formed by a rope stretched across the Crevasse – was not
such a daft idea. It might take a day or two to rig up, and
would involve descending into the depths of the chasm and
climbing up the overhanging wall on the far side, but Ed, our
chief technician, was getting keen on the idea of some more
aid climbing. He had brought with him a huge selection of
sophisticated rock gadgetry. He not only knew the names of
all the bits and pieces, he also knew what to do with them
and had hoped to exercise his special skills on the overhanging rock of the Kangshung Face. To Robert's immense
relief, we had managed to find a route which avoided this
slow method of rock climbing, and Ed's rurps, copperheads,
bashers and bolts had remained unused at Advance Base.
However, the ice had now proved to be more of a problem
than expected and we were all glad that Ed's aid climbing
skills, learned on rock, could now be applied to a different

medium. If he could fix a rope across the Crevasse, we would have a direct route open to the upper slopes. The only alternative was a descent back onto the flank of Big Al Gully, which would be a dangerous detour, wasting our hard-won height of the first week.

Robert was thrilled with our fast progress and kept reminding us that, whereas we had virtually cracked our Buttress in six days, the Americans in 1983 had taken twenty-eight days to fix their Buttress. 'And there were thirteen of them! *And* they had already spent weeks on it two years earlier.' Admittedly, our Buttress was a bit smaller and slightly easier, but we still had some cause for complacency and optimism. The plan for the second phase was to establish Camp 1 on the Cauliflower Ridge, work from there to bridge the Crevasse, then push on to a second camp and continue right through to the South Col, leaving a small cache of supplies there, ready for when we came back up on the final push to the summit.

It was an ambitious plan, but if the weather remained predominantly fine, as the first week of April had been, it ought to be possible. We were so confident that we were even preparing a mail package. The Nepalese side of the Asian traverse expedition and the Australian Bi-centennial team would soon have camps established on the South Col. One of their members could carry our letters down the Western Cwm to the Khumbu Base Camp where Pasang's cousin was the liaison officer. He could send the mail bag down to Lukla, where Pasang's wife would put it on the plane to Kathmandu, to be posted by our agent, Harihar. All we had to do was get the mail to the frontier on the South Col at 7,986 metres and establish a world altitude record for postal collection.

Often when I thought about the character and the scale of our climb I was reminded of the route which Phil Bartlett, Dave Wilkinson and I had attempted unsuccessfully in 1980 on the north side of Kunyang Kish – a massive giant of the Karakoram, nearly a thousand miles north-west of Everest. There had been a similar cirque of three great peaks: Trivor, Disteghil Sar and Kunyang Kish there; Chomolonzo, Lhotse and Everest here. There had been the same Advance Base at the head of a glacier, right under a route rising nearly 3,500 metres to the summit. The route had broken into the same four stages: the first section to Camp 1, followed by a fairly easy-angled spur, draped with folds of hanging glacier, then above Camp 2 a steepening as the spur merged into the main face of the mountain, leading to a saddle on a ridge, and then, from Camp 3, a sharp turn right up the 850-metre ridge to the summit.

There were, however, two important differences: first, each corresponding stage of the Everest route started a thousand metres higher above sea level; second, the first stage, the Buttress, was much, much harder. Once the Buttress was complete we would have climbed the equivalent of a major alpine route which, on account of its technical difficulties, complex route-finding and objective dangers, deserved the top alpine grade, ED – *Extrêmement Difficile*. Perhaps the Andes would provide a better analogy, for the bizarre ice formations were too grandiose for the European Alps and the altitude of the Buttress, finishing at about 6,500 metres, corresponded to the highest Peruvian peaks. The difference here was that once we reached the top of the Buttress, we would still have 2,000 metres to climb to our summit.

Wednesday – April 13th
Back to the fray. On the way up to ABC made a detour up the hill below Peak 38 to take photos of the Buttress. Once again good old Pasang and Kasang carried up loads.

A little snow in the night, but only a smattering, giving way to starry sky at midnight.

Thursday – April 14th
All four of us up to establish a proper Camp 1 at the foot of Webster's Wall. Walking across the glacier before dawn we had brief benefit of exquisite finger-nail moon low in the sky, with the rest of the shadowed globe just showing. Then, just as we stopped to take off duvets, a huge roar over Lhotse, then sudden amplification as the avalanche burst on the floor of the Witches' Cauldron, erupting into a huge cloud which raced across towards us. Just time to close up rucksack, pull up hood and crouch, ready for two mins smothering in snowdust.

Paul said afterwards that he saw a green flash as the avalanche exploded, presumably a static discharge. The speed of the thing, racing towards us in the dark, was terrifying, but in fact we suffered nothing worse than a blasting by ice dust. We continued to the end of the glacier, up the gully and onto the ropes, then started the slow tedious business of breaking a trail up the snow fields and pulling free the ropes, which were often buried a foot deep. It took us seven hours to get from Advance Base to the shelf below Webster's Wall. By this stage Robert and Ed, who were going to stay up here, had caught up and the four of us dug out a platform for one of the dome tents. It was a sheltered spot just under the crest of the ridge. If there were any giant snow avalanches on the spur above, they would almost certainly be deflected into Big Al Gully or the big depression between us and Lhotse. If by any chance they fell down the centre of the spur, they would be swallowed up by the Crevasse. The slopes immediately above us were not big enough to generate serious snow avalanches and it seemed that any collapsing ice on the towers around the Crevasse would tumble down the front of the Buttress or into Big Al Gully.

Robert and Ed had everything they needed to live up here for a day or two. There were also some supplies at the dump above Webster's Wall and Paul and I would be bringing up two more loads from below. We arranged to leave written messages in the tent each day, wished them good luck in the Crevasse and set off back down to rejoin Mimi at Advance Base.

Friday – April 15th
    Paul and I on yak duty again, taking up another load of rope, fuel and food. This time quicker – up in six hours and glad of cool, due to cloud and light snowfall. But even so those last two 100-metre ropes were a real struggle. My fourth time up to Webster's Wall and seventh time up the lower part of the ropes. Sad and annoyed to arrive at 10 a.m. and find Robert and Ed still in bed, lethargic and negative.
    Paul also cross. I spent the descent envisaging total failure due to American apathy and inability to do anything except in perfect Colorado/California weather.

We descended to ABC in 1 hr 40 mins – this is more like it – back for early lunch. Joe up from BC in afternoon. Thank God Robert and Ed finally made a move and we could watch the tiny figures going up to and disappearing into the Crevasse. But why the hell do they have to wait until 1 p.m.?!

Clear evening with huge winds above, sending wonderful misty torrents of spindrift pouring down Lhotse, the Trinity Gullies and down the gully on the left of American Buttress.

On Saturday we did our third carry. It was always brutally hard, jumaring up all those ropes, but I enjoyed the growing intimacy with familiar landmarks amidst such wild scenery – the edelweiss, clinging to a crack in the rock near one of the first anchors, the section of rope that Ed had wrapped in tape to protect it from abrasion, the brilliant crimson mosses on my Headwall, the purple tape anchor above already starting to fade a little in the ultraviolet, the icicles hanging from the wall of the Scottish Gully, the cave above the gully where I usually stopped for a rest and a drink, before the long exposed traverse, then the exhilaration of the steep pull up to the Terrace and the reassurance of seeing Ed's three-piton anchor, so professionally engineered.

After the Terrace came my traverse where you had to lean right out, hanging from waistlines – always two waistlines, so that one point of attachment always remained while you unclipped to cross an anchor. I traversed the dangerous bay of splintered rock, looking up with the usual awe at the stacked blocks and the white mass of the Greyhound Bus hanging out above, then transferred to the next rope and continued up the gully to wait at the top and photograph Paul.

It was a dramatic picture as he appeared from round the corner below. I was happily clicking away, when he suddenly flung himself against the wall, cowering with hands over head.

'Hold it there. That looks fantastic.'

'You're crazy, Venables!' he shouted up angrily. 'It missed me by inches – a cantaloupe!'

'What's a cantaloupe? Don't move – it's a lovely picture.'

'A melon, Dumbo. Put that bloody camera away. It would have knocked my head off. Helmet no good – *Jinjiput*. Now let's get the hell out of here.'

'Just hold it—'

'It could have killed me!'

'Well it didn't, so you're all right. See you at Camp 1.' I continued up to the camp, where Robert had left a note. The previous day he and Ed had both felt lousy after their first night at this altitude, hence the late start. My sanctimonious outrage had been quite unjustified for they had struggled against lethargy and made a successful recce into the Crevasse. Today they were going to explore an 'alley' which might provide a route out of the Crevasse to the left.

When Paul and I returned to Advance Base, Mimi asked us if we had heard the roar. We had heard nothing, so she pointed up to the apex of the Buttress. The Sickle was completely changed. Apparently a huge chunk had fallen off, crashing to the glacier and sending a blast most of the way down to Advance Base. Meanwhile Ed and Robert were somewhere up behind it, hidden in the Crevasse. Unknown to us they too were having their dramas that morning.

They both abseiled into the wide snowy bed of the chasm. Then Robert paid out the rope as Ed set off to explore, treading carefully on the snow floor, wary of thin bridges hiding unseen depths. He crossed to the far wall and started to follow the Crevasse round to the left. To reach the alley he would have to walk under a gigantic leaning block, squeezing between it and the main wall of the Crevasse. The oblong block was about twenty-five metres high and only the very top was attached to the Crevasse wall. Ed was understandably nervous, but Robert shouted cheerfully, 'Don't worry, these things only come down once in twenty years.' Ed moved closer, then stopped a few metres from the leaning tower to place an ice screw, so that the rope would be clipped into something if he should fall into a lower concealed crevasse. He was balanced in an awkward position so, instead of the fiddly screw-in type, he placed a drive-in. This meant hammering violently and driving tremors through the Crevasse wall.

There was a hideous crack and Ed ran in terror, yanking the rope behind him, as hundreds of tons of ice crashed through the air. A few seconds later the leaning tower lay shattered in a thousand pieces on the bed of the Crevasse.

Afterwards Ed said that he was glad he had used a drive-in ice screw. Perhaps if he had used the gentler screw-in type there might not have been sufficient vibration to bring down the tower until he continued to walk right underneath it. Like Paul the same morning, he had had a lucky escape and now had no intention of looking for 'easy alleys' round to the left. He rejoined Robert and almost immediately, before shock could set in, started to climb straight up the smooth back wall of the Crevasse. Down at Advance Base it was late in the afternoon when we suddenly saw Ed's red jacket appear on the smooth snow slope beyond the Crevasse.

Looking through the telescope, particularly in the flat light of that misty afternoon, it was almost impossible to discern any break in the slope between the Fourth Cauliflower Tower and the point Ed had now reached. Mimi and Joe found it hard to believe that there was a crevasse there at all; but Paul had glimpsed it the previous week and I had actually seen the impending far wall, which Ed had now climbed with such efficiency, enabling him to construct an anchor on the far side of the gap and open the way to the South Col.

The Buttress was lost in cloud the next day and we never saw Robert and Ed perfecting the finer details of the Tyrolean traverse. After three consecutive days' load-carrying, Paul and I were having a rest day. It was snowing intermittently and I spent most of the day in my tent, reading, dreaming and listening to music. Mimi was starting to get depressed by the long sojourns at camp and the inevitably subordinate role she was filling at this stage – a non-climbing doctor waiting on healthy climbers who refused to get ill. I needed some exercise, so we took a rope, ice axes and crampons and had some practice on a small ice wall a little way down the glacier. I don't think that I was a very good teacher, but we had good fun, falling off harmlessly and enjoying the air and exercise which, as always, transformed the gloom of a grey day.

At dusk Robert and Ed returned with the good news that they had fixed a rope across the Crevasse and another rope almost to the top of the Hump beyond. With any luck, another rope or two should see us through any difficulties. Paul and I hoped to go up the next day, but heavy snowfall deterred us and we did not go up to sleep at Camp 1 until Tuesday. On Wednesday we woke to more unsettled weather.

Wednesday – April 20th
   Camp 1. Ominous morning. Thick pale clouds below. High, bleak, grey skim above. Very clear silver and gold luminosity on those peaks beyond Kharta. Brooding silence. It reminded me of many similar spring days in the Alps over the last 12 years. Ed and Robert, carrying up from ABC, noticed the same ominous silence. Apparently the choughs even were absent – not doing their usual cheeky acrobatics, diving in to collect the crumbs from our snacks.

The weather was not encouraging, but Paul and I hoped at least to explore for a hundred metres or so beyond the others' highpoint, so at eight in the morning we set off from Camp 1, eager to see the Tyrolean traverse. While they were working at it, Robert had said to Ed, 'We did this at Outward Bound when I was fifteen, but I never thought I'd have to do it again.' Now, fifteen years later, he *had* done it again – for real. They had made a good job of it, stretching a 9mm rope tight across the chasm, anchored at the bottom lip to several ice screws and on the far side to deeply driven snow stakes. The sharp lower lip where I had clung so precariously twelve days earlier was now hacked out to a flat platform, where you could stand comfortably while you tied your rucksack onto a loose rope, ready to be pulled across afterwards, then clipped the karabiner on your waist harness into the tight rope. Having secured the karabiner safety lock, you fixed both jumars to the rope in front, leaned back facing the sky, let your weight come on to the rope, wrapped one leg over for balance and pushed off with the other leg.

Paul recorded it all on Kodachrome and I dragged myself across, hanging horizontally and staring dizzily at the sky-scraper walls around me. The upper lip of the Crevasse was about ten metres higher than the lower one, so the rope was at quite an incline and it was a gasping business to pull up your weight on the two sliding jumars and climb steeply out onto the far bank.

Paul sent the rucksacks and my camera across on the pulley system, then I recorded his journey over the void. Ed had christened this obstacle the Jaws of Doom and from above it looked even more spectacular, particularly on that misty morning – Paul suspended on the world's highest rope-bridge, just hanging there with the serrated lower jaw of the Crevasse behind, apparently poised vertically above the faint grey shapes of the Kangshung Glacier over a thousand metres below.

As always the anchor was backed up, just in case it should fail: as well as being tied off to the two buried stakes, the end of the crossing rope was tied into the rope above, which led up an easy snow slope. I waded my way up this, unintentionally sending down a mini-avalanche which knocked Paul off his feet. A bamboo wand marked the buried anchor near the top of the Hump. Then I continued up new ground. The slopes were already heavily laden, more snow was starting to fall and the clouds were enveloping us completely. The evil threat of dawn was being fulfilled and we both felt nervous. I climbed steeply, straight up, to avoid cutting across the slope and releasing another avalanche. It was hard work, pushing and shoving with arms and legs against piles of snow, pulling in great gulps of air in the effort to rush up and see over the Hump.

There was another crevasse.

Ice, snow and cloud blended into an almost uniform greyness and I had to move warily, avoiding the lip of the great fracture. I walked across to the right, getting just close enough to the edge to see that this crevasse also extended right into Big Al Gully. So I walked back left, dragging the rope impatiently, kicking furiously through the snow, desperate to find a way round. Everywhere above there seemed to be overhanging walls of ice, a great complex of ravines and cliffs completely hidden from the valley. But I was lucky: descending a short way to the left I could see a way through. This had to be it – we couldn't start more complicated rope manoeuvres.

There was a slight crust on the snow now and I could move quickly, striding across to the left, ice axe in one hand, dragging rope in the other. Another huge crevasse ran longitudinally down the slope, but there was a solid snow bridge across it, leading me towards the far left crest of the spur.

I was now walking right underneath a great jumble of ice blocks, dominated by one leaning mass the size of a large house. I had to cross another longitudinal crevasse, sitting down to move astride a jammed block of ice. Glancing nervously up to the right, I saw the cellar of the large house – a turquoise cavern where the ice had been crushed into a chaotic jumble of boulders. Through the boulders I glimpsed dark slits going deep into the mountain. Staring into that cavern I felt the same awful fascination for its dangerous beauty that I had felt as a child, exploring Cornish sea caves. But this place was infinitely more dangerous and I had to hurry on, treading carefully over the jammed snow and ice across the crevasse, then with relief climbing up out of the ravine, kicking steps up steep snow to a safe haven where I could hammer in a snow stake and tie off the rope.

Paul was not amused. Already that morning he had been knocked off his feet by my avalanche. Now I had failed to fix the rope in a straight line and as he followed up on jumars, the rope suddenly twanged tight, whipping Paul ten metres across the slope in a wave of released snow. I heard nothing until he appeared over the crest of the Hump fifty metres away, shouting furiously. I apologized for not flicking the rope over the slope in a straight line but assured him that he was safe, with the rope tied off to a good snow stake. I still had about twelve metres left and I was longing to see a little higher and make quite sure that we really had cracked the Buttress at last, so I rushed up the wall of snow and ice

The author enjoying a rare clear dawn at the Langma La, with the Kangshung Face waiting eighteen miles away. Photo: Ed Webster

Paul Teare watches as Pasang pays the Nepalese porters who carried our luggage across Friendship Bridge to the Chinese border post of Zangmu.

The crest of the Pang La (5,200 m) and our first close view of Everest. The Kangshung Face is still hidden on the left under the usual plume of cloud and snow, blasted off the summit by the prevailing westerlies. Makalu is at the extreme left, Gychung Kang and Cho Oyu on the right.

On 24 March, the porters set off from Lhatse and follow our trail towards the Langma La. The Gyankar range is in the background.

Joe with his view camera on the Langma La, with Lhotse and Everest still seventeen miles away. Most of the proposed route is visible, but the lowest, hardest part is still hidden by an intervening ridge.

Paul awakes to a brilliant morning after another storm on the approach. The main summit of Chomolonzo (7,790 m) is on the left.

Below left: Mimi sorting out sixty barrels of food at Base Camp. The great wall of the Kangshung Face dominates the head of the valley, with our goal, the South Col, on the left and the immense North-East Ridge on the right.   Below right: 3 April — our first day's climbing on the Buttress. The author has fixed eighty metres of rope up the Headwall and Robert now follows on a jumar. About a mile away an avalanche crashes down off Lhotse into the Witches' Cauldron.

Above left: *Ed reaches the cave anchor at the top of the Scottish gully, with the glacier 400 m below.* Above right: *An avalanche thunders down Big Al Gully, between the 1983 buttress and our 1988 buttress on the left.* Photo: Joseph Blackburn

Ed, high on the left, leading Webster's Wall, at the point where the ice starts to overhang.

Nearly 1,000 m above the dark crevasses of the Kangshung Glacier, Ed jumars up to the complex ice screw anchor on the lower lip of the Crevasse. It has to support this downward pull and then an opposing pull from the Tyrolean traverse (below). Each day the rope got slightly tighter as the Crevasse widened.

Above left: *Ed climbing the overhanging wall of the Crevasse to fix the Tyrolean traverse.* Above right: *1 May. Ed on the upper slopes at last. Ice terraces off Shartse behind, with Chomolonzo in the distance.*

Ed at Camp 1. Snow is melting in the hanging gas stoves.

The four climbers on 5 May, about to set off on another abortive summit attempt. L to R: Robert, Paul, Ed and author, with the Lady of the Lake, the expedition snow woman, who later sank in a mass of bubbles when the ice broke up. Photo: Joseph Blackburn

At sunrise on 9 May Robert takes first turn at breaking the new trail to Camp 2.

Bad weather brewing early on the morning of 9 May, as Ed and Paul follow the trail onto the upper spur.

At 10 p.m. on 11 May, the wind miraculously dropped. Robert has on all his clothing for the summit attempt, but he still has to make the huge physical and intellectual effort to sit up and fit crampons to his boots. Ed, Robert and Stephen are about to leave the South Col.

10 May. Paul and Robert preparing to leave Camp 2, protected by the great ice roof of the Flying Wing. Makalu, the dark pyramid on the left, is 12 miles away.

Left: *The only summit photograph! A Buddhist prayer flag hangs from one of the empty oxygen cylinders left the previous week by the Asian Friendship Expedition. Underneath, amongst discarded television transmission equipment, are the two little envelopes which contained Nawang's and Sonam's flower petals.*

Below: *The immense Kangshung Face at dawn, from Base Camp. (See drawing pp 82-3.)* Photo: Joseph Blackburn

Facing page: *The abandoned Japanese tent where Ed and Robert sheltered on the descent. Ed took this photo at dawn on the way up. The huge plateau of the South Col is now about 350 m below. The summits of Shartse and Peak 38 are also below us and we are almost level with Makalu (L) and Lhotse Shar (R).* Photo: Ed Webster

12 May. At 2 p.m. clouds were swirling round the summit ridge as I approached the famous Hillary Step. There are remains of tracks left by Nepalese climbers two days earlier and two fixed ropes hang down the Step. The summit is about 300 m horizontally beyond the highest point in the picture.

I did not manage a smile for the camera, but this was one of the happiest moments of my life – rejoining Ed and Robert after my open bivouac at 8,600 m. The iced-up sunglasses, pulled off to find my way down the Hillary Step the previous afternoon, were still hanging round my neck. I had also not found the strength to pack away my headtorch. Before taking this photo, Ed handed me the last trickle of half-frozen juice in his water bottle. Photo: Ed Webster

Above: *Ed and Stephen post-Everest*

Left: *Robert and Stephen celebrate leaving Karta with a beer, 29 May, 1988.*

L to R: Wendy, Norbu, Mimi and Robert with two boys from Xegar, at the start of the expedition.

L to R: Paul, Stephen, Robert, Ed, Joe and Mimi at Advance Base, just before the summit push.

above, with just enough rope to reach the top, where I hammered in the last snow stake and stopped for a rest.

We had done it. I was right on the crest of the main spur standing at the start of comparatively smooth slopes which would lead us up the remaining 1,350 or so metres to the South Col. Below me now was the fractured chaos of seracs and crevasses, where the hanging glacier was stretched and wrenched apart as it curved over the top of the Buttress. Once again I had the unnerving sensation of standing on the crest of an enormous wave, in a place where human beings were not intended to go.

It was snowing now, we were alone in the cloud and from every direction we could hear the muffled roar of avalanches. Although we were on the crest of the spur, safe from big snow avalanches, there was a feeling of menace in the air and Paul's melodramatic shouts intensified my fear. Twice on the precarious crevasse crossing the snow collapsed under his feet and he yelled up, 'Fucking hell, Venables, where are you taking me?' The shouting continued intermittently as he edged across. 'This is crazy . . . Let's get the hell out of here . . . Venables – you're mad!'

Suddenly I felt a horrible tremor go through the ice. A moment later there was a grinding crash up by the house-sized ice block and another great slice of ice tumbled into the cavern.

'Look, Stephen, this is dangerous!'

'Of course it's dangerous. Hanging glaciers *are* dangerous – they're always moving downhill. You come ten thousand miles specially to climb a hanging glacier and now you complain it's dangerous!'

I felt equally awed by it all, but from my high viewpoint I could see that there was no other route. If we wanted to climb the East Face we would have to climb through this jumble of ice. It was a nasty place, but if we fixed the rope properly now, it could be crossed in two minutes on any future journeys and there would probably be only four more trips to make. Compared to the risks which hundreds of people take every year on the other side of the mountain in the Khumbu Icefall, it seemed quite reasonable.

I came down to Paul, we fixed the rope to make a secure handrail across the Jumble, then hurried back down to Camp 1. By 2 p.m. we were back in our bright yellow haven and snow was melting on the gas stove for the first brew.

Paul was his usual solicitous self, urging me to keep drinking. 'Five litres a day, you're meant to have.' Dehydration is the scourge of high-altitude climbers and we were taking great pains always to take in as much liquid as possible in the form of soup, coffee, cocoa, fruit juice and a bewildering variety of teas. Of course, healthy rehydration had its reverse side – the need to pee frequently – so we all carried quart pee bottles to avoid the horror of leaving the tent during the night. Ed had even explained the art of peeing without leaving your sleeping bag.

'It's quite simple – you just lie on your back and hold the bottle between your legs, tilted very slightly – like pouring a very fizzy beer.' It required nerve and concentration for the consequences of poor aim or a clumsy spillage would be dire indeed, inside $500-worth of luxurious down sleeping bag which one had to continue using for several weeks.

Our virtuoso techniques had been polished up during all those tentbound delays on the walk-in. One day Mimi had turned to Wendy and said, 'Hey, listen to these men. They're just *so* strong and clever: they can carry sixty-pound loads, they can climb Everest *and* they can pee in bottles. Isn't that fantastic?'

Robert's riposte was to reminisce about Heidi, the girl on the West Ridge in 1985, who used a pee bottle 'at twenty-four and a half thousand feet!' The challenge had been set. Mimi found a suitably wide-necked bottle and appeared beaming and triumphant at breakfast the next morning.

Paul and I treated ourselves to Hypnovol tablets and slept well that night at Camp 1. When the alarm rang at four in the morning I was reluctant to sit up and light the stove for breakfast. I unzipped the tent door to look down the valley to the east, where there seemed to be a lot of cloud on the dark horizon. By dawn clouds were again closing in from above and below and we started to discuss our plan of action. I was reluctant to descend, particularly as I had recently lambasted the others for their reluctance to climb in bad weather, as if they were on 'some poncy climbing holiday in California'. By working stubbornly at the route in mediocre weather we had solved the crucial problem of the Crevasse and then pushed on to the end of the major difficulties. All the same, it was now thirteen days since I had discovered the Crevasse and in that time we had only gained a hundred metres height. I was anxious to push on and reconnoitre the route up the spur. I was convinced that it was going to be quite easy, but there might be small awkward steps or crevasses to fix. The sooner we discovered any problems the better.

Paul disagreed: 'It's been snowing several inches every day. Those slopes are getting loaded. You saw what they were like yesterday.'

'Come on – they weren't that bad – just small slides. And it hasn't actually been snowing that heavily. If we're only prepared to climb in immaculate weather, we'll never get up this mountain. Let's at least wait here a day and see what happens.' The tent was extremely secure and comfortable and still had some stocks of food and gas, but Paul was quick to point out the disadvantages of waiting. 'If we sit here we're just burning fuel, eating food . . . all that stuff has to be carried up here. And we'll burn ourselves out at this altitude. Much better to wait at Base Camp.'

I agreed reluctantly that to stay here would probably mean wasting our supplies and energy in fruitless wallowing up dangerous slopes. At 7.30 a.m. we left for Advance Base. The others were very relieved to see us safely down and agreed that we should all return to Base Camp to sit out the bad weather. Paul and I had raced down the ropes in record time. We were extremely fit and by midday we were back at Base. After lunch I put on clean warm clothes, retired to the comfort of my sleeping bag and settled down to read Somerset Maugham's *The Razor's Edge* for the first time in thirteen years.

7
Snakes and Ladders

Friday – April 22nd
Lovely line in *The Razor's Edge*: 'American women expect to find in their husbands a perfection that English women only hope to find in their butlers.'
It snowed most of last night and most of today.

Saturday – April 23rd
Cloudy and blustery. Kasang stole a mutilated Tibetan snow cock from the eagle that was trying to pick it up.

Sunday – April 24th
Snow. Ate Charlie for lunch.

CHARLIE belonged to one of the flocks of ramchakor which lived in the grassy haven of the ablation valley. These snow cocks are as common to the Himalaya as the ptarmigan is to Scotland and, when the mists came rolling up from the Kangshung valley, the strange tootling of the birds heightened the mysterious atmosphere of our isolated home. On the Saturday morning of our second interlude at Base Camp Kasang was up at the stream collecting water, when he saw an eagle swoop on one of the snow cocks, killing it with a single blow of its talons, but failing to pick it up. As the eagle came in for another attempt Kasang dashed across the ground and snatched its prize. As a good Buddhist he knew that it was wrong to take life, but he had let the eagle do the killing for him and could bring the dead bird back to the kitchen with a clear conscience, confident that its death would not bring bad karma.

Kasang plucked and gutted the bird. On Sunday Pasang boned it, and fried the small pieces of meat in onions and spices. It made an excellent meal with curried potatoes and vegetables, but Mimi refused to attend lunch and warned of dire consequences from this sudden abandonment of our vegetarian diet. Ed and I did suffer some indigestion, but I do not think it was induced specifically by meat. Indigestion seems to be a common problem when you are living for weeks above 5,000 metres, particularly at Base Camp when you are trying to lay in reserves of food to combat the drastic deterioration of body tissue higher up.

Everyone seemed preoccupied with worries about the climb. After our brilliant opening move on the Buttress we seemed to have reached stalemate. All that talk of finishing the climb before the end of April had been a little premature and even my secret wish of reaching the top on my birthday, 2 May, now seemed unrealistic. Reading accounts of all those pre-war attempts, we realized just how much they had been thwarted by bad weather. On the other hand, some of their experiences gave cause for optimism. In 1924 they had been frustrated for weeks in their attempts to establish a camp on the North Col, but their patience had eventually been rewarded in June when they reached the col and established two camps above it, from which Norton made his inspiring summit attempt, reaching 8,600 metres on a perfect day. We had still not reached the end of April, we had enough food for several more weeks and, provided the Monsoon did not strike early, we ought surely to be allowed some fine weather during the next month?

I was also inspired by *White Limbo*, the account of the Australian 1984 expedition led by Tim McCartney-Snape. He and his friends had waited nearly three months in the Rongbuk basin, nibbling away at the lower part of their route before they got the chance to push through to the top. From their final camp at about 8,300 metres, near the top of the Great Couloir, four climbers set out for the summit.

Lindsay Hall abandoned the attempt when he realized that he was moving too slowly, but the other three pushed on. Andy Henderson had badly fitting crampons and had to halt several times during the day to take off mittens and adjust the cold metal. By the time he stopped at dusk, only fifty metres short of the summit, his fingers were badly frostbitten. The other two, though, had just reached the summit to witness sunset from the top of the world. Late that night, after an epic descent in the dark, leaving their only rope behind to safe-guard the precarious pitch which had deterred Norton sixty years earlier, the three men rejoined Hall at the tent. Two days later they were all safely off the mountain, completing one of the most spectacular successes in the history of Everest.

There were many lessons to be learned from their ascent. Robert had met Henderson in New Zealand.

'He was starting to think about how to cope with life after his injuries. Things like using a knife and fork are quite difficult when you don't have any fingers.'

It was a macabre reminder of the risks and of the import-ance of having all equipment in perfect working order, ensuring that once one left on the summit day mittens would only have to be taken off for the briefest moments. Another member of the team had started to develop symptoms of cerebral oedema on the way down and the descent for him had become a struggle for life.

There was no doubting that it was a dangerous game and, unlike the Australians, we would have no climbers below, capable of coming up to help in an emergency. However, despite all the manifest dangers, I was thrilled and encour-aged by the description of Tim McCartney-Snape and Greg Mortimer emerging onto the final summit slope, driven on by fanatic determination and the euphoric realization that now nothing could stop them. I had always been inspired by the great fighters – Hermann Buhl pushing on alone to the summit of Nanga Parbat, Haston fighting his way out of the Eiger Direct, Bonatti on the Walker Spur in winter, Kurtyka and Schauer forcing their way so boldly up the immense

West Face of Gasherbrum IV. Perhaps it was arrogant of me, but I had always aspired to that kind of climbing and I was fascinated by the idea of pushing myself way beyond the normal frontiers of tiredness.

This is not to suggest that we were deliberately seeking danger for its own sake. We had put a lot of thought and effort into finding the safest route possible up the Buttress. We were laying in stocks of food and fuel on the mountain so that we could survive a difficult extended retreat. And we were constantly discussing tactics and timings. We had planned to have reached 8,000 metres by this stage, but the projected cache on the South Col had been thwarted by bad weather and we had still not been higher than about 6,500 metres. Now we revised our plans: we would reconnoitre the route to Camp 2, at about 7,450 metres, leaving tents, food and fuel there, ready for the final push. When we came through the second time, after sleeping at Camp 2, we would lift the tents and carry everything straight through to the South Col, make our third camp there, then travel light to the summit.

I had always thought that one's best chance lay in going once to 8,000 metres, descending for a rest, then pushing straight through. However, Ed pointed out that this may not be the best way to acclimatize. Messner on his solo ascent never went above 7,000 metres before setting off on his summit push. The Australians had only reconnoitred as far as 7,400 metres before their final climb, and in 1986 Ed had been on the Rongbuk with Troillet and Loretan, who never went above 6,500 metres until they left on their phenomenal dash up and down the mountain. The message seemed to be: get really fit and well acclimatized between 6,000 and 7,000 metres, but don't waste energy burning yourself out at 8,000 metres before the final push. That would be like climbing Annapurna, then trying to climb Everest a week later.

The final stage of our climb would be easier than the Australians' for there is little doubt that the South-East Ridge is the easiest way of surmounting the final pyramid. However it would also be longer for, whereas the Australians camped at about 8,300 metres, we would be starting our last leg at 7,986 metres on the South Col, with an 862-metre height gain to the summit – almost 3,000 feet to ascend and descend in a day. Pasang had been at the South Col, the world's most notoriously bleak campsite, in 1969. He advised that we should arrive on the col ideally at midday, spend all afternoon in our tents melting snow and forcing down liquid, rest a little in the evening and then set off for the summit at midnight.

Talking analytically in this way, it was easy to believe that our ambitions were realizable. We had already put so much into the climb, proving that this new route up the East Face was feasible, that we wanted desperately now to complete it and reach the summit. It is hardly surprising that, with success so demonstrably possible, we were depressed and irritated by the continuing unsettled weather.

Monday brought a respite. Ed, Joe and I walked up the hillside above the camp in brilliant sunshine. On the northern side of the Kangshung Glacier there is no great wall of mountains, just grassy slopes leading up to lakes, ancient moraines and the vestigial remains of tamed glaciers, that have shrunk significantly since Mallory's visit. We took hundreds of photographs and walked up to the foot of Khartse, the peak which Mallory described as the most lovely he had ever seen. He climbed it in 1921 to try and gain a clear view of the north-eastern flank of Everest. It would have been fun to attempt this or one of the other comparatively low peaks dividing the Kama and Kharta valleys with Joe and Mimi. It would have been fun also to cross the high passes to the Rongbuk Glacier, use the Japanese satellite telephone and see how my British military friends were doing on the West Ridge, but we had neither the time nor the equipment to spare. As soon as the weather looked properly settled we would have to concentrate all our energies on completing the new route up the East Face which sponsors had paid us nearly $200,000 to climb.

However, for that day at least we were free to wander through some of the most delightful walking country in the world, accompanying Joe to his altitude record of 5,600 metres at a little pass which we named the Blackburn La, then running back down by a different route to Base Camp. On Tuesday the waiting game continued.

Tuesday – April 26th
5th day down at BC. 5 p.m. Still cold fog and a little snow, but birds outside making spring noises. Green shoots suddenly multiplying on ground after melting snow of last few days.
Went for evening walk down to the lake about 40 mins below here. Came back in an excellent mood. Saw lots of redstarts – a type I haven't seen before – brown with bright pinkish orange head and chest. Also have seen white-capped redstarts.
Birds, evening light on Makalu and apparent improvement in weather put me in a good mood. At BC kitchen Pasang and Kasang doing a great double comedy act.
In the evening Robert discussed plans. He and Paul will go back up to ABC tomorrow and probably continue on Thursday to C1. Ed and I, still recovering from suspect guts, will follow a day later. I fear inevitably that we are being fobbed off as B Team, hanging back while Robert and Paul forge ahead.

Wednesday – April 27th
Robert and Paul left in the morning – the first clear morning for ages. Mimi, Joe, Ed and I remained here with P and K. I continued with the biography of Hemingway – what an obnoxious shit.
Very windy here at BC. Big cloud build-up in evening and some snow. Anxious about weather and my own health – legs feel unduly weak, pain in chest nagging . . . if only we could finish this job quickly.

I had been through all this so many times before on expeditions, the needless anxiety and hypochondria after spending too long at Base Camp. There was nothing wrong with my health and the next morning I raced back to Advance Base in a record three hours, enjoying the familiar journey through the wasteland of Everest's detritus. The rocks littering the glacier were a shifting mosaic of slate, quartzite and marble, pale granite studded with garnets, rose quartz and some beautiful olive green crystals, all testifying to the geological complexity

of the Kangshung Face. The route was marked with our
cairns, not the shapeless heaps of rock which you find in
Wales or the Lake District, but beautiful, funny, idiosyn-
cratic sculptures designed to show up amidst the gargantuan
mounds of rubble. On the last mile or two to Advance Base
the route passed huge glacial lakes, enclosed by hollowed
walls of ice, carved and marbled in every shade of green and
blue. The water of one lake had escaped through a submerged crevasse, causing the surface ice to collapse and shatter
into a jigsaw of jagged slabs. I remembered Monet's 'Break-
Up of the Ice at Lavacourt' and thought what a field day he
could have had on the Kangshung Glacier.

The A Team was still at Advance Base, as it had snowed
heavily during the night, prohibiting a dawn departure. By
the time Ed arrived in the afternoon it was snowing yet again
and I wrote in my diary: 'Dreaming of wine, gardens, piano
playing and women.' Robert dispelled my worries about
being paired off into unequal teams. I have always preferred
to keep changing the combinations on a big climb, and I was
glad now to hear that Robert envisaged a summit push with
all four of us going together. As he pointed out, it was
unlikely that all of us would make it up the final stretch and
having four people together allowed for swapping partners
to suit circumstances. Also, if the four of us stayed together,
at least as far as the South Col, there would be some hope of
evacuating an injured climber in the event of an accident.

If everything went well, four of us would climb together
to the South Col, but for the moment Robert and Paul would
start the recce to Camp 2. When the weather allowed, the
plan would be: Day 1 – Ed and Stephen do final load carry to
Camp 1 and descend; Robert and Paul sleep at Camp 1. Day
2 – Robert and Paul start wallow to Camp 2 then descend to
Camp 1; Ed and Stephen carry up remaining personal gear to
sleep at Camp 1. Day 3 – Ed and Stephen take over lead and
complete route to Camp 2. After day 3 we would play it by
ear.

The sky started to clear after midnight and by dawn the
next morning Ed and I went on our way, excavating the

lower ropes from a metre-deep avalanche debris. Only a few more supplies were needed at Camp 1, so we carried light loads and, in spite of the laborious trail-breaking, reached the camp in five and a half hours. On the way down we passed the other two jumaring up.

That evening Ed and I selected the final food supplies to supplement the store at Camp 1 and discussed exactly what high-altitude clothing to take up. We really hoped that this time we might be leaving on the final push and the next morning, Saturday 30 April, Joe set up his flash equipment in the pre-dawn darkness to record what we all hoped was the departure for the summit. Joe's photography and Ed's slow preparations delayed us by an hour so that we were still safely down on the glacier when a monstrous avalanche blasted down Big Al Gully just before dawn. Most of the force had been dissipated by the time it hit us, but perhaps if we had been up on the Headwall, as planned, we would actually have been hurt as the avalanche spilled over the sides of the gully. It was another reminder that each time we made this journey up the Buttress we were inevitably exposing ourselves to some risk.

When I arrived at Camp 1, Robert had just left and was jumaring up the ropes 150 metres above the Jaws of Doom. He and Paul returned at dusk, tired and content. Ed and I had cut a huge pile of snow bricks and had three stoves going at once, so that we could hand out a steady supply of hot drinks to the other two, as they told us about the day's discoveries. Robert was euphoric.

'It's all clear now.'

'No more horrible crevasses?'

'No – just one awkward place; but there was a good bridge, nothing serious enough to need a fixed rope. It's really straightforward up there.'

'It's easy, man,' Paul gasped between gulps of fruit juice, 'just easy. You could ski it. Really easy-angled. "Other men, less wise . . ." We were right up there, above Big Al, looking down on his loose denture. But *deep* snow –'

'No crust?'

'No crust anywhere. All the way it's like this' – he cut with a mittened hand at his knee – 'real high-altitude wallowing.'

The snow conditions had been exhausting, but Robert and Paul had made a good start on the trail to Camp 2 and were convinced that there were no obstacles ahead. If the weather remained fine in the morning Ed and I would forge ahead up the others' track, and complete our share of trail-breaking to Camp 2. We would carry fairly light loads and the other two would follow with the rest of the supplies. Between us we would take up two tiny dome tents, two stoves, twelve gas cylinders and food for three days, caching it all at a safe campsite ready for the summit push. Later we would return with personal high-altitude clothing and sleeping bags. Because of the huge height gain – over 1,000 metres – and the deep snow between Camps 1 and 2, it would have been impossible to carry up everything on one journey, sleep at Camp 2 and still be in any fit state to continue to the South Col and the summit.

May Day dawned clear and I was away up the ropes. The free-hanging jumar up Webster's Wall was brutal, but my runnel on the Fourth Cauliflower Tower was gentler. Already our East Face was flaming pink and gold, and purple light was creeping across the Kangshung Glacier a thousand metres beneath my feet. I reached the snow stakes and transferred to the next rope for the traverse up to the Jaws of Doom, hurrying past the tottering menace of the Gargoyle. There was a pause to photograph Ed as he followed, then more photographs on the Tyrolean traverse, where the rope was now taut as a fiddle string, pulled ever tighter by the widening jaws of the Crevasse. Then on through the Jumble to the end of the fixed ropes, where we left our jumars and roped together on a short length of our lightest 7mm line to safeguard the journey through the labyrinth of crevasses on the upper spur.

Two hours later we reached the end of Paul and Robert's tracks. Now the hard work started. Rhythm was paramount and I timed each step to coincide with a full breath in and out, counting out the steps patiently, forcing my lungs and legs to keep going through seventeen, eighteen . . . only two more to go . . . nineteen . . . *twenty*. Rest weight on lower leg. Clutch at the air with gaping mouth. Resist the temptation to bend over and lean on knee – no, stay upright, allowing the lungs room to expand, extracting every possible molecule of oxygen from the thin air, forcing them into those red blood cells to reinvigorate shattered leg muscles for the next twenty kicks through the relentless deep snow.

The great secret is to get the rhythm. Once that is right, you can plod on for hours. I was almost enjoying myself, kicking doggedly forward, so when Ed shouted for a photo stop for what seemed the hundredth time, I turned round and yelled furiously. 'For Christ's sake, why do we have to stop all the time? I've spent the whole of this trip waiting for you – waiting on the ropes, waiting for you to get your arse out of bed in the morning and waiting for you to take your bloody photos. We've got a mountain to climb.' Gasping and apoplectic, I turned round, yanking the rope obstinately, and stomped off for another twenty paces.

Later we stopped for a rest and I apologized to Ed. He explained that he had always been slow and had been called the Tortoise in 1985. He also wanted and needed to pause for pictures. Photography was one of the most important things in his life and there was no reason why my impetuousness should stop him recording this brilliant morning high on Everest. Looking out over the Kangshung valley, we were in a new dimension. The glacier now seemed to belong to another world. The American Buttress of 1983, which for so long had been our gauge of progress, was now below us and when an avalanche broke loose from the face of Lhotse, on our right, we found ourselves looking down on it.

We trudged on, weaving a line through hummocks, trying to avoid steep exposed avalanche-prone slopes and marking crucial junctures with bamboo wands. When the slope steepened, I had to slow my pace, taking two full breaths to each step and resting every ten steps. Infinite patience was required and I tried to avoid looking too far ahead. The South Col seemed so close and attainable, yet it was still over a thousand metres above us and I had to limit my ambition to the few metres ahead.

The sun blazed down mercilessly, heating the great white furnace of the East Face, forcing us to stop again and unpack water bottles. Then we continued, zigzagging through a zone of crevasses. We were almost stopped by one enormous gash, which seemed to cross the entire slope, but after a detour to the right we found a natural bridge leading safely to the far side and a traverse back left to the main slope. Now the afternoon cloud was closing in and we were alone on an interminable grey slope, weary from the long hours of trail-breaking. All the joy had gone out of the day and I was now only managing four or five steps between ever longer rests, leaning dejectedly on my ski stick and ice axe.

Our goal was the Flying Wing – a vast wing-shaped slab of ice about 500 metres below the South Col, where we hoped to find a safe campsite. It now looked very close, but I had been trail-breaking for nearly six hours and I was only managing one step at a time. I could do no more, so Ed took a turn in front and for a while I enjoyed the luxury of following in someone else's steps. But even that became a struggle as he pressed on relentlessly. It was late and snowing. I shouted up, 'Ed, how much further are we going? What are you doing? Why can't we stop here?'

Robert and Paul had now caught up and were joining in the shouting, trying to persuade Ed to stop. But he was determined to continue, always shouting down, 'Just a little further. Look it's just up there – the Flying Wing. There's nowhere safe to leave the stuff here.'

'Please, can't we dump it on that ice cliff over there?'

'No, it's no good. Just a little further.' The tortoise was getting his revenge on the hare, ruthlessly dragging me up through the swirling cloud.

The final section was a nightmare of collapsing steps up steep powder snow. Then came relief and thanks to Ed for making us come all the way to this haven of a campsite, protected by the huge roof of the Flying Wing. We fixed some ice screws to the roof and left all the equipment hanging from them, confident that here it would be quite safe until we returned. We all felt wasted and dehydrated after eleven hours' hard labour, but not one of us had a headache and we were all breathing with ease at our new estimated altitude of 7,450 metres. It had been a good day's work and now everything was in place for the summit bid.

The descent to Camp 1 only took one and a half hours. Suddenly it was all so easy, rushing down with gravity on our side, leaping crevasses, sitting down to slide at exuberant speed down the steeper sections, then clipping into the fixed ropes for the abseils, the whizzing slide over the Jaws of Doom, down my runnel and over the edge of Webster's Wall, to tumble by the last glimmer of daylight back to Camp 1.

The clouds had vanished, the weather was fine and Robert wanted to go straight back up the next day to continue through to the top, but Ed and I felt exhausted from the long day of trail-breaking. I just wanted to sink into the warm oblivion of my sleeping bag and I had to struggle to stay awake for the long session of snow melting to produce our supper. Eventually at midnight I gave up, even though we were not yet sufficiently rehydrated, and sank into a profound sleep.

At dawn I sat up to continue the work of melting snow. Robert still wanted to push on, arguing that we could leave fairly late, because with the trail now broken it would only take about six hours to reach Camp 2. Ed, however, was still very weary and was adamant that he needed more rest. Paul and I were loath to waste what might be one of a limited ration of fine days sitting here, then arrive at the South Col to discover that we were one day late for our summit attempt. On the other hand, I also felt desperately tired and I really wanted to be in perfect condition before I left on a gruelling summit push. In the end we agreed to delay our bid for a day.

It was 2 May, my birthday, and the others presented me with a cake consisting of a Mars Bar with a cigarette lighter stuck in the top for a candle. My wish, needless to say, was that we should reach the summit of Everest. A year earlier I had spent my thirty-third birthday climbing on one of the Derbyshire gritstone outcrops with Henry Day, who was now somewhere on the north side of Everest with the British Services Expedition. I wondered how far they had reached on their long route up the flank of the West Ridge. It would be wonderful to meet them on the summit. We were already hoping to meet the Three Nations Asian team on top, for if we left the next day and the weather held, we would reach the summit on 5 May – the day planned for their summit crossing. It would be fun to gatecrash their live television broadcast. However, by mid-morning snow was falling and our plans seemed less secure. The snowfall was only light and it abated in the evening but the next day flakes were again falling thick on the tents, blotting out our hopes for an immediate dash to the summit:

Tuesday – May 3rd
Snow started again early in the morning and was to continue non-stop for over twenty-four hours. No point in staying, so we bailed out and abseiled down in cloud and snow to Advance Base. Mimi had come up from BC with news from the Radio Nepal bulletin, announcing that eighteen named members of the Asian Friendship Expedition were all poised ready for the summit crossing on May 5th.

Wednesday – May 4th
After a long night of the familiar depressing pitter-patter, the snow stopped at 8 a.m. Day of some sunshine and constant avalanches, building up to a great barrage of roaring in the evening. Ed and Paul down at BC. The rest of us up here, hoping for a four-day fine break. Longing so much to complete this climb.

Thursday – May 5th
Sunny morning. Robert shouting at Joe: 'Get that telescope out! Can you see any Asians up on that ridge?'

It was a perfect morning and only the tiniest wisp of snow blew off the summit two miles above us. A silver aeroplane was circling in a sky of deepest blue, photographing the

Asian summit climb for the Japanese press. Sitting so close under the mountain we could not see the climbers, but at Base Camp Ed and Paul, squinting through binoculars, saw three tiny figures against the snow near the South Summit. Pasang followed it all on the radio, reporting that the figures belonged to one of four teams, each made up of one Japanese, one Nepalese and one Chinese climber. With all the advantages of huge support teams and high camps stocked lavishly with food and oxygen, the two teams on the north and two teams on the south side had been able to sit out the preceding days of bad weather and leave for the summit before dawn today. At about 11 a.m. Nepalese time the twelve climbers met on the summit, transmitting live satellite pictures to televisions all round the world.

Robert and I longed to be up there too. As soon as Paul and Ed returned from their brief rest at Base Camp, we told them that we were leaving that very afternoon. Once again Mimi and Joe saw us off on our departure for the summit, but it was already snowing when we started up the fixed ropes. Ed and Paul returned to Advance Base, but Robert and I continued obstinately, jumaring in the dark, with snowflakes dancing in our torch beams and spindrift pouring down onto our heads. Late that night we dug out one of the tents at Camp 1 and crawled in to sleep.

Friday morning brought more snow and cloud, as we vacillated, first lying in bed, then attempting to trail-break, wading laboriously and pointlessly up to the Jaws of Doom in driving wind and snow, then returning to Camp 1, packing up the tents and setting off back down to Advance Base, passing on our way Ed and Paul, who had come up to watch our futile heroics. They dumped their loads at an anchor, turned round and fled with us, back down through the murk.

On Saturday we procrastinated at Advance Base, waiting for the latest dump of new snow to do its worst, crashing down off the face in a series of huge avalanches. Once again the sky was deep blue and it was hard to remember the evil weather of the previous day. Robert and I were fretting to be away, and Mimi and Joe were growing impatient with all our

hanging around. 30 April had passed the previous week and
Angchu had walked over from Kharta, as arranged, to find
out about our porter requirements for the end of the expedition. He had been sent back with a message for Mr Yang and
Mr Shi that we still had no definite date for departure and
that porters might not be required till the middle of May or
later. Mimi wanted to get back to her own life in New York
and Joe was missing his wife and daughter terribly, but still
we had not even made our first attempt on the summit.

Hardly a cloud dare creep up the Kama Chu that day, and
the evening was perfectly still and clear. When my alarm
went off at 2.30 on Sunday morning the sky was jewelled
with stars and there was not a hint of cloud over Lhotse and
Everest. Robert and Paul wanted to go up later, but Ed and I
made our traditional early start, setting off in the darkness yet
again, once more shouting, 'Goodbye Joe, goodbye Mimi.'
It was my tenth trip to Camp 1 and I managed it in a record
time of four and a half hours. I was bursting with strength
and confidence and longing to be given the chance to complete our route.

I enjoyed our day of rest at Camp 1, eating plentifully,
drinking every half hour, photographing the surreal snow
formations on the far side of Big Al Gully and pottering
about with vital small tasks like sharpening crampon points.
If this really was it – our chance at last – we had to be
perfectly prepared. Up there, above 8,000 metres, we would
probably climb unroped, for at that altitude, with reactions
dulled by hypoxia, we could do little to help each other. It
was up to each one to ensure meticulously his own survival,
and on an icy patch sharp crampon points could make all the
difference between life and a stupid meaningless death.

We made yet another brew of raspberry tea and Ed
enthused about our chances.

'You know, I really think we might do it. This is the best
day we've had for weeks.'

'Yes, no clouds coming up from the Arun, just a few over
the summit from Nepal –'

'Hardly moving. Look! There's just no wind up there, a

perfect summit day. If only it would just hold for three more days. That's all we need.'

There was a movement on the fixed rope to our left, and soon Paul's purple helmet appeared from out of the depths of Big Al Gully, so I put more snow blocks on to melt.

At five o'clock on that evening of 8 May, the tenth anniversary of Messner's and Habeler's historic oxygenless ascent of Everest, all four of us were in bed at Camp 1, drugged with Hypnovol to calm our excited racing brains and help us to catch some sleep on the eve of our summit bid. If all went well we would be on the South Col in two days' time, but first we had to break a new trail, through even deeper snow than the last time, to Camp 2. It was going to be a long hard day and the more of it we could do in the cool before dawn the better. For once the Americans, even Robert, had agreed to a really early start and the alarm was set for midnight.

8

South Col

IT WAS my turn to make breakfast on 9 May. That meant having to sit up at midnight, reach over for a cigarette lighter, ignite the gas stove hanging from the apex of the tent, lie down again, then wake up every fifteen minutes to take another brick from the bag of snow blocks at my side, make hot chocolate, make tea, cook and eat with apathy a bowl of instant porridge, top up water bottle for the day ahead. Eventually one had to face the fact that breakfast was coming to an end, and that it was time to emerge from one's down chrysalis and stuff it tight into a rucksack, struggle into the sewer man's outfit, pull socks tight and smooth, put on inner boots, then plastic shell boots, then neoprene overboots.

The finer details followed: a base of Kiehl's wind cream spread thick on the face, climbing harness buckled round the waist, jumars attached, another belt fitted with SLR camera and Instamatic, then the final packing of the rucksack, checking that everything is there – monochrome film, colour film, sunglasses, sunhat, first-aid kit, sun cream, water bottle. 'Ed, are you bringing the lighters? Three. Good, I needn't bring one then. And you've got the mail packet?'

Then it was time to open the tent door, swing my legs out into the cold darkness and clip on crampons. At three o'clock I started up the ropes, kicking steps to the base of Webster's Wall, where I tied my rucksack into the end of a spare rope to be pulled up when I reached the top of the wall. I slid up my waist jumar as high as I could, pulling down with the weight of my body to stretch the main rope tight, then held the tautness with the foot jumar, slid up the waist one again and eventually I was moving up, dangling free in the darkness. It was always hard work, this section, taking all my weight alternately on the waist harness and the right foot, stabbing out at the overhanging ice wall with the left foot to maintain stability and stop myself spinning round on the rope. In the dark of a moonless night it was bizarre, hanging in my pool of torchlight, isolated from the yellow glow of the tents beneath my feet.

I stopped on the terrace above to regain breath before hauling up the rucksack. The view out to the east made me gloomy, for dark bands of cirrus confused the outline of the horizon and over to the right a lenticular cloud was nosing round the back of Chomolonzo like some malignant shark.

I continued up the Fourth Cauliflower Tower. Each time we came this way a few more tons of ice had fallen off the right-hand side and now I could look straight over the edge into the abyss of Big Al Gully. I continued through the darkness, wading and burrowing my way underneath the Gargoyle, the top half of which had now toppled onto the terrace below. The Jaws of Doom were gaping even wider and the rope was now tuned an octave higher, straining tight on the securing ice screws.

Hanging on the rope bridge I stared up at the stars and noticed that already wisps of cloud were drifting across the sky from the South Col. When I had completed the exhausting crossing I looked back to the east, where the cirrus was streaking the sky thicker by the minute and valley cloud was billowing up from the Arun. It looked so hopeless that I was almost tempted to turn back but we had to continue in the forlorn hope that this break in the weather would only be a temporary nuisance, not a dangerous storm; so I started kicking steps up towards the Hump, pulling the rope out of the deep powder as I went, then wading laboriously along the next rope, extricating it metre by metre towards the perilous Jumble. By the time I reached the final anchor beyond the Jumble the sky was lightening.

The weather looked increasingly ominous but as I stood at the top of the ropes waiting for Robert it did treat me to the most outrageously beautiful dawn I have ever seen. The whole sky to the east was rippled with waves of orange, pink, purple, yellow and green. Behind me a cloud shadowed the wall of Lhotse dark purple against an ultramarine sky, while a soft peachlike radiance crept down the snows of Everest. As Robert appeared over the Hump, the light spread down to him, illuminating the snow with Robert's dark figure poised minute above grey and silver clouds billowing up from the Kangshung basin.

All the signs of an impending front were there and when Robert arrived I said gloomily, 'I suppose we might as well continue?'

'Of course,' he replied cheerfully. 'Yes, of course we're going up.' So we prepared, each leaving our descendeur and one jumar clipped into the anchor. Weight was now crucial and we only took one jumar each, for using on the fixed rope over the Hillary Step, up near the summit. If we had to do any abseiling we would have to manage without the heavy luxury of a descendeur. My long 80cm ice axe was the lightest available and I had followed the others' example of dispensing with an awkward safety sling, attaching the axe to my body just with a simple wrist loop. With the long axe in one hand and ski stick in the other, I followed Robert who had now led out the thirty metres of light safety rope, starting his first laborious stint of trail-breaking.

It was eight days since our recce to Camp 2. There was no sign of our tracks and this time the new snow was even deeper. At least it seemed stable. I had always been worried that these huge upper snow slopes might prove to be a lethal avalanche trap but only the steeper hummocks seemed suspect; and our route ensured that the steep sections we climbed were always underpinned by flat hollows which would quickly arrest any small slides. I was reassured too when I looked out to the left, towards the face of Lhotse. Our route followed a very distinct spur which we had not really discerned in our first awed view from the Langma La, nor in the photographs we had examined in New York all those weeks ago. My fears had been unnecessary, for a huge depression separated our route from the freight trains rumbling down Lhotse.

I felt reasonably safe, but what a labour that day was! We moved so slowly, Robert and I, swapping the lead every forty minutes or so, resigned to ploughing our interminable furrow, metre by tedious metre up the endless slope to Camp 2. Some time later, perhaps at midday, Ed and Paul took over.

It was snowing now and we were lost in a shapeless grey world. Only the dull green of bare ice was distinguishable from the greyness and as we approached the big Crevasse bridge we noticed that the ice cliffs on the right had begun to collapse. Ed was in the lead. Suddenly there was a loud crack and a huge block fell into the Crevasse a few yards to his right. A moment later there was another louder roar and a larger section of the cliff erupted, crumpling and bellying outwards in slow motion as it tumbled into a pile of debris. I watched entranced as a large delivery van slid past us, gathering speed through the snow then disappearing over the edge on the long trundle down to Big Al Gully. We hurried over the bridge, thankful that our route had just avoided obliteration.

The treadmill went on and on, up the long uniform slope above, only broken by our occasional marker wands with their fluorescent orange flags. We stopped to eat some chocolate, drink some Carboplex solution and put on our down clothing. Then we continued. Robert and I took over again. Paul complained, 'This is crazy. This is dumb. These slopes are loaded and it's still snowing and we just keep going.'

'Stop being such a gloom bag – it isn't that bad. Now we've come this far we might as well go all the way to Camp 2. We'll be safe from any avalanches there.' I was secretly worried that perhaps Paul was right, but if we were very lucky this might prove just to be an afternoon storm. We had to maintain our momentum as long as there was still some hope of completing the route.

It was now getting late. After a long spell in the lead, Robert stopped moving for an age, so I shouted reluctantly, 'Shall I take over?'

'All right,' he answered wearily.

The final slope took me about an hour. On the last steepening I had to burrow with my hands to clear the snow in front of my chest, then lift each leg, kicking hard to gain purchase, and drawing in three or four deep breaths for each step. Like Ed a week earlier, I found a perverse satisfaction in that battle at the end of a fourteen-hour day, wallowing my way proudly up those final gruelling metres to Camp 2.

Under the canopy of the Flying Wing we were safe and sheltered, but the day's work was not over. We had to level platforms in the snow, unpack and pitch the two tents, hang up all the climbing gear for the night and chop ice blocks, collecting them in a bag ready for the night's cooking. I swore at Ed for taking photographs when there was work to do and when we finally settled in the tent he came as close to anger as I had ever seen him.

'Look – let's get it clear: the one thing that really bugs me is you complaining about my photography. It really pisses me off – especially when I turn round a moment later and see *you* taking photos. There's not that much hurry.'

That was the end of it. I knew that one day we would all be glad of the photos and I apologized. We organized the tiny two-man tent, each of us resolving our private chaos of clothing and equipment while the other person steadied the swinging gas stove. Each time a little water spilled out of the pan we thanked Ed's friends in Boulder, who had coated the sleeping bags with water-resistant Gore-Tex fabric.

After much thrashing around we settled down. The only remaining task was to continue producing the drinks vital to rehydrate our bodies after the day's work. We also ate well that night – biscuits and cheese, chocolate, noodles and an unusually good freeze-dried chicken casserole. It now looked as though we might be continuing to the South Col in the morning. The snowfall had stopped at dusk and much of the cloud had cleared by the time we pitched the tents. We needed to stock up well with food and liquid, so that if the weather did improve we would be in a fit state to make the most of our luck.

We were lucky. At three o'clock the next morning I looked out of the tent and saw that the sky was completely clear. Late at night we had given up melting ice, too exhausted to complete our target number of drinks, and had collapsed into a deep sleep. Now we had to continue, dozing while we waited for each panful of ice to melt. Just before dawn, cursing at the nuisance of it all, I had to put on boots and go out into the cold to relieve myself. There was still no sound from the other tent and when I woke Paul and Robert they were not enthusiastic about an early start. It seemed that they had reverted to American decadence.

I was anxious to reach the South Col early in the day but I had to resign myself to a late start, not leaving until the sun had transformed the sheltered East Face into a burning white furnace. However, it was a beautiful morning to be kept waiting – not the threatening beauty of the previous dawn but a morning of transparent blue tranquillity. The air was quite still and our veranda under the Flying Wing was a perfect sun trap, so while Robert and Paul procrastinated we were able to dry all our equipment thoroughly and brew numerous cups of tea, sitting in the sun and looking out across the valley. Pethangtse now looked squat and insignificant, far below us, whereas Makalu, fifth highest mountain in the world and twelve miles to the east, had grown to its full stature, transformed now into a magnificent towering pyramid.

We made leisurely preparations, deciding how much of our tiny stock of food to take with us. We only had enough for two days' meagre eating but we took, I think, five gas cylinders per pair – enough to provide us with liquid for three or four days if necessary. About three cylinders and a tiny amount of food were left at Camp 2 for the descent. The weight of our rucksacks was depressing for, unlike Messner and Habeler in 1978, we had no Sherpas helping us to establish a camp on the South Col. We had to carry everything ourselves – food, gas, stoves, pans, tents and all our personal gear. Because of the blazing heat we could hardly wear any of our clothing and as well as my sleeping bag and Therma-Rest, I had to pack away down bibs, down jacket, pile jacket, spare high-altitude gloves, spare socks and my bulky windsuit – the infamous sewer man's outfit. I wore just my long thermal underwear, my fibre pile suit, a single pair of mittens and my sunhat, and even then I was far too hot.

At 7.45 Ed and I shouldered our crippling rucksacks, roped together and set off to find the way to the South Col. The only possible start was to traverse under the Flying Wing, so Ed led the way northwards, following the ledge underneath the huge overhang for about a hundred metres until he reached the end of the Wing and could head up through an alley. We were still not certain that there was a way past the Wing, so I felt a great wave of relief when he shouted down, 'It's OK – there's a route. Just watch the rope on this bit – an awkward crevasse, then we're through.'

Soon we were on the big slope above, sitting in the sun and waiting for the other two to catch up and discuss the options ahead. A few days earlier Mimi had asked why we could not head diagonally right from this point, completely missing out the South Col and emerging on the summit ridge much higher, close to the South Summit. Back in America, Robert had considered this possibility, but we had all decided that those huge open snow slopes looked horribly avalanche-prone. We would probably be less exposed to risk on the shorter slope to the South Col. In a sense the left-hand route was also more logical. As Paul pointed out, 'That's our route, the East Face of the South Col. That way, even if we don't make it to the summit, we'll complete our new route.'

We had all agreed on the logic of this first ever ascent of the South Col from Tibet – our special contribution to the history of Everest which we had variously named 'South Col Direct', the 'International Buttress' and, in a less pompous vein, the 'Neverest Buttress'. Now it only remained to decide on the final details – either a steep open couloir directly above us, leading to a snow ledge breaking left through rocks, or the bigger snow and ice face further left still, towards Lhotse.

Ed and I had always favoured the first option, on the grounds that it seemed less avalanche-prone and would provide rock anchors if we needed them. However we had not actually managed to bring any heavy rock gear up here and now, looking more closely at the ledge above, I imagined reversing it, exhausted on our descent from the col, and thought how easy it would be to slip and fall over those rocks. Paul seemed to agree.

'We should do whatever's easiest. That's the only thing that counts up here. When we come down we're going to be zombies.'

Everyone agreed. The more left-hand route was easier and probably safer, with no rock cliffs to tumble over. I was sent off to do the next bout of trail-breaking, diagonally left towards the bergschrund, the crevasse where the slope steepened into the final face leading to the col. To my utter delight and surprise I found a firm wind crust, where I could walk on the surface, managing at least thirty steps between each rest.

It was all too good to be true. I had to stop and wave exuberantly to Mimi and Joe, who would be sitting at breakfast over 2,000 metres below, watching the ant figures against the snow. Once again, as had happened so many times on this expedition, I felt incredulous at my good fortune – being right up here on this brilliant morning, under this blue sky which grew ever more intense as we climbed further out of the earth's atmosphere, completing our new route, so close now to the South Col and hoping, praying, believing that tomorrow we would be up on that ridge, climbing towards the famous summit cornices which looked so absurdly close.

Paul took over the lead and cursed me for my good fortune. 'Typical – as soon as I start leading it's back to wallowing.' Our brief respite was over and Paul found the snow increasingly intransigent as he kicked, pushed and waded his way through the deep mounds of powder bridging the bergschrund. The face above was nearly fifty degrees steep but contrary to our expectations the deep snow had not sloughed off. Frequently Paul had to change course to make any progress at all, searching out the firmest snow, and generally trying to stay close to the right-hand containing wall of the slope, minimizing avalanche danger.

Ed and I followed the line of bucket steps, admiring Paul's and then Robert's work until, soon after midday, it was Ed's turn to lead. Once again the Tortoise came into his own, plodding stoically upwards, doing a longer stint than any of us and, wise as ever, staying close to the rocks on the right, the first rocks we had seen since below Camp 1. The usual afternoon cloud was now boiling about the face, but in spite of the encroaching greyness, the mounting wind and the repetitive drudgery of our climb, I still felt intensely happy. The South Col now looked so close. We could see the rocks on the left, leading up the ridge of Lhotse, and the prominent rock buttress on the right. Snatches of wind blowing through from Nepal were starting to reach down to us and one squall blasted down a scrap of paper – a small token of litter to remind us that soon we would be on known ground. A couple of choughs, those brilliant black high-altitude scavengers, also danced in the wind. I wondered if the Asian expedition still had people up there on the col and whether the Australians would be around, inviting us into their tents for mugs of hot tea. It would be marvellous to see the looks on their faces when we suddenly stuck our heads over the rim of the col, appearing unannounced from Tibet.

After a long magnificent effort, Ed stopped and let me take a turn in front. I started off well but became increasingly sluggish, weighed down by the heavy sack and frequently stumbling when steps collapsed. When I stopped to look down the view was stupendous: a steep drop to the huge detached Flying Wing, with our spur stretched out below it to the point where it disappeared over the top of the Buttress, then a mile and a half below, partially obscured by cloud, the dark lines of the Kangshung Glacier. Soon, however, the clouds enveloped us, the familiar snowfall started and the blasts of wind grew fiercer. We stopped to put on down clothing. Later, while Ed was in the lead again, I put my windsuit on as well, anxious to have maximum protection when we reached the col.

The foreshortening was cruel, tempting us upwards with the promise of quick release but always holding back our reward. We could see the curved line of the col now, looking so close that when I took over the lead again I really thought I was going to reach it. But I had to lower my goal to a little clump of rocks where I slumped down, weary and deflated, to wait for Ed to come and do the last section.

The rope tightened and reluctantly I stood up to follow Ed. We were now climbing out of the cloud as we approached the wind tunnel between Lhotse and Everest. Paul drew level with me and we staggered up together, following Ed's steps. All three of us were now higher than we had ever been before, and our route was almost complete. Just above us Ed was battering at the little cornice with his fist, releasing lumps of snow, which were flung up by the wind to flash white in the evening sunlight. Finally Ed climbed up into the light and disappeared. Paul and I followed neck and neck, pushing, stumbling, gasping our way up the last slope, to emerge breathless from the East Face.

It was ghastly. There were no welcoming tents, no smiling faces, no mugs of steaming tea. There was nothing – just Ed bent into the screaming wind, staggering across a desolate plateau of rock and ice, with the rope bent out behind him by the wind. Beyond was the famous summit pyramid, the black rocks seamed by lines of snow, the couloir which we would have to take to the summit, the snow shoulder disappearing into the cloud plume. It was as bleak as all the books had warned, yet, burning through the fear and shock and loneliness, I felt a small glow of pride, stepping at last from Tibet into Nepal on this historic mountain pass.

I staggered after Ed, pulled forward by the rope. The wind was cruel, whipping snow against my face and snatching my breath away. Talking was impossible. Shouting was no use. Everything was obliterated by the wind. Our minds were numbed, our bodies were battered and we wandered in a daze, four of us now, ropes crossing as we stumbled backwards and forwards pointing at possible campsites.

We found a level patch of snow and rock, untied from the entangling ropes, took off rucksacks and unpacked tents. Soon I was inside one of the Gore-Tex shells, fighting the flailing fabric as I tried to fit the long sprung poles, battered and disorientated as the wind blew the tent against rocks.

'Ed,' I shouted, 'can you help?' He sat in the entrance and added his weight to the groundsheet. 'That's better. Just sit there. I was being blown all over the place. Just a sec, my fingers are completely numb.' It was fiddly work, forcing the long bendy pole into one corner, flexing it and fighting to get the other end into the opposite corner of the tent, then forcing the other pole into position. At least with this design the poles were *inside* the tent so we had some shelter for the job, but it was still finger-numbing work to get them in place then secure them with Velcro tabs, transforming the flapping fabric into a stretched elongated dome.

Paul and Robert now had their tent up and were starting to lash both tents down with the ropes. Luckily we had had the foresight to fit strong loops to all the corners the previous evening, in the shelter of the Flying Wing, so that now we could secure each corner with heavy rocks. We moved fast and efficiently, knowing that without the tents we would die, and soon they were both secure, all our survival equipment was inside and we could crawl in too and organize ourselves for the night.

It had taken eleven hours to do a climb of about 500 metres, which we had hoped to complete in four hours. The weight of our sacks and the depth of the snow, coming after the exhausting fourteen-hour day from Camp 1, had slowed us to a crawl so that now we had arrived late on the col, only settling down as darkness fell. Ed and I had talked of leaving for the top really early, at 10 p.m., to arrive on the summit mid-morning the next day, but now it was already 8 p.m. and there was no hope of continuing that night; in any case it would be pointless trying to climb in this wind. For the first time now, after weeks of sheltering in the Kangshung basin, we were experiencing the full force of the prevailing westerly.

It was an unhappy night, our first night out at virtually 8,000 metres. The wind buffeted the tent, shaking the gas stove violently, and frequently spilling water. I was on the windward side, pushed and pummelled by the inward bulging fabric. The strongest gusts bent the dome right out of shape and I was sometimes terrified that the seams would rip. And of course the Gore-Tex did not breathe as it is supposed to; as usual in extreme cold, even with the door slightly open, it just clogged up with thick hoar frost which was shaken in our faces by the wind.

Ed and I managed to organize some food and drink and at least we were warm in all the down gear which we had carried up so laboriously. However, we both suffered headaches and shortness of breath. I had to discipline myself to control my breathing, lying still, taking deep rhythmic breaths, resisting the claustrophobic panic I always suffer on these airless nights. I had felt the same in Africa sixteen months earlier, camping on the crater rim of Kilimanjaro on Boxing Day night – much lower than this at a mere 5,700 metres – but I had not been properly acclimatized and the night had been a long struggle against panic. And it had been the same six months ago, just sixty miles from here on Shisha Pangma, crawling into the emergency snowhole on our abortive summit attempt.

There was no rest that night on the South Col, not the genuine rest where you go to sleep at the end of one day and wake refreshed at the start of another. We hovered on the edge of consciousness, frequently drinking from our water bottles and swigging down pain-killers to relieve nagging headaches. When the light came I saw how haggard and pained Ed's face looked, half-buried amongst boots, cameras and water bottles. His voice too sounded weak and I wondered whether he would consider continuing to the summit.

At about 6.30 Robert appeared at our door. 'Paul's ill. Someone will have to go down with him.'

'What's wrong?'

'Really bad headache – it just won't go away. And he was vomiting badly. He's lost all his liquid. He agrees that it's not safe to stay up here.'

It was a cruel blow for Paul, who had put as much as any of us into this climb, and I knew that one of us should volunteer to escort him down. Robert, whose expedition this was, deserved first chance at the summit; that left Ed or me to go down with Paul. However, I was starting to feel a little better now and I secretly hoped that Ed might want to descend, leaving me with a chance to try for the summit if the wind dropped the next day. But as we ate our breakfast and Ed became more lively, I realized that he too wanted very much to stay at the South Col. He was also feeling better now and the sun was transforming the night's claustrophobic prison, filling the tent with light and warmth and quickly sublimating away the hoar frost. The wind too had relented slightly, allowing us to relax a little. We evaded the question until nine o'clock, when Paul himself appeared at the door.

'Ed, Stephen, goodbye – I'm going down –'

'But don't you want –?'

'No, I'll be all right on my own.' There were tears in his eyes as he excused himself. 'I was sick. Now I've got nothing left – just dried out. And the headache just won't go – the pills did nothing. Maybe it's cerebral oedema? I have to go down . . . I mean, if I stay here I'll die. I did the route – finished the East Face. But I got sick. I hope you guys get to the summit. Yes, make sure you get to the top. Good luck. Goodbye.'

He turned his back on us and hurried away, disappearing quickly over the eastern rim of the plateau. I was dazed by emotions: sadness for Paul's bad luck, guilt at allowing him to descend alone, thanks for his generosity which had pervaded the whole expedition, sorrow at losing him and losing our chance of getting all members of an unsupported four-man team to the summit, by a new route without oxygen – an unprecedented feat which would have stunned the mountaineering world.

We knew that Paul had made the only possible decision,

starting down while he was still in perfect mental and physical control. The sky was mainly clear, the route was well
marked and there would still be traces of our steps from the
two previous days. He would almost certainly be fine, but
there was always a chance of something going wrong, a
concealed crevasse, an avalanche, a careless mistake on the
ropes. He had volunteered generously to descend alone but
perhaps one of us should have insisted on accompanying
him.

Ed and I discussed our summit hopes. Unless the wind
dropped significantly we would have little chance, and I
knew that it would have to drop soon. 'I think we can afford
to wait here for one day,' I said. 'Today we're actually resting
but any longer and we'll start to deteriorate. If the wind
hasn't dropped by tomorrow morning we'll just have to go
down.'

'Do you think you could wind yourself up for another
attempt?' Ed asked.

'I don't know. Maybe.'

'I think I could, but –'

'We'd need several days' rest at Base Camp. Then,
assuming the weather's right, we'd have to flog all the way
back up here – more food, more gas . . .'

'Well, let's just hope the wind drops tonight. And we need
to try and sleep today.'

Ed was right about the sleep. We had hardly slept all the
previous night. At Camp 2 there had only been time for
about four hours' proper rest and we had been similarly
deprived at Camp 1. So we spent the day resting. Once I had
to go out to relieve myself, fumbling with zips in the cruel
wind. Over the rim of the col I could see a plume flying off
Makalu. Lhotse, just above us, was also streaming cloud and
snow and on the other side of the col our ridge to the summit
of Everest was a maelstrom of spindrift. The huge plateau of
the col was apparently deserted and there was no sign of the
other climbers we had hoped to meet and give our mail
packet to.

It was a desolate lonely place and after chopping more

snow blocks for the stove I was glad to return to the warm
companionship of the tent. The day passed quickly. We ate a
little, forced ourselves to make several hot drinks and dozed
in our sleeping bags. My headache had now gone and I was
breathing properly, but occasionally I had relapses of claus-
trophobia as the wind pushed the tent wall against me.

Robert came over for a talk at about five o'clock in the
afternoon. Once again we were cheered by the optimistic
determination which had pervaded his planning for the last
two years. He felt, and we agreed, that the wind seemed to
be dropping slightly. We had to grab our chance, leave really
early and hope that the wind would continue to drop. He
suggested a midnight start and we put it forward to 10 p.m.
Tonight we would leave for the summit.

Soon Ed and I were preparing for departure. First we
cooked what was virtually the last of the solid food, Chinese
instant noodles in soup. Then we melted snow for our water
bottles, adding Rehydrate powder and Carboplex. Getting
dressed at this altitude, having to pause frequently to regain
breath, was a long tiring operation, even though we already
had on most of our clothes. For months now I had thought
about my protective shell for the summit bid. I wore loop-
stitch long thermal underwear and a tight-fitting fleece balaclava. The second layer was a Helly Hansen fibre pile suit,
like a furry romper suit, with a balaclava of the same material
sewn on. Over this I wore my powder blue fleece jacket from
Bolder Designs. The next layer was goosedown, the
wonderful Bolder Designs bibs insulating my legs and coming right up to my chest, overlapping with my Mountain
Equipment duvet jacket which had a hood, providing a third
layer for my head. The final layer, into which I now had to
struggle, was the windproof shell of heavy duty Gore-Tex,
Mountain Equipment's drab but eminently functional sewer
man's outfit.

I decided not to wear inner gloves, but keep my fingers
free to be rubbed and wriggled against each other inside
warm down mitts I had bought in Kathmandu, fitted inside a
brand new extra large pair of Wild Country mitts of fibre pile

with an outer layer of heavy duty Gore-Tex. For my feet, Ed had lent his spare size twelve Koflach boots, with inners of closed cell Alveolite foam. After all my ridiculing of the Americans' surplus equipment, I had been more than glad to borrow boots that might be slightly warmer than mine. I decided to wear just one pair of socks, leaving my feet as loose as possible inside the foam inners and rigid plastic shells. I had been keeping the boots warm inside my sleeping bag and as soon as they were laced on my feet I pulled over the Javlin overboots, giant stretchy socks made from Neoprene, the same material as wet suits.

The wind was dropping all the time and the tent had stopped flapping. Ed and I talked little, each of us busy with our patient preparations, but when we did speak it was with an excitement quite different from the previous night's numbed lethargy. All the experts say that it is impossible to rest properly in the 'death zone' above 8,000 metres, but our day's waiting had clearly done us good. I was now making a tape waist belt, to replace the proper harness that I had left behind at Camp 2. We had each now rejected the weight of even one jumar, replacing it with a short length of thin line, to make a prusik loop for safeguarding ourselves on the fixed rope we expected to find at the famous Hillary Step.

We had to save weight ruthlessly and Robert had dissuaded me from my original intention of carrying emergency bivouac equipment in a rucksack. We all agreed now that our only hope of doing this final climb without oxygen was to travel virtually unburdened, leaving before midnight to ensure our return to the tents by the following evening. I had my improvised waist belt, prusik loop and two karabiners. I also had my two cameras on another belt. In my pockets I carried spare mittens, the full quart water bottle, spare film, sun cream, sunglasses and two bars of chocolate. That was all.

When I stepped out of the tent at ten o'clock the wind had died away completely. There was no sign yet of the waning moon, so the stars shone with unchallenged brilliance. On the col beside me, Robert's silhouette moved inside his glowing tent, as he struggled with boot laces. Above us the summit pyramid was dark, but I could just make out the white line of the couloir over to the left. Up near the South Summit all traces of the wind plume had vanished. We really were lucky to be given this rare gift of a windless night on Everest.

The sublime beauty of that dark night on the South Col was soon sullied by profane cursing as I tried to fit my crampons. Ed was now outside, so I lay in the entrance of the tent, laboriously re-warming my fingers inside the tent after each abortive attempt to fit the crampons to my feet outside. It was crucial to make sure that the toe binding was biting through the foam overboot, gripping on the plastic welt of the boot proper and in the end I had to ask Ed to hold it down while I fought, panting, with the heel binding. Robert was up now and starting to make the tents safe, checking that the rope lashing was really secure. If the wind rose again, these tents had to be standing when we returned, so I walked around looking for large rocks and carried them one at a time to the tent to place inside the corners, lying down to rest after each journey.

Ed was sorting out the spare rope, surprising Robert.

'I thought we were going to go unroped?'

'I'd like to rope up,' Ed insisted. His meticulous attention to safety had been a good influence throughout the climb, but at this altitude I was sceptical about my ability to use a rope effectively. However, for the moment I said nothing. The companionship in our tent had been so good that day that I did not want to shatter it by refusing this symbolic link.

At 11 p.m. 11 May, an hour later than planned, everything was ready. We zipped up the tents, tied ourselves onto the rope, put mittens back on and grabbed our ice axes. Robert set off in the lead. Ed followed in the middle, then the rope tightened and it was my turn to start walking across the wide expanse of the South Col.

9
Summit Fever

SOON AFTER we left Camp 3 on the South Col I asked to take over the lead. Robert was moving haphazardly, as if in a daze, and I needed desperately to establish a rhythm. I was feeling strong after our day of rest and once I took over I was able to manage twenty paces at a time, heading slightly left towards the big couloir.

There was a firm wind crust and I walked easily on the surface of the snow, counting out twenty paces, resting for a couple of minutes, then walking another twenty paces, resting, walking, repeating the process over and over again as the slope steepened very gradually towards the big couloir. However, the other two were starting to drag on the rope and I was anxious to maintain the momentum at the start of this long climb to the summit.

Soon after midnight, I shouted down, 'It's no good. We need to go faster and the rope's just a nuisance – just another thing to trip up on and no one's going to fall off here.' There was some muttering below and I think that Robert said, 'Yes, I agree – we should unrope.' I said that I would trail the rope ready to be used higher up if necessary.

Perhaps it was selfish of me to push on alone, as if rejecting the friendship and teamwork which had sustained this expedition for nearly three months. However, we had always known that on this final stretch we would be unlikely all to move at the same speed, or to use a rope effectively. Robert, in particular, had always said that above the South Col we would each be on our own. I know that at this

altitude, now higher than Annapurna, Shisha Pangma, Man-
aslu, the Gasherbrums, heading up to the highest summit of
all, which only twenty people had ever reached without
supplementary oxygen, a streak of egotism was essential for
anyone to reach the top. Too many times over the last sixteen
years I had been slowed down or forced to turn back by
others, but on this occasion I was determined to give myself
every possible chance of success.

It was good to move unfettered. My only worry was for
the toes of my left foot which, in spite of my careful preparations, were going numb; but I decided that I was prepared to
be a little irresponsible and risk my toes for this climb. I was
now in the couloir and occasionally there were reassuring
crampon marks left by the Asian expedition the previous
week. For a short stretch there was a line of good steps to
follow, then my torch beam picked out the detritus of other
expeditions – an old oxygen bottle, a length of rope, some
tattered tent fabric. After weeks of exploration on the
Kangshung Face, we were now following a known route.
This was not the Himalayan climbing I was used to. It was
more like being on some Alpine classic like the Matterhorn
or the North Face of the Eiger, following in the steps of
history and legend.

The route from the South Col, which Norbu's father had
pioneered with the Swiss in 1952 and which was completed
by John Hunt's 1953 expedition, traverses right on to the
crest of the South-East Ridge. Nowadays most parties seem
to take a big couloir well to the left of the ridge, following it
up the centre of a vague broad triangular face. After 150
metres the couloir was broken by bands of rock and I followed an easy line leftwards up snow patches between rocks,
led on by occasional crampon marks. There was now a faint
glow of moonlight behind the ridge in Tibet, but here on the
Nepalese side we were in deep shadow. It was almost impossible to judge distances and gauge the size of features like the
dark rock tower above me. I wondered if I should turn it on
the left, then decided to move back right. Surely the route
tends to the right, not left? But why were there marks so far

left? And why was Ed shouting? His torch was quite far below now, and Robert's was lower still. I shouted, 'Are you all right?' There was more incomprehensible noise below and I realized that it was directed at Robert, not me.

I picked my way across slabby bands of loose rock, then more snow patches and more rock, dragging the rope behind me, until I arrived on a large snowfield. It seemed to narrow above and lead onto the ridge, so I headed that way, having now to kick steps in softer snow. There was more shouting, so I waited till a torch light appeared below and could see where I was, before I continued. I was moving more slowly now and I was starting to lose all sense of time, lost in a dream, hardly believing that we really were climbing up the summit pyramid of Everest.

It was so dark. If only I could be sure that this was the correct way. Was that the ridge just above by that big boulder? I kicked slowly towards it, wondering if there would be a way through. The boulder assumed a reddish colour and then I found rope protruding from the snow. I pointed my head up again and the torch beam picked out 'Dunlop' stencilled on a large red dome tent. It was pitched at a crazy angle on a precarious shelf of ice but it was in good condition and was presumably the top camp used for the Asian traverse on 5 May. On our oxygenless attempt we never could have carried a camp this high.

Now that the boulder had metamorphosed into a tent, reassuring me that I was on route, I relaxed and stopped for a rest, eating a little chocolate and drinking some of my precious Rehydrate juice. I also untied and coiled up the tiresome rope, leaving it prominent beside the tent, in case Ed and Robert wanted to use it. Then I turned off my torch to see better into the distance. I had not in fact reached the crest of the ridge, which was still some distance to the right, and it was now obvious that the couloir continued straight above. It was already about 3.30 a.m. on 12 May, we had a long, long way to go and I realized now that we were unlikely to achieve our aim of reaching the summit by eleven in the morning.

I rested for five minutes, then continued up ankle-deep snow. The slope was about forty degrees steep and I used the old tested method of climbing in slow zigzags, tacking my way patiently up the mountain, forcing myself to kick hard through the floury crust to make firm steps. At the end of each rising diagonal I made sure that the upper foot was firmly planted on the new track and that my ice axe was transferred to my upper hand before resting. With that psychological advantage, it was easier to start again after each increasingly long rest.

Soon, far too soon, I became aware of grey light. Facing out to the south-west I suddenly became conscious of jagged forms below me. For the first time in my life I had a close view of the famous peaks of Sola Khumbu and almost immediately I recognized Ama Dablam amongst a cluster of surreal shapes floating, completely detached, above the valley mists. Time was rushing on and soon our ridge was in the sun and the summits below me were touched by gold light. I spotted Kantega, the peak Paul had climbed in 1986, and again Ama Dablam, one of the most photographed mountains in the world. I was looking at the characteristic North-East Face, climbed in 1985 by Carlos Buhler who had been with us in the Karakoram in 1981. In 1983 he had made the first ascent of the Kangshung Face and now he was on Kangchenjunga with another Everester, Peter Habeler. Perhaps they too were up on their summit ridge today. Turning round to the east I could see Kangchenjunga for the first time since that brief glimpse near the Langma La all those weeks ago. Yes, there it was again, close to the rising sun, seventy miles away on the horizon, and that lower, sharper, more elegant peak to the right must be Jannu. I had to photograph that wonderful sunrise, slanting gold light across the huge mass of Kangchenjunga, the closer pyramid of Makalu, and Lhotse just opposite – the third, fifth and fourth highest peaks in the world. I framed the picture on the SLR camera and managed to take one exposure before my fingers stuck numb to the metal. I quickly put the camera away and brought my hands back to life before using the warmer plastic compact camera to take a shot in the other direction, looking down on the Sola Khumbu peaks.

It was exciting to see Sola Khumbu. Somewhere down there, to the right of those famous peaks, was Pasang's home in Namche Bazar. Immediately below me was the secret valley of the Western Cwm, the normal route to the South Col. Ed had told me that the famous Yellow Band of rock which shows so prominently on the North Face of Everest also reappears in Nepal. Now I could see the squiggly parallel lines curving round the wall of Nuptse on the far side of the Western Cwm. At the head of the bowl, between me and Lhotse, was the South Col. Now that I was looking down on that barren plateau of rock and ice I could see that it was as big as an Olympic stadium. I suddenly noticed tiny red tents at the official campsite, several hundred metres to the west of our site and hidden from it by the slight undulations of the plateau.

I saw no sign of people by the red tents, but afterwards we learned that four Nepalese members of the Friendship expedition were resting there that morning. On 10 May, the day we reached the South Col, the famous Sherpa Sundhare had made his fifth ascent of Everest, accompanied by a Nepalese Army officer, Padma Bahadur. The other team – Ang Rita, also attempting his fifth ascent, and Narayan Shreshta attempting his second – had turned back when Ang Rita decided that they were climbing too slowly. They had waited for the other two to descend to the South Col and all four climbers were still there on 12 May, waiting for Sundhare's companion to recover from snow blindness.

However, as I trudged on up the couloir there was little sign that people had been here only two days earlier. On this section nearly every trace of their passage had been obliterated by the wind. In places the wind had helped me by packing the snow down, but for much of the way I was breaking through the crust. I sat down frequently and often failed to complete a whole tack without a rest. A crippling lethargy was seeping insidiously through my body, draining the power from my legs and dazing my mind, so that I became almost oblivious of time.

Hours must have passed in that upper couloir, but I can remember few details. All I know is that for the last hour or so I tired of the sideways slither on breakable crust and took the slope straight, facing into the snow and collapsing far too often to lean on my ice axe and draw great sobs of air into my lungs. I saw Robert or Ed starting up from the tent below and hoped that they might catch up, but I was essentially alone, struggling unquestioningly upwards.

My goal was the crest of the ridge. Several times I had to abandon it for intermediate goals, stopping for more sobbing gasps of air, before I could continue for a few more steps up the tantalizing foreshortened slope. Eventually I narrowed the distance to a few yards, forced my rubber legs up to the skyline, stepped over and collapsed on the flat shoulder of the ridge.

I think I drank some Rehydrate juice. I know that I rested a long time, perhaps half an hour, perhaps waiting for Ed and Robert, perhaps just delaying the reality of continuing. It was good to take the pressure off my feet and keep them out of the cold snow, wriggling life back into the toes and discovering that I would probably escape without frostbite after all. I was now back on the Kangshung side of the ridge and I wondered if Joe and Mimi could see me. Immediately above was the big snowslope leading up to the curved hump that must be the South Summit. It looked very close and easily attainable. Soon I would reach it but for the moment I needed to rest. It would be good to take some photographs now that it was warmer, but that would require such a huge effort. At least I had managed to put on sun cream and sunglasses, but that was different for they were essential to survival. Photography, which I normally found almost as compulsive as Ed did, had become a superfluous task beyond my will; all my energy had to be directed now to moving my body uphill.

I stood up and moved forward. At first it was easy – there was a hard crust and the ridge was almost flat. But as soon as the snow steepened just a little I felt tired again. I had to stop every few steps, tucking the long ice axe under my arm and leaning on it, like some wounded soldier on his crutch. All the power and determination seemed to have flowed out of me and for the first time since leaving the South Col it occurred to me that we might not reach the summit. Nevertheless, I continued, dimly aware that we would not get another chance.

I was climbing quite steeply now but the South Summit looked no closer and the snow crust was breaking again, sliding away under my feet. Why couldn't they look after it better? It was in shocking condition. Must be Spain – lazy Mediterranean types. Can't look after their land properly. Everything crumbling under the white sun . . . sleepy sun . . . siesta time . . . No, you're not in Spain. Why Spain? You've never even been there. This is the South-East Ridge of Everest and there's no time to sleep . . . have to keep moving if we are to reach the summit.

Tenzing Norgay and Raymond Lambert had reached a point somewhere up here in 1952, climbing up into the unknown after a miserable night at their high camp without sleeping bags. Threatening weather and their slow progress had forced Lambert to insist on retreating but Tenzing, according to his son Norbu, had wanted to continue. A year later he had returned with the British expedition. This time Tenzing was not on the first bid and it was Charles Evans and Tom Bourdillon who were given first try at the summit on 26 May. Somewhere up here they had forsaken the slabby snow-slope for the rocks on the left. Now I did the same, tired of slithering on the unstable powder.

It was at this stage that an imaginary old man first appeared. I never identified him, but this alter ego was to accompany me on and off for the rest of that day, sometimes comforting me and advising me, sometimes seeking my support. I do not know what he looked like – few of the hallucinations that day were visual – but at moments I was acutely aware of the presence of this other older person. As I reached up to the rocks I told myself that the old man would approve: the solidity and security of rock would appeal to his sense of tradition. In fact the rocks were quite loose and, balancing up on scratching crampon points, I had to concentrate hard, aware that a fall would be serious. But I also had to hurry, tiptoeing precariously, gasping furiously, desperate to reach a ledge and sit down before my legs gave out. The old man had to rest, I had to get to that ledge . . . here grab that old fixed line . . . so thin and frayed – I wonder who brought it all the way up here . . . never mind – grab it for balance and step up quick, turn round and sit down.

After a long rest I decided that the rocks were too precarious and traversed back onto the snow. Weeks later I reread the 1953 account and realized that Hillary and Tenzing had done the same. Bourdillon and Evans, climbing all the way from the South Col, had been forced to turn back from the South Summit when they found that they had neither enough daylight nor enough oxygen to reach the top and descend safely. They had almost certainly been higher than Mallory and Irvine – higher than any man before – but the final prize of the summit was left for Tenzing and the New Zealander, Hillary, starting from a much higher camp above the South Col on 29 May. When they reached this slope below the South Summit they decided to stick to the snow, finding it easier than the Englishmen's rocks. Hillary knew that it was in dangerous slabby condition, liable to avalanche, but had already decided that for the Everest prize he was prepared to contemplate greater risks than usual.

Now, almost thirty-five years later, the snow was in similar nasty condition, but by keeping close to the anchoring rocks I felt safe enough. It was just hopelessly slow. Every step required a slow winding up of effort, followed by a long rest. My whole body was crippled by lassitude and I longed to sleep. My goal now was never further than the next step and as I bent over my ice axe, staring despairingly at a drift of powder, a crumbling yellow rock or a wind-whirled snow crust, I drifted back to the neglected fields of the indolent Spaniards. Occasionally I would remind myself that I was on Everest, then I would be back in Spain, an incompetent drunken tourist, staggering and swaying in the heat of the day.

It was no use. I had to stop, cut a ledge in the snow and

slump down to rest. Time had raced on, leaving me behind, and now it was already eleven in the morning. We were still below the South Summit and my rate of climbing had slowed to about thirty metres an hour. Perhaps I was not good enough after all. I was now higher than Makalu and I was level with, even looking down on, the 8,500-metre summit of Lhotse. But perhaps that was my limit; perhaps the last 300 metres was too much for me; perhaps you *did* have to be a physiological freak to climb Everest without bottled oxygen.

Robert and Ed were climbing up the long slope now. Robert, who had always seemed so strong, was still down near the shoulder, only moving occasionally between long rests. Perhaps he was just having an off day. Ed was closer and I decided to wait for him, hoping that he might take over trail-breaking. I slumped forward on my ice axe and dozed for a while. When I opened my eyes Ed was only slightly closer. I dozed again, sinking into blissful semi-consciousness, perhaps even falling asleep. This time when I opened my eyes Ed too was sitting down; but after a while he stood up and moved a few steps closer.

I had been dozing intermittently for an hour when Ed finally arrived at a spot just below me. I had been alone for nearly twelve hours and it was good to have company again. I asked Ed if he would do a spell in front. He replied sleepily, muttering something about not being able to stay awake. I cannot remember the exact words, but the message was that he doubted whether he could go much further. Days later I told Mimi that I had just shrugged my shoulders, whereupon Ed reminded me that actually I had shouted back, 'So I've waited here a whole bloody hour for nothing.'

In fact I had longed to sleep, the hour's rest had probably done me good and it had been another chance to let my toes rewarm, but now I was alarmed at having to wake up and make a decision. Robert and Ed seemed even more tired than me and I realized that no one could help me. Either I had to get a grip on myself and go all out for the summit on my own, or I would have to turn round and descend empty-handed. It had taken me twelve hours to climb this far, and I was still a long way from the top, whereas Messner and Habeler had climbed all the way from the col to the summit in nine and a half hours. I would either have to move faster or accept failure.

It was midday. If I really pushed myself I might reach the South Summit by one o'clock. That would give me three hours to reach the main summit and turn round by four o'clock, leaving another three hours of daylight for the descent. That ought to be enough time. As Ed had often reminded us, once you were on the way down hypoxia – oxygen deprivation – was not such a problem; you just let gravity do the work for you.

The biggest problem at the moment was staying awake, so I took two of the caffeine pills which Mimi had given us. I do not know whether it was the pills, or the hour's rest or some inner determination that had been lying dormant but, whatever it was, from the moment I decided to continue I felt transformed. Now I took firm balanced steps, kicking deliberately into the snow and keeping going for four, five, maybe six steps at a time, stopping only for short rests. I was no longer a passive observer of my body: I was controlling it, directing it confidently towards the South Summit.

Ed was still following and I think he shouted up to ask, 'Do you think that's the South Summit up there?'

I replied, 'Yes, I hope so! It must be less than an hour from here.'

I had now passed the rock outcrops and was zig-zagging up the final long snowslope, knowing that soon I would be on that curved top. But the curved top only led to another steeper slope. Then there was a bergschrund, like a horizontal cave barring the way to the final steepening. Now I had to do real climbing, cutting a step on the upper lip of the bergschrund, plunging the axe shaft in as high as I could reach, stepping up, pulling on the axe then falling back down again as the step collapsed. That made me angry and I swung the axe violently, cutting a better step. This time I succeeded, pulling up on the axe, then delicately shifting weight onto my upper foot and balancing up over the bulge. I stopped to regain breath, surprised at the ease of it, delighted to find that

I could make those familiar moves over the bergschrund, as if all the bergschrunds I had surmounted over the last fifteen years had been a preparation for this test at 8,700 metres.

Cloud was brewing up from the valleys, but I was not concerned. I continued above the bergschrund and arrived at the apex of the slope. But it was not the South Summit. That was still about twenty metres ahead, marked by a great triangular cornice, jutting out over the Kangshung Face like a lopsided pyramid. I turned round and shouted, 'Five minutes!' to Ed, hoping to encourage him, then continued out of his sight along the narrow ridge to the South Summit.

It was like the Eiger again. It was like that moment in 1986 when Luke Hughes and I had emerged from the Brittle Crack and looked across to the Traverse of the Gods, seeing for real that ledge which we had already seen in a hundred photographs, and knew that we were on the home run. Here on Everest, six thousand miles from the Eiger, I was at last looking at the final ridge I knew so well from the 1953 photos and the picture Chris Bonington took in 1985 – the descent to the gap, the rocky corniced knife-edge, the steep rise of the Hillary Step and the snow ridge beyond, bulging out to the right in huge cornices, flung by the westerly winds over the Kangshung Face.

I looked back round to the south, trying to absorb it all – Lhotse half-obscured by cloud and the Western Cwm, so far below, curving round towards the invisible Khumbu Icefall. Clouds were boiling up from the valley but I could see the famous summit of Pumori and as I turned back to the north I could see part of the turreted West Ridge of Everest, still quite a way ahead on my left, rising up to meet my South-East Ridge, out of sight, at the summit. Was I going to the main summit? Or was I going to turn back now, settling for the 8,765-metre South Summit?

I looked again at that final quintessential mountain ridge, the rocky knife-edge, the tantalizing sting-in-the-tail which Bourdillon and Evans had been first to see, thirty-five years earlier. The actual summit was hidden. I could only see the hummock above the Hillary Step and I knew that there were

three or four similar hummocks beyond. But the distance
from the top of the step could not be more than about three
hundred metres. The weather was still reasonable. I was
healthy and strong, I had recovered from the morning's
depressing lassitude and the summit of Everest was only
eighty-three vertical metres above me. If I did not do it now I
might return on four expeditions and never get another
opportunity like this. I continued to stare towards the Hillary
Step and the dip in the ridge leading to it. It looked hard, that
narrow crest crossing the gap, the bridge to the summit.
Perhaps I would be unable to get back across the bridge.
Perhaps I would lose control, like those Japanese climbers in
1983 who reached the summit without oxygen but dropped
off like flies on the way down. I would have to watch myself
carefully.

The time was 1.30 p.m. I was behind schedule, but that
was because I had not realized the extent of hidden ground
leading up to the South Summit. Now that I had covered that
ground and could see the final part of the route, I reckoned
that I could reach the main summit and turn back within two
and a half hours, sticking to my 4 p.m. deadline. (Later I
discovered that Messner and Habeler had climbed from the
South to the main summit in just one hour; but they were
fitter and stronger after an easier Sherpa-assisted climb to the
South Col.) I was almost certain that I could do it. At the
very least I should descend into the gap and see how long it
took to reach the Hillary Step.

It was time to cross the bridge. I took out two more
caffeine pills, swigged them down with Rehydrate juice,
replaced the bottle in my windsuit and started down the far
side of the South Summit. Suddenly I saw red and green
spots against the snow. Not now! Please not – I must not be
ill! Could it be a retinal haemorrhage? That was a common
and relatively minor problem at altitude. Or was this the
killer – cerebral oedema – water on the brain? Vision problems are often the first sign. Please not. I can't turn back now
and I don't want to die. I blinked hard and saw with immense
relief that my vision had cleared.

I climbed down steep snow for about fifteen metres to the gap. The red and green spots had not recurred so I continued along the horizontal ridge. I noticed a huge rock overhang under the South Summit with discarded rope and oxygen bottles lying in its shelter. Then I looked down the South-West Face on my left. My brain was dazed by hypoxia but it managed a flicker of excitement, recognizing the huge upper snowfield where Doug Scott and Dougal Haston had traversed out towards the summit in September, 1975. I could see all the way across to the site of their Camp 6 and I could just make out the top of the Rock Band gully. But it all looked much drier in these pre-Monsoon conditions with far more brown rock showing than in Scott's pictures.

I kept well to the left of the crest, moving now across rocks. This was wonderful: I was doing real climbing, placing feet on little ledges, pushing up with one mittened hand, reaching high with the other, shifting weight – real technical moves, two or three together, and breathing at the same time. I could do it – I could climb these rocks 8,750 metres above sea level! I looked back up at the deserted South Summit. Still no sign of Ed, but perhaps he would arrive soon. Perhaps he would get dramatic photos looking across to me on the Hillary Step. What vanity! What presumption to be crossing this bridge . . . for I had now decided definitely that I was going to the summit and I had decided with total conviction that I would be able to return. However, just in case Ed did not arrive in time, I forced myself to take one photo on my compact camera, my first photo since dawn, looking up at the Hillary Step with clouds blowing off the bulbous cornice above. Then I continued, enjoying the solidity of the rock, but moving with patient care, determined not to slip and tumble out of control down the 2,500-metre South-West Face.

I arrived at the Step. Why didn't Hillary climb round to the left? Those rocks don't look so bad. Quite steep, but . . . no, maybe he was right. Maybe it is easier up here, right on the crest, treading on this almost vertical snow plastered to the Kangshung side of the rock. And this way is now safeguarded by a fixed rope, three ropes in fact.

I took off my double mittens, stuffing them safely inside my windsuit while I unclipped my safety loop and arranged a Bachman knot, twisting the loop round a karabiner against one of the fixed ropes, so that the karabiner could slide up like a jumar. The other end of the loop was clipped into my waist belt. If I fell the twists would jam round the karabiner and hold me to the fixed rope.

Hillary had jammed his way up a crack between the rock and the snow. This year there was no crack, but the snow on the right was firm and there were remnants of steps left by the Asian expedition. I felt quite secure, with my right foot kicked firmly into the snow and right arm plunging my ice axe deep above my head. My left foot found what holds it could on the rock and my left hand alternately held the rock and slid the Bachman knot up the fixed rope. Again I was delighted to discover that I could really climb at this altitude. Of course the conditions were good, and when I remembered the photos of Haston in 1975, flailing his way up seventy degrees steep powder snow, I thought how lucky I was to have firm steps. Nevertheless it was a wild place to be, this twenty-metre cliff where I climbed up within inches of the cornice overhanging the immense Kangshung Face and everything was so cold and grey, like a November afternoon.

Suddenly I was in a pub – a proper pub with no imitation plastic beams, quasi-rustic horseshoes or flashing video games – just a simple unpretentious room with an open fire. I was sitting next to a girl with long golden hair, glowing in the firelight, and someone was bringing two pint glasses of warm dark rich Guinness, topped with pale creamy foam. The vision brought a brief moment of warmth and comfort; then I was alone again on the Hillary Step. At the top there was a chimney where I squeezed between the snow and the rock pinnacle securing the ropes. I stopped behind the pinnacle to rest and unclip my safety loop then continued across the easier slope above.

Nothing could stop me now. There were clouds below and above, but here on the curved roof of Everest the visibility was still reasonable and the snow underfoot was crisp and firm. All

I had to do was walk gently upwards, picking my way from rock to rock, well to the left of the dangerous cornices, moving patiently across the first great hump, stopping every three or four steps to lean slightly on my ice axe and draw extra gulps of air into my lungs. I cannot remember how many humps I had to cross. All I can remember is the unquestioning certainty that soon, very soon, I would be on the summit.

I continued steadily across the convex roof and finally saw over the crest of a hump to a final higher hump where three figures sat in the snow, silhouetted against the grey sky. What a wonderful surprise – other people on the summit, waiting only about a hundred metres away. They sat still and erect and only their hats moved slightly in the breeze. Perhaps it was the British Services, successfully completing the West Ridge. Perhaps there would be people I knew there – Henry or Nigel or Luke? I shouted excitedly: 'Oi!' No answer. I shouted again: 'Hallo!' then bent over in a fit of coughing. The thin dry air was irritating my throat and the shout had exhausted me. I would be able to make a little joke about giving up smoking, when I met them on the summit. A joke at 29,000 feet – not bad. But why didn't they answer now, or wave at least? Lousy soldiers. Better speak to them in their own language: 'Are you going to fucking talk to me or not?!' I erupted into another fit of coughing and the three figures watched impassively. I looked up again and they were still sitting there, thin and straight. I started to move and as I walked slowly closer the three figures looked increasingly lifeless and I realized sadly that they were not people at all.

I was now descending into a slight dip. All that remained was the final snowslope, perhaps ten metres high. I just had to step up that slope. Don't rush. Don't try more steps at a time than you can manage. Don't bring on another fit of coughing – it's too exhausting. Just keep those lungs and legs synchronized – slowly, patiently up the last few feet.

The slope eased back slightly, I climbed out onto the curved crest of the West Ridge, turned right and took the last few steps to the top of the world.

★

I allowed myself ten minutes on the summit. Now, writing three months later, I find it almost impossible to recall the emotions of those precious moments. Even at the time, I found it hard to know exactly what I was feeling. There was a dreamlike sense of disbelief at being in this special place, sitting so utterly alone beside the three yellow French oxygen cylinders which the Asian expedition had left upright in the snow. The empty cylinders were labelled CNJ for China–Nepal–Japan and were decorated with the prayer flags that I had mistaken for hats. The cylinders and bits of discarded radio equipment were the only signs that people had ever been here. When I could find the strength to stand up again I looked down the West Ridge, which disappeared into swirling clouds. There was no sign of the British Services Expedition. Then I turned to the right, where the North-East Ridge – the 'Mallory Route' – also dropped away into the clouds. I could not see the Rongbuk Glacier, nor the Kama valley and to the south there were yet more clouds, completely hiding Lhotse from view. It was like being alone on the apex of some huge grey roof. At this point on the ridge the ground drops away slightly to the giant cornices overhanging the Kangshung Face, so that one can keep well clear of danger, yet stand right on the crest of the ridge, on a real unequivocal summit.

I had work to do. First I had to photograph myself. I took off the camera belt, removed the big camera, cocked the self-timer, and, gasping with the effort, knelt down to prop it on its case about three metres from the summit. I was too tired to lie right down and frame the picture in the viewfinder, so I just put the zoom on wide-angle and pointed it in the general direction of the summit. Then, as the self-timer whirred, I stepped back up and sat by the ornamental oxygen bottles. I thought that I heard the shutter click. I knew that I should take more frames, bracketing the exposures for safety, but I did not have the mental or physical energy to reset the camera.

Robert had the summit flags and trinkets from Norbu, but there was one small ritual for me to carry out. I reached into one of my inside pockets and pulled out a tiny polythene bag. Inside it were the two miniature envelopes given to me in Bombay by Nawang and Sonam. I carefully took out the flower petals and scattered them in the snow, then placed the two envelopes beside the oxygen bottles. Then, panting with the effort of concentration, I took two pictures on the compact camera.

The film in the SLR with the self-portrait was either not wound on properly or was lost on the journey home, for I was never to see the photo of myself on the summit. However, I do have a picture showing the little envelopes. Each envelope is decorated with the face of one of the teachers at Geeta's ashram in Pondicherri, staring up from amongst the radio boxes, yellow cylinders and wisps of prayer flag on the summit of Everest.

I rested again, slumped in the snow. The air temperature in this second week of May had been getting steadily warmer and even at 8,848 metres there was still very little wind. I felt comfortable and I was almost tempted to linger, for I was aware that this was a terribly important event in my life and I wanted to savour that precious moment, storing away what memories I could in my feeble oxygen-starved brain. It would be nice to say that it was the happiest moment of my life and that I was overwhelmed by euphoria; but that would be a gross exaggeration, for at the time there was only a rather dazed feeling of – 'Isn't this strange? You really have done it, after all those weeks of watching and waiting and worrying. It would have been better if everyone had made it but at least someone has actually reached the summit – and a rather special summit . . . So this is what it's like.'

It was a turning point. Even in my befuddled state I knew that this would inevitably alter my life. But I also knew that it was far more urgently critical as a turning point in the climb, the point where I no longer had to struggle upwards but had to start down immediately, fleeing from this bewitching dreamlike place and hurrying back down to Earth before it was too late. It was now 3.50 p.m., Nepalese time. I was just ahead of schedule, but the clouds were closing in fast and in three hours it would be dark. I stood up, took the ice axe in my mittened hand, had one last look down Mallory's ridge, then hurried away back south.

After descending a short way I stopped for my final summit task. Just below the top there was an exposed outcrop of shattered rock, where I knelt down to collect some pieces of limestone and stuff them in a pocket.

The wind was mounting now, starting to blow spindrift in my face. I hurried on, using gravity to speed myself back towards the Hillary Step. As I came over the last hump the clouds enveloped me completely. Suddenly I realized that I was heading too far to the right, down towards the South-West Face. I headed back up to the left, peering through my iced-up sunglasses at the swirling greyness. I was utterly alone in the cloud and there was no sign of the South Summit. I felt disorientated and frightened, remembering the tragedy of 1975 when Mick Burke, the last person to complete the South-West Face, went alone to the summit and never came back. Somewhere up here, in conditions like this, blinded behind iced glasses, even more myopic than me, he had made an unlucky mistake, probably falling through one of the fragile cornices overhanging the Kangshung Face. I suddenly noticed the dim outline of one of those bulbous overhangs just in front of me and veered back right. For God's sake don't do a Mick Burke. Just concentrate. You've gone too far left now. Head for that rock – must be solid ground there. Now I could pick out some tracks – my tracks almost filled with spindrift already, but tracks none the less. This is right. But it's so difficult. Must have a rest. I sank down and sat in the snow. Then I continued wearily, too slowly, legs sagging, head bowed. I stopped after only a few paces but forced myself not to sit down, leaning instead on my ice axe. Then I took a few steps again, willing my legs not to sag and crumple.

It was snowing now, stinging my face and encrusting my glasses. I had to wipe them with a clumsy mitten, clearing a hole to peer through, searching for landmarks. I recognized clumps of rock and followed them to the pinnacle above the

Hillary Step. Then came the hard part, taking off mittens, pulling up some slack in the fixed rope and clipping it into my waist belt karabiner with an Italian hitch. I pulled mittens back on and started to abseil down the cliff. Even though I was moving downhill it was exhausting. Possible the waist belt was pulling up and constricting my diaphragm, for I had to slump and rest during the twenty-metre abseil, gasping for breath. I continued in a frantic blind struggle to the bottom of the Step where I fell over and collapsed on the side of the ridge, hyperventilating furiously.

It had never happened before and I was terrified. This was quite new – this ultra-rapid panting, like a fish out of water incapable of getting oxygen into its gills. I panted harder and harder, clutching at the air, frantic to refill my lungs. But nothing seemed to get beyond my throat and for a ghastly moment I thought that I was going to suffocate. Then the air started to get through, and I gasped great sobs of relief as my breathing slowed to normal again.

I had to move. Get off that rope and continue. Take mittens off and unclip from the rope. Now, quickly get those mittens back on again. The first one is always easy but the second one won't go. I can't grip it – can't make those useless numb fingers work. It's all too difficult. I'll never get it on and my fingers will freeze solid. No more piano playing. But I must get that mitten on or I'll never get down. Concentrate. That's it, ease it up the wrist.

I slumped over again, gasping with exhaustion. The wind was flinging snow at me and I was starting to shiver. I was completely blind and tore at my sunglasses, letting them hang down round my neck by their safety leash. At least I could see a little now, only blurred shapes, but better than nothing. There's a bit of a clearing. That's the South Summit up there on the far side of the bridge. No sign of Robert or Ed. They must have gone down by now. Crazy to continue to the top in these conditions and no reason to wait for me. There's no one to help me. Either I get myself down or I die. It would be so easy to die – just lie down here and rest and soon the wind would kill me. It would be the easiest thing in the world but I'd look bloody silly. No use to anyone climb-ing Everest then lying down to die. No, pull yourself together and move. It's not possible to get out the other pair of glasses without taking off mittens again, so we'll just have to move very carefully on half vision.

My invisible companion, the old man, had reappeared and together we moved forward, determined not to die. We stumbled half-blind along the ridge, crouched over the ice axe, peering anxiously through the driving snow, almost on all fours, laboriously dragging ourselves across the rocks, clinging carefully to avoid the death slide down the South-West Face. Fear and instinct kept me moving over the rocks. Then I recognized the dry hollow by the overhanging rock where Boardman and Pertemba had waited in vain for Mick Burke to return. I wondered briefly whether I should bivouac there, but decided to continue, determined to get right back across the bridge to the South Summit. That was the critical point beyond which I was confident that I could survive.

The visibility was still atrocious and I strayed too close to the crest on the left. Suddenly my left leg shot down into a hole and I collapsed in another fit of hyperventilation. I may have trodden on the cornice fracture line, but I think it was just a deep snowdrift. Whatever it was, the jolt almost suf-focated me; but I regained my breath and forced myself on up the fifteen-metre climb to the South Summit. I collapsed again and this time, as I regained my breath in great anguished gasps, I was filled with pity for the poor old man who was finding it all a bit too much.

We floundered eventually up to the crest of the South Summit where my mind must have gone almost blank, for I can only recall blurred images of snow and cloud and the gloom of dusk. I can remember nothing of the descent of the knife-edge ridge, I only have the vaguest recollection of slithering back over the bergschrund and then I was back on the big snowslope, sitting down to slide, because it is easier to sit than to stand.

We were racing the darkness, using gravity to hurry down towards the safety of the South Col. But even sliding is hard work, because you have to brace your legs and brake with your ice axe. It was somewhere down here that Peter Habeler, during his phenomenal one-hour descent, from the summit to the South Col, spurred on by his fear of permanent brain damage, almost flew out of control down the Kangshung Face. I was anxious about the big slope below me and kept stopping to walk further right towards the ridge. Then on one slide the old man became very frightened. We were gathering speed in a blinding flurry of powder snow. The surface underneath felt hollow and unstable and seemed to be breaking off in avalanches. We were sliding faster and faster down to the east and the old man was hating it. He had suddenly become a musician. Musicians hate this. The composer is sliding on his cello, riding the avalanche to his death. Please stop! Now!

I dug my heels in and leant over hard on my ice axe, dragging the ferrule deep into the snow, and came to a halt. We were about to collapse and had to rest as soon as possible, but we could not sit down here. Too steep and insecure. Quick, cut a ledge. Ice axe and burrowing hand – that's it. Quick. Just enough of a hollow to sit down. Must rest. Must have a pee. The old man says do it in your pants – it'll keep you warm.

I could wait no longer and with one last frantic effort I plunged the ice axe deep into the snow and used it to heave myself up onto the ledge. Then my strength gave out and I collapsed, wetting myself and suffocating in another fit of hyperventilation.

Poor old man . . . that's better now, he's breathing again. He just needs to rest. What was all that business about music – cello music? What has that got to do with avalanches? Who is this composer? Dvorak wrote a cello concerto. Kate plays the cello – but she's a woman. It's all too confusing. Better to concentrate on reality – on me sitting here on this precarious ledge in the snow. And why did I believe that nonsense about peeing in my pants? All wet now. It must have been the shock.

I was getting chronically exhausted and it was now virtually dark, so I decided to stay where I was. I sat there for about an hour, shivering as the cold pressed through from the snow. Then I decided that my precarious perch was too dangerous and that I should try to continue down to the South Col where Ed and Robert would be waiting in the tents. I lowered myself to my feet, faced into the slope and started kicking steps carefully across the snow, back towards the crest of the ridge. There I tried to orientate myself, climbing backwards and forwards over the rocks, trying to recognize individual out- crops from the morning. But it was dark, there was no moon and, although the afternoon storm had blown over, there were still drifting clouds to confuse my vision. Even after putting on glasses and switching on my headtorch, I found it very difficult to judge shapes and distances. I started to worry that perhaps my glissade had taken me lower than I thought and that I was now below the point where I had to turn right into the couloir.

After about half an hour of wandering about, the old man suggested that we should stop here for the night and wait for daylight to re-orientate ourselves. I decided that he would be warmest sitting on a rock and soon I found a ledge on the ridge where we could sit down. But it was precarious and sloping and we both longed to lean back properly, so we traversed back out onto the snow and dug a horizontal ledge where we could lie down properly. At about 9 p.m. we settled down for the night.

The emergency bivouac had many precedents. During the American traverse of Everest in 1963 Willi Unsoeld and Tom Hornbein completed the first ascent of the West Ridge, reach- ing the summit just before dark at 6.15. Two companions had reached the summit by the normal route the same afternoon and were waiting near the South Summit when Unsoeld and Hornbein started to descend the South-East Ridge. When they met, Hornbein tried to persuade the other three to continue down to the top camp but they soon became lost in the dark and had to resign themselves to a night out in the open at about 8,500 metres. They survived the intense cold and descended safely the next day, but afterwards Unsoeld had to have nine frostbitten toes amputated and one of the South-East Ridge duo, Barry Bishop, lost all his toes.

In 1976 two British soldiers, Bronco Lane and Brummie Stokes, were also forced to bivouac on the same slope just below the South Summit, descending in bad weather. Twelve years later in Kathmandu, Stokes was to show me his mutilated toeless feet. Lane had to have fingers as well as toes amputated, but at least both of them were alive, unlike the German climber, Hannelore Schmatz, who in 1979 insisted on stopping to bivouac before dark, even though her Sherpas were urging her to carry on down to the safety of their top camp. She died sitting in the snow and for several years her frozen body was a grisly landmark on the South-East ridge, until it was recently buried or swept away by an avalanche. I also knew about the Bulgarian climber who had died whilst descending the difficult West Ridge in 1984. Meena Agrawal, who had been doctor to another Everest expedition that year, had later told me how she had talked to the Bulgarian on the radio, trying to comfort him and persuade him to live through the night; but eventually the man had been unable to hold up the receiver any longer and had presumably died soon afterwards.

I had no intention of dying that night. I was alone just above 8,500 metres (about 28,000 feet) but the wind which had frightened me so much by the Hillary Step had now died away and the air temperature was probably not much lower than −20°C. I was lucky with the conditions and I knew that I could survive in the excellent clothes I wore, but I had to resign myself to the probable loss of toes. Six months earlier, caught out high on Shisha Pangma, Luke and I had dug a snowhole and crawled inside to take off boots and warm each other's toes. But now I was nearly a thousand metres higher, I was alone and I barely had the strength to cut a ledge, let alone a proper cave where I could safely take off boots. I had climbed with the specific intention of not bivouacking, so I had no stove to melt snow. Only a trickle of half-frozen juice remained in my water bottle and in the last twenty-four hours I had drunk less than a litre. Dehydration was thickening my blood, already viscous with the concentration of red blood cells necessary to survive at altitude, and circulation was sluggish to the remote outposts of the vascular system, particularly my toes.

If the weather had been worse, I would probably have found new reserves of strength, either to dig a snowhole or to search harder for the correct descent route. But as the air was calm I lay inert, huddled up in the snow with my spare mittens providing meagre insulation under my hips and my ice axe plunged into the slope in front of me, like a retaining fence post.

I was not really alone. The old man was still with me and now there were other people as well, crowding my tiny ledge. Sometimes they offered to look after parts of my body. At one stage during the long night the old man became rather patronizing towards a girl who was keeping one of my hands warm. Perhaps it was then that Eric Shipton, the distinguished explorer so closely involved with the history of Everest, took over warming my hands. At the end of the ledge my feet kept nearly falling off where I had failed to dig a thorough hollow in the snow. I was aware of several people crowding out the feet, but also trying to look after them. They were being organized by Mike Scott.

I had never met Mike Scott but I knew his father, Doug, who had bivouacked even higher than this, right up on the South Summit in 1975. He and Dougal Haston had been half-prepared for an emergency bivouac, carrying a tent sack and a stove. When they emerged from the South-West Face late in the day, they had started digging a cave and had made a hot brew before climbing the final ridge to the summit. After photographing the magical sunset from the summit they returned to the snowcave where their oxygen ran out and they settled down for the highest bivouac ever. Scott had no down gear – only the tent sack and a rucksack to sit on, yet on that bitterly cold autumn night he had the strength not only to survive but to concentrate on 'the quality of survival', warming and talking to his feet throughout the night. When he and Haston descended to the haven of Camp 6 the next day, neither of them had any frostbite.

I drifted in and out of reality, occasionally reminding myself that I was actually alone, before returning to my confused hallucinations. Towards dawn, as I started to long for warmth, my companions teased me by announcing that there were some yak herders camping just round the corner with tents and food and hot fires. They left me alone with the old man and went to investigate. It was good to be left in peace for a while and I reminded myself that yak herders could not possibly be living up here at 8,500 metres; but later the people returned to tell me that while the insidious cold of the snow had been creeping through my body they had been enjoying hot baths and food. Now I longed even more desperately to be warm.

At some stage during the night I stood up to enlarge my ledge. After that I felt slightly more comfortable and less precarious. Eventually I think that I must have slept, for I remember an actual awakening and sudden realization that the long night was finally over.

I sat up shivering. There was pastel light in the sky and only a soft blanket of grey cloud remained in the valley far below. All the people, even the old man, had gone but I had survived my night out. My body was stiff and my feet were dead, but my fingers were still alive inside their down mittens. The hairs on my eyebrows, moustache and beard were stuck together with great lumps of ice and a frozen film encased my wooden nose. My iced sunglasses still hung useless round my neck, but my other glasses were clear, so that I could see the route down.

I could not believe that it had all seemed so strange in the dark, now that I could see the shoulder just below me, with the little dip where one had to turn right into the couloir. If only I had seen better in the dark I could perhaps have descended to Camp 3 and saved myself all that shivering!

The sun was rising over Kanchenjunga as I stood up shakily, picked up my ice axe and set off wobbling and sliding down the slope. Soon I was back in the couloir, daring myself to sit down and slide wherever possible. Once I went too fast and gave myself another alarming attack of hyperventilating, but after that I stayed in control. The world was sparkling in morning sunlight and life was wonderful. I was alive and warm again, I had climbed Everest and soon I would be back in the valley.

Suddenly I saw two people in the couloir, down by the Dunlop tent. It took a while for my dulled mind to realize that they must be Ed and Robert, who had also failed to reach the South Col in the dark and had taken shelter in the Asians' abandoned tent. They turned round and saw me sliding towards them and a few minutes later we were reunited. I cannot remember what we said. Only a few words were spoken and they were probably banal; but I remember vividly Ed and Robert's relief at seeing me alive and a deep warmth of friendship as the three of us roped together for the final descent to the South Col.

10

Escape

*R*OBERT led the way down to the col. I followed, sitting down to slide whenever possible, and Ed came last. On the bottom easy section of the couloir we unroped to slither and stagger independently. Then we just had to walk across the plateau.

Ed photographed Robert towering over me with a welcoming arm over my shoulder, then me on my own, with my torch still on my head and camera equipment and sunglasses tangled round my neck. I just managed to rise to the occasion, forcing a smile out of my iced-up face and holding up the ice axe in my left hand. Before Ed put his mittens back on he showed me his fingers: 'I think they're frostbitten. I didn't really notice yesterday, but I think it must have happened at sunrise. I took about twenty frames. Wasn't that light amazing? Kangchenjunga, Makalu . . . They're going to be some brilliant pictures.'

We continued towards our two tents. Robert and Ed were moving quite strongly but on this last stretch I sank every few metres to my knees or just sat down, waiting for the willpower to move my legs again. We knew that we should really continue straight down the East Face to the safer altitude of the Flying Wing, but we were desperate for liquid and sleep and by the time I reached Camp 3 on the South Col Robert was already crawling into his tent. Soon Ed and I were nestled amongst down sleeping bags in the warmth of our tent, with the first batch of snow melting on the stove while we started to remove our mittens and boots to inspect the damage.

My fingers were fine, apart from a touch of frostbite on the right thumb; and the right foot looked all right apart from slight discoloration on the big toe and heel. The left foot was worse but I was relieved to see that the damage was limited to the heel and toes, which were starting to turn a purplish colour. The demarcation line between live and frozen tissue curved from the base of the big toe to the tip of the little toe. By some inexplicable coincidence Ed's right foot was also virtually undamaged and the injuries were much worse on his left foot, almost identical to mine. However, it was the fingers that were now worrying him. He explained again how he had exposed them at sunrise the previous morning.

'I had on liner gloves but even so my fingers must have been frozen by the metal camera. I thought that they had just gone numb and would warm up again. What do you think?'

'They'll be all right,' I assured him. 'They're certainly frostbitten but they don't look much worse than Luke's did on Shishers and he didn't lose anything. What does my nose look like? It feels completely dead.'

'It's a sort of purplish grey colour.' As soon as the melted snow was ready, Ed started to bathe his fingers in warm water. With considerable difficulty I did the same with my toes, twisting my foot to get it in the mug. Later I was to be reminded that one should avoid thawing frozen tissue until one is safely down; but at the time we lacked the sense to realize that our digits were about to be refrozen descending the East Face. After our thirty-two-hour ordeal on the summit ridge we just wanted warmth and comfort and it did not occur to us to keep our damaged digits firmly frozen, which would have meant keeping our left feet and both Ed's hands out of our sleeping bags.

The tent was a haven of bright warmth seducing us into staying on the South Col. We knew that this was our third day above 8,000 metres and that we should leave the 'death zone' as soon as possible, but we decided that we would wait till the next morning, by which time we would have rested and rehydrated a little. It felt wonderful just to lie back, warm and content, drinking the remains of our tea, sugar and hot chocolate.

Ed told me a little about what had happened to him and Robert up on the South Summit, but we were too tired to talk properly and it is only now, three months after our summit climb, that he has searched his memory for the details and written from Colorado to tell me what happened.

Like me, he kept falling asleep on the long slope up to the South Summit, but always forced himself to wake up and continue, drawing closer to me. When I pushed on again he followed at a distance. Ever professional, he tried to photograph me on the final slope, but by the time he had the exposure adjusted I was disappearing over the crest. That was the last he or Robert saw of me until the next morning.

Ed eventually reached the false top just below the South Summit. The clouds were now closing in and, like me, he remembered Mick Burke. He stared along the final precarious snow arête leading to the South Summit and decided that he did not like it. If the three of us had been together, giving each other moral support, he might have considered it; but he was alone, Robert was about an hour behind him and it was too late. He had a strong gut feeling that if he continued he would either lose control and fall off, or at the very least have to face an open bivouac near the summit. However, if he turned round now, at about 3.30 p.m., he could descend safely to our Camp 3 on the South Col.

Ed started back down and soon met Robert, who announced that he wanted to go a little higher. Ed replied that he would wait on the shoulder at the top of the couloir leading down to the South Col. Robert, with his usual determination, forced himself slowly up to the South Summit. He arrived at about 4.30 p.m., while I was battling to find my way back down from the summit to the Hillary Step. Everest was enveloped in swirling cloud and Robert became disorientated. As he explained later, 'After I'd walked round in a circle once, I realized that if I tried to continue I wouldn't come back.' In 1985 he had retreated from the West Ridge

250 metres below the top, after weeks of hard work. Since then he had spent three years dreaming of his return to Everest and now he had to take the same painful decision less than 100 metres below the summit.

Ed had a long wait at the shoulder, staring up at the murky slope leading down from the South Summit. Frequently he hallucinated, seeing Robert and me descending out of the mists. Sometimes the two figures were too far to the right or had already descended past him and Ed would yell to them, trying to warn them of danger. But there was never an answer and the figures always disappeared. Ed grew steadily more cold, tired and frustrated until, at dusk, Robert finally appeared in bodily form. Ed was angry with him, because they now had only about fifteen minutes of daylight left.

They thought that they would be unable to reach the South Col in the dark, so they were resigned to a night out without sleeping bags. However they remembered the Asians' tent and rushed off down the couloir, peering through the fading light to find the way and race the darkness. Ed just managed to find the tent before it became totally dark. A few minutes later Robert arrived and they both crawled inside. There was no insulation other than the tent groundsheet, but Ed managed to sleep intermittently. Robert had a worse night and kept waking Ed, asking to go down to the col; but Ed told him each time that it was too dark and cold outside and that they should wait for the sun. Finally the sun appeared and Ed gave permission to leave. They crawled out of the tent and a few minutes later saw me 'staggering down the gully like a drunk'.

The extraordinary thing about Ed's decision to turn back by the South Summit the previous afternoon was that he felt no regret. Having analysed the dangers so rationally, he set off down with the patently absurd notion that he would simply rest a day at the South Col, then come back up for another attempt. Now, a day later, we were back on the col. We felt warm and secure, but Ed certainly realized now that there was not the slightest chance of another summit attempt and we were both becoming dimly aware that even the descent was going to be a hard struggle.

We talked idly and dozed and soon it was dark. By the evening our last gas cylinder was now empty and I had to quench my thirst by sucking lumps of ice. It was a strange confused night and, although there was nothing to compare with the hallucinations of the previous night, I slept badly, wandering in and out of troubled dreams. In the morning I lay half-conscious, waiting for Robert to bring us water. Time was moving with unchecked speed and several hours passed as we waited for our drink. Occasionally we would shout: 'Robert, what's happened to that water?' and he would answer from the other tent in a dreary slurred voice, 'Just wait. It's coming soon. The stove's not working properly.'

It must have been nearly midday when he eventually brought over the water to relieve our thirst; but still we delayed our departure. It was pitiful to witness our own deterioration as we sprawled on our backs, mumbling feebly about the imperative need to descend but failing to do anything about it. Eventually Ed forced me to start the first exhausting task – sitting up, getting out of my sleeping bag and, with many pauses for rest, packing it into my rucksack. Then I lay down for half an hour, delaying the awful effort of putting on boots.

I knew that this was all wrong. It was now the afternoon of 14 May and we had spent almost four days above 8,000 metres. We had broken the rules and we were asking for trouble. We should have left early that morning to descend all the way to Camp 1, but now we would be pushed even to reach Camp 2 before dark.

It was nearly 4 p.m. when we eventually left. A combination of laziness and the intention of glissading most of the way down meant that we did not bother to rope up. We did not have the strength to take the tents we had carried up from Camp 2 and left them standing on the bleak plateau; we would have to manage without them when we got down to the Flying Wing. I left my Therma-Rest, my spare mittens, my down sleeping boots and the windsuit which had saved my life two days earlier. I could manage without it now and I had to keep weight to a minimum. Before he left, Ed asked, 'What shall we do with this?'

'Ah – the mail packet. Perhaps the Australians will wander over here and pick it up, if they're still on the mountain.'

'I'll leave it here in the tent. You never know, even if no one picks it up now, the tent might still be standing in the autumn, when the next lot comes up here. Right, I'm going. Make sure you and Robert come soon.' He left quickly, determined to escape to a safer altitude.

Robert was still nurturing his last few ounces of gas, making one final brew of tepid water. I concentrated on my crampons. When they were safely on my feet I sat drinking half a pan of water, watching Robert staggering over to the edge of the plateau to start down the East Face. About ten minutes later I managed to stand up, put on my rucksack, pick up my ice axe, fit its safety loop over my wrist, put one foot forward and start walking.

I did not get very far before sinking to my knees to rest. That was better than sitting down, because it required less effort to stand up again from a kneeling position.

The afternoon had closed in, it was snowing and the South Col seemed even more forlorn than usual. I knew that if I failed to follow the other two I would die, but still I dallied, stopping to rest every few steps. When I reached the brink of the plateau and looked down the East Face Robert was resting far below. I saw the furrow where he had slid down and yelled, 'Is it all right?' I took his garbled shout to mean 'Yes' and jumped over the edge, landing in a sitting position and glissading off down the slope.

It was steeper than I remembered and I accelerated rapidly. I leaned hard over to one side, braking with the ice axe, but it made little difference. I was sliding faster and faster, then suddenly I hit submerged rocks. The ice axe skidded on the rocks; then it was plucked up in the air. I felt a sharp crack on my hipbone, I bounced faster and faster and then I was flung up in a rag doll somersault, spinning over and landing on my back to accelerate again. I was shooting down the slope, but now I was on snow again and could dig in my heels, braking desperately and finally coming to a gasping halt, coughing and spluttering in a shower of powder snow.

I lay there, battered, bruised and helpless, almost succumbing to terror before finding the courage to stand up. Luckily I had broken no bones but my one ice axe had been wrenched off my wrist, almost taking the Rolex with it, and now I had no tool to safeguard my descent. I was blinded by snow and frantically took off mittens to wipe clear my glasses, irretrievably dropping one mitten in the process. Now I had to split the remaining double mitten, wearing the flimsy down mitt on one hand and the outer on the other.

Robert was still a long way below watching impassively and Ed was far ahead, out of sight. Again I felt weak and helpless and in a fit of terror I yelled down, 'Robert, wait. Please wait! Don't go without me.' Then I started to kick shaky steps down towards him, holding my useless penguin arms out to the side.

Robert waited patiently and when I reached him he explained that he had also slid out of control. 'I never saw those rocks at all. Then the snow below avalanched, carrying me all the way down here.'

'Can I borrow your spare tool?' I asked. 'You had two tools with you, didn't you?'

'Sorry, I've lost both of them. The ice axe was ripped off my wrist and the spare ice hammer fell out of my holster. Now I just have this ski stick. I could break it in half . . .'

'No, it's all right.'

We carried on down, Robert leaning on his ski stick, I holding out my mittened hands for balance. Dusk was falling as I followed the others' tracks across the big slope above the Flying Wing. That traverse seemed an interminable purgatory. Robert and Ed were now out of sight and I was sitting down every few steps, finding it harder and harder each time to stand up again. Snow was still falling and everything was cold and grey.

I suddenly remembered a winter evening in 1976, in Italy, returning exhausted to the roadhead after an abortive climb above the Val Ferret. I longed to be back there, taking off snowshoes and walking into the little bar where I had sat on a high stool and made myself gloriously dizzy with a tumbler-ful of dark sweet Vermouth and a cigarette. Then I thought about skiing in bad weather, succumbing to temptation and ordering an overpriced Swiss glühwein. Which took me back to the soft green twilight of an evening in January 1986, camping amongst the primeval tree heathers of Bigo Bog in the Ruwenzori Mountains of East Africa. It had been a long wet day and after changing into dry clothes we had lit a fire to make mulled wine. Soon the air had been infused with the hot steam of wine, lemons, Cointreau and spices, sweetened with heaped spoons of sugar.

Darkness fell and there was no restorative hot drink. I wanted help to remove my sunglasses and I shouted out to Ed and Robert; but they were too far ahead, so I had to manage on my own, fumbling with wooden fingers to take off sunglasses, open the zipped lid of my rucksack and take out clear glasses and headtorch. Now I could see where I was going but I still felt lonely and frightened that I would not make it to Camp 2. I kept shouting 'Robert! Ed!' as I trudged laboriously over the little crevasse, past the marker wand, down into the dip, then back right, following the shelf under the Flying Wing, longing for warmth and rest and the reas-suring company of my friends.

At last I saw their lights at the site of our Camp 2. They had already fitted one of the cached gas cylinders to the burner Robert had carried down and the first brew was on the way. The instant coffee and milk which they had found in the Asians' tent two nights earlier tasted disgusting but we drank it anyway, hoping that it would give us some strength. For an hour I just lay in the snow, too feeble to get into my sleeping bag. When I eventually made the effort I kept boots and overboots on my feet, deciding now that it would be best to disturb the frozen toes as little as possible. I had left my inflated Therma-Rest on the South Col but my down sleep-ing bag kept me warm enough in the snow. Robert produced one or two more brews before we all fell into a deep sleep.

*

Thirst and a croaking cough woke me at dawn on 15 May. For ages I lay inert, coughing up foul lumps of phlegm from my throat. Then I tried to rouse Robert and Ed, begging them to light the stove. I tried several times but there was no response. In the end I had to do it myself. It was a big effort, leaning up on one elbow, scooping snow into the pan, setting the stove upright and struggling with my slightly frostbitten right thumb to work the flint of the lighter. Fifteen minutes later I had to replenish the snow, then I dozed again. Eventually we had a full pan of dirty tepid water but the stove fell over and we lost it. I started the laborious process again, forcing myself to repeat the whole exhausting routine, but after about forty-five minutes the stove fell over again.

The day was now well advanced. The weather was fine again and the open cave under the Flying Wing was a blazing suntrap. The heat was appalling, pressing down on us and intensifying our thirst. I managed to haul myself out of my sleeping bag and unzip the legs of my down bibs but I could not find the energy actually to take them off.

The third attempt to make a drink was successful. Then Robert's slurred zombie voice suggested that we should eat some food. The bag we had left here five days earlier contained chocolate, freeze-dried shrimp and clam chowder and potato powder. 'No – I couldn't,' croaked Ed. 'Not the chowder.'

'Can you make some potato then, Stephen?' Robert asked.

He managed to eat a reasonable helping, and I forced down a few spoonfuls but Ed could not face it. He was more concerned about getting off the mountain and kept urging, 'We must go down! Soon we won't be able to move.' We knew that he was right, but each of us was lost in his own private world of dreams, sprawled helpless in the stultifying heat, powerless to face reality.

'We should signal to the others.'

'Yes, we should stand up so that they can see us.'

'Maybe they saw our lights last night. Anyway, they'll see us when we start moving.'

'We should go soon.'

'But I want to sleep.'

'We'll go soon.'

'We need another drink. It's so hot!'

The heat grew worse as the East Face was covered by a layer of cloud, thin enough to let the sun through, but also just dense enough to reflect the white heat back onto the snow. We were imprisoned in a merciless shimmering glass-house and it was only in the afternoon, when the cloud thickened and snow started to fall, that we felt cool enough to move.

Ed urged us on as usual. His frostbitten fingers had now ballooned into large painful blisters, but he still managed to be ready first. Again we had wasted nearly a whole day and it was after 3 p.m. when Ed set off, wading through the deep heavy snow below the Flying Wing. I followed last, nearly an hour later. It was snowing and visibility was bad. After I had descended about 150 metres I heard Ed's voice further below, shouting up through the cloud to Robert.

'This is scary – I can't see a thing and I've just slipped over a cliff. We're not going to make it to Camp 1 tonight. If we try and continue we're just going to get lost. We'll have to go back up to Camp 2, where we've got shelter and gas. We'll just have to spend another night there and make sure we leave early in the morning.'

I knew that Ed was right but groaned with despair at the horror of having to force my body uphill. It was a slow painful battle to climb back up that slope and Ed quickly overtook me. He had our one remaining ice axe and moved alongside me as I balanced my way up a fifty-degree bulge of ice which we had slipped over on the way down, sweeping off the snow. Ed would drive his pick into the ice as high as possible, then I would use it as a handhold to step up higher, before letting go and balancing on my tiptoe crampon points, with the mittened palms of my hands just pressed to the ice, while Ed moved up alongside and placed the axe higher. Robert was approaching the bulge from below and shouted gloomily, 'What am I supposed to do?'

'I'll leave it here – half-way up!' Ed shouted encouragingly.

'Thanks a lot. How am I meant to reach it?'

'Jump – I suppose.'

It was dark by the time Robert eventually joined us under the Flying Wing. Ed and I were sprawled once again in our sleeping bags and I was starting to melt snow. We had no tea, coffee, Rehydrate or sugar – nothing to flavour our water except the remains of the potato powder. After the first cup of water I promised to produce another solid meal of potato, knowing how desperately our bodies needed fuel, but the meal never materialized for I fell too soon into an exhausted sleep.

When we woke at dawn on 16 May, we knew that this was our last chance. If we stayed another night at this altitude with virtually no food we would probably become too weak to move. It was now five days since Paul had left us on the South Col. We knew that he and the others would be worried, but once again we were too apathetic to take advantage of the cloudless morning and stand up to wave; instead we lay hidden under the Flying Wing, reasoning that the others would see our tracks of the previous evening and realize that we were on the way down.

Ed's blistered fingers were now agonizing and Robert's finger tips, though less badly damaged, were also painful, so I prepared the morning water. Everything smelled and tasted disgusting and the other two refused to eat the chocolate-coated granola bars that I had found. However I managed to sit up and eat two bars, concentrating stubbornly on the unpleasant task and swilling them down with sips of dirty melted snow. All this took time and we failed to leave before the sun hit us. This time I found it even harder to struggle out of the stifling oven of my sleeping bag and the down bibs. Beside me, Ed looked like an old man. His face was lean and haggard, his hair hung lankly and the light had gone out of his eyes as he stared in horror at his swollen blistered fingers. His voice too was the dry croak of an old, old man, repeating over and over again, 'We've got to go down. We *must* go down. If we don't go down today we're going to die.'

Robert, like me, was almost silent, fighting his own private battle against lassitude, building himself up for the great effort of departure. Ed, the most sensitive member of the team, seemed more deeply affected by the trauma of our descent and actually said that it was going to take him a long time to get over the psychological shock of this experience. However, because he was so sensitive to the danger threatening us and because he so urgently needed to reach Mimi's medical help, he had become our leader.

The only help Ed could give us was his insistent croaks of encouragement. We were powerless to help each other physically and I thought with detachment how our situation was starting to resemble the 1986 tragedy on K2, when the storm finally cleared, allowing the Austrian climbers, Willi Bauer and Kurt Diemberger, to bully their companions into fleeing the hell of Camp 4, after eight days at nearly 8,000 metres had reduced them all to emaciated wrecks. Julie Tullis had already died in the storm. Alan Rouse was only semi-conscious, incapable of moving, pleading deliriously for water. Diemberger and Bauer could do nothing and had to leave him lying in his tent. The other two Austrians, Immitzer and Wieser, collapsed in the snow soon after leaving the camp. The Polish woman, 'Mrufka' Wolf, managed to keep going but died later that day on the fixed ropes. Only Bauer and Diemberger, both large heavy men with enormous bodily reserves, crawled down alive.

Our experience had not approached the horror of K2: we had only spent four days, not eight, above 8,000 metres; we had been hindered slightly by poor weather, but we had experienced nothing to compare with the horrendous storm on K2; we had failed to make adequate brews but we had at least been drinking something, our gas at Camp 2 was still not finished and there were further stocks at Camp 1; nevertheless we were now in danger of re-enacting the K2 tragedy and as I lay flat on my back, delaying feebly the moment of departure, I realized how easy and painless it would be just to lie there until I died.

'Come on you guys, we've got to move! It's clouding over

already.' Ed was right: it was only 9 a.m. and the clouds had arrived earlier today with their crippling greenhouse effect. I reached out for the things I wanted to take – cameras, torch, down bibs and jacket. The sleeping bag would have to stay here, like Ed's and Robert's. It seemed monstrous to litter the mountain with $1500 worth of sleeping bags, but they weighed two and a half kilos each and the less weight we carried the greater chance we would have of reaching safety.

At 10 a.m. Ed was ready. Again he urged me to move. 'Don't wait long, Stephen. You've got to get up and move: if you don't get down alive you won't be able to enjoy being famous.' Then he left.

Robert made his final preparations, and I fitted my crampons. Everything was now ready but I wanted another rest so, while Robert set off, I sat on my rucksack. I sat there for nearly an hour, bent over with my elbows on my knees and my head cupped in my hands. My eyes were shut and I swayed slightly, almost falling asleep as I dreamed of life after Everest. Ed was right: life would be fun when I returned to earth. People would be surprised and pleased by our success. I would be so happy and everything would be so easy. I would be able to eat delicious food and I would have that sweet red Vermouth, with great crystals of ice and the essential sharpness of lemon. And I would drink orange juice, cool tumblers full of it, sitting in the green shade of a tree. That life was so close, so easily attainable; all I had to do was reach Advance Base – just one more day of effort and then the others would take over.

I tried to stand up and failed. It was a feeble attempt and I told myself that next time I would succeed. After all, I *wanted* to descend, didn't I? I was just being a little lazy. I would have to concentrate a little harder on the task: lean forward, go down on my knees, shoulder the rucksack, stand up and away! Easy. Let's try now.

Nothing happened.

I began to worry. It was nearly an hour since Robert and Ed had left and I knew that they would not have the strength to climb back up for me. It was 11 a.m. and I had to leave now and catch up with them. I just had to take that simple action to save my life but I was finding it so hard. I was also frightened now that when I stood up my legs might be too weak to remain standing.

There was only one way to find out and with a final concentrated effort I started to move. This time it worked. I went down on my knees, reached round behind me and pulled the rucksack onto my shoulders. Now came the hardest part. I pressed a mittened hand to one knee, pushed up with the other knee, held out both hands for balance and stood up. I managed to stay upright and took a few wobbly penguin steps to the edge of the shelf under the Wing. It was so tempting to sink back down onto the shelf and fall asleep, but I forced my mind to concentrate on directing all energy to those two withered legs. The effort succeeded and I managed six faltering steps down the slope, sat back for a rest, then took six steps more, then again six steps. It was going to be a long tedious struggle, but I knew now that I was going to make it.

Ed led us down the mountain. Paul's tracks had long since disappeared, obliterated by successive afternoon snowfalls. The warm air currents which heralded the Monsoon's approach from the Bay of Bengal had made the snow damp and heavy and there was no possibility of sitting down to slide, as we had done in the dry powder two weeks earlier: this time we had to descend on our feet, wobbling down the deep furrow which Ed ploughed for us.

Ed also had to navigate, guessing his way through a confusing blur of half-remembered shapes shrouded in mist and falling snow. He was terrified of losing the way and plunging irrevocably down towards the ice cliffs of Lhotse, because each time he reached an orange marker wand he had to continue blind for quite a distance before the next one came into view. Then he veered too far to the right and I heard his voice calling out of the mist, 'We've got to go back up left, to the snowbridge.'

I started to break a trail back left, wading through the

clogging knee-deep snow. This was hell – having to climb up round this crevasse, step by laborious step, resting sometimes for three or four minutes between steps. It was my fifth day with virtually no food and I craved for rich flavours. I dreamed that someone organized a lunch stop. We came across the crevasse and there was a striped pavilion, cool and clean inside, with a large pink-faced Frenchman welcoming us. There was a huge tray of cheeses – Camembert, St Nectaire, Gruyère, Roquefort and, out of deference to my Englishness, a slab of Stilton. Our host had already opened bottles of rich dark claret but he knew that we would be thirsty, so he had also laid on a great jug of fresh orange juice.

Fantasies like this were to continue all day. Sometimes I would be coming in after a day's climbing to sandwiches and unlimited cups of tea; at other times it would be pints of beer on a summer's evening in Wasdale. Meanwhile, on Everest, we ploughed our way down. Ed caught up and led across the snowbridge. For a long time I sat in the snow, wondering whether one of these times I really would sit down and find, like those Austrians on K2, that I could not stand up again. I also worried about Robert, who was out of sight behind, but I decided to continue and give Ed a break from trail-breaking.

Once we crossed the snowbridge the route-finding was easier and the visibility improved, so we became almost certain that we could reach the safety of the fixed ropes. Nevertheless on several occasions we reached a marker wand and asked, 'Where the hell do we go now?' Then Ed or I would wade off down some steep bluff, horribly laden with unstable snow. At the top of one bluff I dithered on the brink before waddling down over the edge, with my useless penguin arms held out either side, waiting for the snow slab to give way. Suddenly the surface cracked with a horrible breathy 'hhrmmmphh' and I was away, riding a wave of snow, all arms and legs as the wave flung me over a steeper ice bulge and poured me down into the hollow below, where I came to a standstill, buried up to my thighs.

Fear was a thing of the past. I calmly dug myself out,

looked up at the little silhouetted figure of Ed, fifty metres above, and shouted, 'Yes, this is the right way,' before ploughing manically onwards towards the ropes.

The snow fall had stopped, the clouds were clearing and the daylight was fading when Ed joined me at the wand marking the first anchor.

'Let's dig out our stuff,' I suggested.

'We didn't leave anything here, did we?'

'Of course we did. We need our harnesses and descendeurs!'

'But we're not at the rope yet.'

'Yes, we are. Look – down there. Can't you see that little bit of rope sticking out of the snow? That's the bit past the Jumble.'

Then Ed realized that we had made it to safety. Nothing now would stop him descending the ropes that night and he started to dig feverishly with his frozen claws, while I watched feebly, too lazy or too stupid to stop him damaging the delicate blisters on his fingers. Robert had lent me his spare mitts at Camp 2, but my hands were cold, and I found it very hard to buckle on my harness and organize my descendeur. God knows how Ed managed.

Soon Ed was away down the first rope. I was anxious about Robert, but he appeared a moment later, wading down our trench a few hundred metres above. I asked, 'Are you all right, Robert?'

'Yes,' he shouted. 'See you at Camp 1.'

'No, we're going all the way,' yelled Ed, digging his way across the Jumble. 'All the way to Advance Base!'

I followed across the Jumble and the Hump. Then I looked down the twilit slope to the Jaws of Doom and saw with immense relief that the lower jaw was intact, for I had been terrified that it might have gone, ripping out our safety line as it crashed down the Buttress and cut off our retreat. However, Ed was now sliding safely across the dark gap and a thousand metres below him the clouds had drifted away from the Kangshung Glacier. It was almost dark, but surely the others would be up and looking, seeing our figures against the snow? Surely they would see us and know that everything was all right? In a few more hours, by 10 p.m. we would be down with them, drinking buckets of fruit juice and tea.

For the last time I made the exciting whoosh across the Jaws of Doom, transferred to the rope below, slid, fell and rolled my way across to the next anchor, transferred ropes again and abseiled down the Fourth Cauliflower Tower. It was almost dark now but I could see that more of the tower had disintegrated, littering the terrace below with great ice boulders.

Ed was busily searching for the rope over Webster's Wall. It was buried deep in the snow, so we advanced unprotected right to the brink of the wall, hoping to unearth the rope there. For a few minutes I suffered the torment of believing that it must have gone, leaving us stranded above the over-hanging wall, but eventually Ed hacked it out with his ice axe and clipped in his descendeur.

He rushed on past Camp 1, but I stopped to collect some things. While rummaging in the sack of cached gear I noticed a huge furrow, gouged by a falling ice boulder right through the spot where our tents had been pitched, but I hardly took in its significance. I grew bored with searching for my equipment and the thriller which I had been reading a week earlier, but I did make a point of collecting my helmet. It would make the final descent safer and in any case I was damned if I was going to leave it behind: it was a good helmet and it had cost a fortune, even with the Alpine Sports discount.

Before leaving on the final climb, Paul, Ed and I had always argued that we should make every effort to clear all our equipment from the mountain. Now, faced with the reality of our nightmarish descent, all those good intentions had to be abandoned. We were only just managing to get ourselves off the mountain alive, and there was no question now of removing the detritus of our climb. Not only that – I was not even waiting for Robert. Like the Polish girl, Mrufka, on K2, he was being left to find his own way down the ropes. If he chose to stop at Camp 1 that was his problem;

Ed and I were rushing on headlong to Advance Base and nothing was going to stop us now.

I buckled on my helmet, waded across to the next rope and clipped in for the first abseil into Big Al Gully. Ed was waiting at the anchor fifty metres below, unable to clip his descendeur into the next section of rope. It was ridiculous for him to go first and I insisted, 'I'll have to go first and clear the ropes; otherwise you're going to shred your fingers.' It was hard work, straining on the rope, pulling and pulling, until it came unstuck from the ice below and gave me enough slack to clip in my descendeur.

I abseiled down that rope, clipped my safety loop into the next anchor and shouted up, 'OK, Ed, you can come!' Then I was off again, excavating the rope below, down to Paul's letterbox, where I perched for ages, pulling desperately on the next rope. I could not get enough slack to feed into the descendeur, so I had to go down with the rope just wound round my wrist, until I could free more slack from the imprisoning ice. Then I could abseil normally, down, down the big icefield to the next anchor where everything was buried and confused. I searched and searched for the next rope but could not find it and, as the snow was compacted by wind, I had to wait to dig until Ed arrived with the ice axe. His torch had gone out, so he asked me for my spare bulb, but in the numb-fingered confusion we lost both bulbs. Now we had to descend in total darkness.

We never considered stopping. We were too close now. We would just fight on down the ropes, groping our way by memory along the 1,600-metre lifeline. It was weird, repeating all those familiar changeovers, section by section, relying just on feel and the faintest glimmer of starlight. Nearly every metre of the ropes had to be pulled out from the snow and ice, as I fought my way back across the shattered wall to the Terrace and down to the big traverse, and on, slithering sideways on my knees, past all Paul's anchors to the cave above the Scottish Gully. It had been slower than I expected but I hoped at least to be back by midnight, and I shouted as loudly as I could, 'Mimi. Joe. Paul. TEA!'

The gully was hideous. The ropes were buried in knee-deep soggy snow and every few metres I had to stop and pull out the next section before I could continue. We had now been on the move for twelve hours without water and we had hardly eaten for five days. I was struggling again, stopping repeatedly to close my eyes. But I had to get down, had to fight just a little longer and soon we would be lying in our tents, drinking all the fruit juice and tea in the world.

'Joe. Paul. Mimi. TEA!'

Columns of ice ensnared the rope over the Headwall. There was no hope of feeding it into my descendeur, so again I had to rely on the friction of the ice hawser wrapped round my wrist. Midnight passed and I was still on the lower part of the Buttress. Once I stopped for half an hour with my head lolling on the snow and almost fell asleep before continuing the painful excavation, metre by metre, fighting the heavy snow until at last I reached the bottom of the last rope, and there was the spare ice axe for the glacier, which I had left clipped into the end of the rope nine days earlier.

When I reached the glacier I lay down and waited for Ed. He arrived at about 1.30 a.m. and we tied on to the short length of rope we always left here for the crossing.

The fight with the fixed ropes was over now and all we had to do was plod. We thought happily that we would be back at Advance Base in an hour; but the mountain would not let us escape that easily. Soon we lost our way, strayed from the usual easy route and started to wander through a maze of hummocks and crevasses. The darkness was confusing and we stumbled back and forth, pulling each other in and out of crevasses, crying and cursing with misery as we staggered about like impotent drunkards.

At last we fought our way out of the maze and reached the final smooth section of glacier. Surely now it would be easy? But no, it was a warm night and the snow had not frozen properly. Time after time the crust gave way and suddenly I would plunge waist-deep into a pit of slush. I screamed with rage as I flung myself back onto the surface, yanking furiously at my trapped feet until I could crawl out on my hands and knees, displacing my weight to try and avoid another collapse. Then I would stand up gingerly and walk again, waiting for the next unannounced plunge.

Ed followed slowly, dragging on the rope, and taking an intolerable age to crawl out of each pit. Now I seemed to be even more desperate than him to reach camp and eventually I grew tired of waiting, so I just untied from the rope and left him to follow at his own pace. I was sure that the glacier here was safe, but it was still a callous thing to do and I tried to assuage my guilt by telling myself that I had to hurry on and find the others.

Where were they? Why hadn't they come out to meet us? I tried shouting again.

'Joe, Paul, Mimi. TEA!'

Surely they could hear us? Surely they would have water heating by now? We must be nearly there. I can't go on for ever. I just want to be comforted and cosseted.

'Mimi! MIMI! Why don't you answer?'

Where are they? Do I still have to walk? At Camp 2 I thought that I might not be able to stand up and yet now, sixteen hours later, I'm still coping; but surely there comes a point when the body stops? At least the snow's better now, no more heffalump traps. And the air down here is so rich and thick. Just as well, otherwise I would have given up long ago. There's that buttress on Peak 38. Almost level with it now. And this strip of frozen lake on the left. It's all collapsed at the edges so I must keep my distance. It would be so stupid to get down this close to safety then die of drowning or hypothermia in a puddle.

Now this is it, surely? The moraine on the left curving slightly. 'MIMI! JOE! PAUL!' Please be there – if they've left Advance Base we'll never cope. It must be up on those rocks to the left. Just got to drag the legs a little further. First a little rest: bend over and lean on knees, but don't sit down – fatal. Now up the hill, dragging one leg after the other, stumbling on the rocks, left . . . right . . . left . . . right . . . almost there . . . Now, we're on the crest of the moraine. It's somewhere round here. But why is there no sound? It all looks different.

What's happened to the lake? Are those lumps over there tents? Please – they must be! I can't go any further. 'WHERE ARE THE BLOODY TENTS?!'

I heard a scuffle, then, at last, the sound of startled voices. A dark shape materialized, a torch was lit and Paul came rushing across the rocks towards me. I remembered all those pre-dawn departures from this camp, the shivering break-fasts and dark journeys across the glacier, in that other life when we climbed the Buttress; I remembered my impatience on all those load-carries, and now that it was all finally over I shouted out a feeble joke, 'Four o'clock in the morning, Paul. Time to go up the ropes!'

Paul reached me and put an arm on my shoulder. He shone his torch in my face, stared in disbelief at my sunken eyes, swollen lips and lumpy black nose and he gasped, 'Venables! Where the hell have you been?'

11
A Gentler Spirit

P_{AUL} tried to help me over to the tents, but I insisted on hobbling the last few steps unaided; only then would I let him take over.

'Just sit there, Venables,' he ordered. 'We've got to get your boots off.'

Another dark shape moved in the tent and I asked, 'Is that Joe?' But Joe was at Base Camp and it was Mimi, still dazed and saying nothing, who came out of the tent.

'Hey, Mimi, look at his nose, it's a black snout!' Paul tugged at one of my frozen overboots and asked, 'Did you get to the top?'

'Yes, we did it. The others are coming. Ed will be here in a minute. I think Robert's at Camp 1.'

'Well done, you made it!' he exclaimed, then continued emotionally, 'We thought you were dead. We saw nothing for five days. Mimi was crying and crying. We didn't know –'

'What about tonight? Didn't you hear me shouting?'

'Nothing. We were on heavy sleeping pills, double doses. It was the only way. Night after night, just waiting –'

'But, didn't you see –?'

'Just some tracks below the Wing, but only a short section. I thought they must be left from *my* descent.'

'So you got down all right?'

'He was so fast,' Mimi answered. 'He was just flying – got down from the South Col in seven hours. But I think he *was* ill. He had signs of oedema.'

She and Paul helped me into the tent and at last I could ask for some orange juice.

'I think there's only grapefruit left.'

'That's fine. Will you make some, please? Then lots and lots of tea.'

Mimi went to heat water and I asked Paul to go and help Ed off the glacier. I was left alone to enjoy the wonderful sensation of being safe and alive and knowing that at last the fight was over. However, my enjoyment was shadowed by sadness. I had travelled far beyond the frontiers of any previous experience, drawing on enormous reserves of willpower and endurance to reach the highest point on earth and return alive; but right at the end of our journey, in my impetuous headlong flight to safety, feverishly craving warmth, drink and rest, I had left Robert alone on the ropes and then I had abandoned Ed on the glacier, only half an hour from the camp.

I was relieved when Paul brought in Ed, and promised that he would leave soon to escort Robert down the ropes. Now I could drown my guilt in waves of happiness, revelling in pure exquisite sensation: the wonderful relief of cold fruit juice and the sweet anticipation of tea to come; the softness of the air mattresses where Ed and I lay back while the others took off our snow-encrusted fibre pile suits; the cathartic release of tension and the tearful smile in Mimi's eyes as she kept repeating, 'I'm so happy that you guys are alive.'

A new day was dawning as she bathed our feet in a bowl of warm antiseptic solution, knowing that down at this altitude there was no hope of keeping them frozen any longer for the walk back to Base Camp. Neither Ed nor I had taken off our boots for three days and it was a relief to see in the grey light that the damage to our feet had not spread beyond heels and toes. But Ed's fingers were wrecked. Even though he had kept on his mittens, the eight hours of fighting with the frozen ropes had burst the delicate blisters inside, leaving his fingers shredded raw. Mimi did what she could, dressing each finger separately and instructing Paul to fit the regulator valve and mask to our one bottle of medicinal oxygen. Ed really needed all the resources of a modern hospital at sea level, but a short blast of oxygen now was at least a token effort to save his fingers.

We drank some tea then lay down to rest. After a while I became vaguely aware of shouting outside and asked Mimi what was going on. Apparently Robert was just starting down from *above* Camp 1, having failed in the night to find the rope over Webster's Wall. Now Paul was setting off to meet him, while I sank into the blissful warmth of a sleeping bag. Ed was lying next to me, with a mask on his face, and the gentle hiss of oxygen soothed me as I drifted off to sleep.

I woke an hour or two later to a feeling of pure content-ment. I felt quite detached from the voices outside and it took a while to realize that Paul was back, annoyed that he was now unfit to help after twisting his knee on the glacier. However he could see Robert up on the Buttress, making his own way slowly down the ropes. Now Mimi noticed people coming from the opposite direction. A few minutes later there was a sound of running outside and Kasang knelt down, panting, at the door of our tent. It was incredibly moving to see his face, which we had grown so fond of, not smiling, but staring with a profound look of shock, pity and relief, as he took in our emaciated faces, my blackened nose and Ed's bandaged fingers. Then Pasang arrived and again I was deeply moved by his sympathy and love and obvious delight at seeing us alive. Joe arrived last with a huge smile on his face. He explained that they had virtually given us up for dead, but had suddenly noticed our tracks on the East Face early that morning, and had immediately set off for Advance Base to see whether their hopes of our survival would be justified.

The previous day Angchu had been sent to Kharta with a note for Mr Shi and Mr Yang, announcing that Anderson, Venables and Webster were missing and requesting a search of the Rongbuk and Khumbu Base Camps. Paul had exhaus-ted all the possible reasons for delay and concluded that we were probably dead. However, there had been the faint possibility that we might for some reason have descended from the summit by the North Ridge to the Rongbuk Glacier, or descended the Western Cwm on the Nepalese side of the South Col.

I was slightly surprised that Paul had sounded the alarm so soon, but we were at fault for failing to signal clearly during our protracted descent. By now the message was probably on its way to Beijing and to the Rongbuk Base Camp, where the British Services Expedition would fear the worst. There was a huge risk that the false news would leak to the press, causing unnecessary anguish to family and friends. (Later we discovered that Wendy *had* been informed by Beijing that three of us were missing. She suffered five days of torment in New York, keeping the news to herself and fending off friends and relatives with vague answers while she awaited further details.)

We had to cancel the message quickly, so now Paul wrote another note, stating that we had descended safely but needed urgent evacuation to medical help, ideally by helicopter or if not by stretcher, to minimize damage to our frostbitten feet. Angchu's brother, who had come up with Kasang, was despatched with the note and a plea to run to Kharta as fast as he could.

I floated through the day on a cloud of drowsy content-ment. Paul limped back to Base Camp with Pasang and Kasang, and Joe walked up the glacier to meet Robert, while Mimi worked tirelessly to nurse Ed and me. Neither of us could eat yet, but she helped us to sit up and drink bowl after bowl of liquid. She had threaded on string a piece of Robert's equipment – an alloy belay brake – to wear round her neck, thinking that she would never see him again. Now after all the days of dwindling hope, she could hardly believe that we had just been a trifle slow and that Robert was almost down off the mountain.

He finally arrived some time in the evening. I was barely awake and only discovered later that Mimi was up most of the night nursing him and listening patiently to his hallucina-tory ramblings. The next day, 18 May, I went to visit him in his tent. Now that the pressure was off I discovered the full

extent of my exhaustion. After putting on shoes it took me
several minutes to find the energy to stand up. I only had to
cross about ten metres of stony ground but it was a slow
wobbly journey. When I reached the tent I felt too tired to sit
upright and had to lie flat on my back. During the descent I
had been living off my own muscle tissue and now my whole
body was withered. Unlike Frank Smythe on the North
Ridge in 1933, I could not quite get a single hand round my
thigh, but I did look and feel extremely scrawny.

Robert was recovering quickly from the ravings of the
previous night and looked healthier than either Ed or me.
Already he was discussing how we should best announce the
news of our success. There was no trace of resentment about
my pushing on alone to the summit and he did not blame Ed
and me for leaving him behind on the ropes. On the contrary, he just laughed about his extra night out on the
mountain.

'I just couldn't find the pink rope over Webster's Wall. I
kept searching and searching in the dark, but I didn't dare go
any closer to the edge. Then I decided to cut down the rope
above and use that to safeguard myself right to the edge. So I
wallowed all the way back up the shelf. Then I couldn't find
my penknife, but I had this brilliant idea to cut the rope with
a crampon. So I took one off and there I was – at midnight,
holding this blunt crampon in my numb frostbitten fingers,
trying to saw through the rope. Eventually I decided to give
up and wait till the morning. It was really cold, curled up in
the snow without a sleeping bag, but I wasn't too worried:
after getting down that far I knew that I wasn't going to die
now.'

I returned to my tent to sleep again. Later that day Mimi
brought me my Walkman and tapes. I chose the Brahms
Horn Trio, and immersed myself totally in its glorious rich
texture and bitter-sweet harmonies which spoke so much
more eloquently than any words of the joy and beauty and
sadness of life.

The following day we felt strong enough to move. Paul's
knee had recovered and he was back from Base Camp,

laughing, joking and chivvying us into action. He, Joe and Mimi organized all the luggage and helped us get our bandaged dead toes into loose-fitting boots. We did not have to carry anything and our only job was to get our bodies down across the glacier, but it took me six and a half hours to cover the distance that normally took only two hours.

Each day was bringing new sensations: first drink, then deep sleep, then a little solid food and the luxury of music. Now, as I climbed over the moraine and returned to the hollow of Base Camp for the first time in three weeks, the afternoon drizzle released the most beautiful smell in the world – the sweet smell of warm damp earth.

We waited three days at Base Camp before leaving for Kharta. Between meals I spent most of the time horizontal, sleeping, resting and occasionally finding the strength to read. On the first day a group of smartly dressed American trekkers appeared in camp, the first other Westerners we had seen for over two months. Two members of the party were physicians from prestigious East Coast teaching hospitals. The vascular surgeon was particularly fond of Mimi, flirting outrageously with her and virtually offering her a job on the spot. Both he and his colleague were full of praise for her competent handling of our injuries.

On the day when we crawled back into Advance Base Mimi worked without a break for twenty-two hours. Since then she had continued to work almost constantly and now she spent a whole afternoon with our medical visitors. They gave every encouragement but we heard cries of pain as Ed's dressings were changed and I think we all knew that, however tender and careful Mimi was, by the time Ed reached a hospital the end joints of most of his fingers would have to be amputated. Only the very tips of Robert's fingers were blackened and the skin had not been broken. With luck he would lose nothing from his hands and on his feet only one big toe was seriously affected. The toes of my left foot were worse. Although they were not torn and shrivelled like Ed's fingers, they were rapidly turning black. Mimi obviously encouraged me to be optimistic, but looking at the depth of discoloration I was already resigning myself to amputations.

One evening we opened the last bottle of whisky. Robert proposed a toast to me for getting to the top. I proposed a toast to John Hunt, who had given me the opportunity of joining the expedition. Then I proposed a toast to The Yanks – my American team mates who had become such good friends in the course of an unusually happy expedition. We toasted The Support Team and The Woman, who had suffered our male company with such tolerance and even, dare I suggest it, pleasure. We toasted Our Leader and the sponsors who had made it all possible. We toasted John Hunt again and George Mallory for good measure. Pasang and Kasang had some chang which they preferred to whisky. Now they refilled their glasses while Robert thanked them for the enormous contribution they had made to the success of the expedition.

Paul and Mimi stayed up late talking with Pasang, reminiscing happily about times they had spent in his Nepalese homeland. Kasang watched and listened to everything while Paul loved to tease him in pidgin English: 'Kasang now very smart man. New clothes, clean hair, much money. All the women in Kharta want to marry him now.' For better or worse, we had changed his life. The gormless boy who had come with the tent eleven weeks earlier was now quick, clean, funny, efficient and determined to charm us into giving him every possible spare piece of clothing and equipment. Already he was thinking ahead to the projected post-Monsoon American expedition to the East Face, because now he would have the confidence and skills to be useful to them and earn money in return, freeing him slightly from the limitations of subsistence farming in Kharta.

'Goomornu. Goormornu, Ishteamy.'

Kasang handed me my morning mug of tea and I enunciated, 'Good morning, Kasang. Thank you. The name is Stephen.'

'Ishhhteamy.'

'No – Stee-Ven.'

'Jhimmi . . . Theev . . . Ishteamy.'

'You'll never learn, will you?' I said, and added to myself, but you're a lot cleverer than me. In three months I had not managed to remember a single word of Tibetan, whereas Kasang already had a smattering of English. As for Pasang, like most inhabitants of the Indian subcontinent, he was, perforce, a brilliant linguist, speaking Nepali, Hindi, English and Tibetan as well as his own Tibetan-related Sherpa language.

It was our last morning at Base Camp. The previous day all the porters had arrived from Kharta. Angchu had preceded them with a note from the Chinese saying, unsurprisingly, that there was no helicopter available. However, to help save our frozen toes they would send stretchers. No stretchers arrived with the porters, but luckily we had just enough timber and rope for Paul and Joe to improvise two excellent ones for me and Ed. Robert, whose toes were in better shape, would manage to walk. Everything was now packed up and all our rubbish had been meticulously burned and crushed and the charred remains buried in deep pits. Pasang and Kasang had also buried the huge mound of rusty cans left by the Americans in 1983 at their Base Camp a short way up the valley. Even if we had desecrated the East Face with our ropes and equipment, we were determined to leave this beautiful ablation valley unspoiled.

The porters gathered round to collect their loads. This time more of them seemed to be young boys and girls. Some of the boys in my stretcher team were tiny and only looked eleven or twelve, yet they carried me mile after mile over rough tussocky ground. Like Ed, I had eight people who could work alternate shifts of four. I was tired and irritable and I always groaned complaints when I had to stand up and hobble over a particularly rough stretch, but my bearers treated me with unfailing kindness and humour, particularly Phuti's young brother, Pinzo, who was always offering me chang and rakshi to make the arduous journey more bearable.

On the second day we reached the junction with the

Rabkar Chu, where we had to leave the Kama Chu and turn left towards the Langma La. Ed and I had to get out and walk through the thickets of rhododendron. All the snow had now melted down here and the rhododendrons were a mass of lemon yellow and pale mauve flowers. There were azaleas in every shade of pink, and the first delicate little blue primulas, where we stopped for lunch in a warm green meadow.

Ed was moved almost to tears and said, 'Whatever happens to my fingers and toes, coming down here makes me realize just how wonderful it is to be alive.'

Mallory had expressed similar sentiments in 1921. Referring to the two Tibetan names for Everest, he wrote: 'When all is said about Chomolungma, the Goddess Mother of the World, and about Chomo Uri, the Goddess of the Turquoise Mountain, I come back to the valley, the valley bed itself, the broad pastures . . . the little stream we followed . . . the few rare plants, so well watered there, and a soft, familiar blueness in the air which even here may charm us. Though I bow to the goddesses I cannot forget at their feet a gentler spirit than theirs, a little shy perhaps, but constant in the changing winds and variable moods of mountains and always friendly.'

It was indeed wonderful to return safely to the 'gentler spirit' of this valley I had been so fortunate to visit. The following day as I hobbled back up to the Langma La, past the Shurim Tso, the lake which had been a frozen white sheet in March but which was now a turquoise jewel set in russet granite, I hoped that I might return one day to this magical valley for a real holiday, with no commitment to high-altitude masochism, free to rock climb and explore and hunt for flowers.

By the time I reached the pass, clouds were already gathering round the now distant mass of Lhotse and Everest, but I was allowed a final glimpse of the Kangshung Face before I turned my back to limp down the far side, where the terrain was too steep for the stretchers. The pain in my left foot intensified on the descent and I was immensely relieved to reach Lhatse, the place where we had waited so long in the snow all those weeks before. Now our campsite was hardly recognizable and I lay flat on my back amongst young green shoots of grass. The others caught up and after a long picnic with much chang my stretcher-bearers were ready to carry me. I felt gloriously helpless, travelling horizontal and feet first, like a funeral corpse, and I enjoyed the drunken undulating motion as the carriers swayed and stumbled over the rough ground. Occasionally my vehicle would suffer a flat tyre as one of the boys tripped. Usually it was the rear outside tyre and I would suddenly sag alarmingly, to find myself staring straight over the edge.

Ed had a stronger team and at one point his vehicle swerved deliberately off the road, abandoning the contouring path for a jubilant headlong descent to the bed of the valley. It was a wonderful sight as his men bore their cargo straight down the forty-degree hillside, careering without deviation through the bushes and boulders. Unfortunately my team lacked competitive spirit and stuck to the boring path, even making me get off to walk again on one stretch.

Paul was already at camp, pitching tents and waiting to help the cripples. From the moment we had come back from the dead and appeared at Advance Base, Paul had taken over, laughing, bossing, cajoling, organizing and nursing. Of course Pasang, Kasang, Joe and Mimi were also working extremely hard, particularly Mimi, but I think it was Paul's selfless energy and humour that galvanized everyone into action.

Ed, with his shrivelled bandaged fingers was particularly in need of help and frequently he would ask, 'Paul, I need to have a pee. Can you help, please?'

But even Paul was finding his kindness overstretched and that evening he insisted, 'Look Ed, this is the last time I'm holding it. You've got to learn to get it out yourself!'

We got pleasantly drunk that last night before Kharta. Angchu had rushed ahead to his house and returned with a huge bowl of *thongba* – fermented barley grain to which boiling water is added, producing instant hot chang – the Tibetan equivalent of mulled wine. It is a very sociable drink, because everyone has a straw made from hollowed bamboo and sits around the same pot sucking from the steaming fermentation.

Pasang, the Nepalese Sherpa, was laughing and drinking and singing with Angchu and Kasang, his Tibetan friends; it was as though we were back in pre-communist days when Sherpas and Tibetans, ethnically almost identical, travelled freely to and fro across the Himalayan frontier. Without Pasang's diplomatic and linguistic skills we never would have enjoyed such a good relationship with Kasang and Angchu, whose brilliant smile and unique dimples charmed Mimi so much as she linked arms with him and Kasang to sway in a complex foot-shuffling dance. I was flat on the ground, only rising with difficulty for the occasional groggy suck at the thongba. Robert was also comatose. But Ed temporarily forgot the horror of his mutilated fingers and some of the brightness seemed to have returned to his eyes as he looked forward to returning to Randa.

In the morning our stretchers lurched and swayed through fields now alive with the first shoots of spring. Robert rode ahead on a tiny pony and Joe, who had run down to Kharta the previous day, came up to meet us with the famous mountain photographer, Galen Rowell, who was doing some work in the area for *National Geographic*. He and his wife had a landcruiser with them and for the few miles down to the government resthouse at Kharta Shika we enjoyed the luxury of motor transport.

Mr Shi and Mr Yang welcomed us with open arms, but soon relations deteriorated again, as we discovered that our Chinese officials did not have enough money to pay the porters properly, were blaming us for the delays and increased charges of the approach and using that as a reason to withhold transport to Kathmandu and Lhasa.

The Rowells had no room for us in their vehicle and for three days we were stuck in a dusty hovel in the compound. Pasang still worked tirelessly to make good meals out of the remains of our food, but I was growing tired even of his excellent cooking, craving new flavours and longing to be pampered in the westernized luxury of Kathmandu. Ed was really desperate to leave. His toes were more painful than mine and the ends of his fingers were shrivelled black claws. He kept staring at them in horror, sniffing the putrefying flesh and one evening, for the first and only time, his placid stoicism cracked and he burst into tears, screaming, 'I can't stand it any more! I've got to get out of here!'

Our landcruiser and a truck for the luggage arrived, three days late, the next morning. Mr Yang and Mr Shi reluctantly made arrangements for our debt with the people of Kharta to be settled from Lhasa. Then we said goodbye.

Jirmi, who had danced in the snow with Mimi back in March, put in a drunken appearance; but such limited charms as he possessed had long since been overshadowed by the winning ways of the dimpled Angchu who had done so much to help us, and, of course, our cookboy. The previous day Kasang had delivered the old bell tent back to his mother. She had observed that it was now even more dilapidated than when she lent it to us, but she was delighted with the transformation of her son. Now, as he said goodbye and scrounged a few more cassette tapes and pieces of clothing to supplement his meagre wages, he seemed genuinely sad to see us leaving.

We drove quickly and comfortably to Shegar in the landcruiser, only stopping briefly on the crest of the Pang La to look back at Everest. Paul, Pasang and I would see it again next day on the way back to Nepal; but for Robert, Joe, Mimi and Ed, who were travelling home via Lhasa and Beijing, this was their last sight of the mountain. It was 29 May, thirty-five years to the day since Hillary and Tenzing had first crossed that bridge beyond the South Summit and reached the top of the world.

At dawn next day I was on my way to the Nepalese border. Paul and Pasang had kindly agreed to follow with the luggage in a rickety truck while I got a lift with two American travellers in a comfortable landcruiser. Our own landcruiser had left Shegar long before dawn, speeding off in the opposite direction with Robert and the others. The previous evening we had drowned the sadness of parting by drinking lots of beer, the provision of which seemed to be the only service that the CMA could guarantee; so it had been a lighthearted occasion, our last evening together before the family, which had grown so close over the last three months, was disbanded.

By tonight the others would be at the Lhasa hotel, where Robert would be able to telex a message to Wendy in New York. She would presumably pass on the news of our success to the British press. Ours was the smallest team ever to climb a major new route on Everest without oxygen and, although I was the 206th person known to have reached the summit, I was probably only the eighth Briton to reach the top and the first to do it without oxygen. It would be interesting to see whether the newspapers, who had resolutely ignored our expedition before departure, would decide now to give it a mention.

If the British press did cover the climb, it would inevitably concentrate on my summit achievement, but I knew that it was the dedicated hard work of *four* climbers that had achieved success. I also knew that, given the physical and psychological strain of climbing on Everest, we never would have managed, nor had such fun, without the help and good company of Joe, Mimi, Pasang and Kasang. I would always have slight qualms about some of our actions, like the decision to let Paul descend alone and my sudden abandonment of Ed on the descent, but the dominant memory would be of the fun and companionship, during the long approach over the Langma La to the Kama Chu, during all the days we spent together at Base Camp and on the Kangshung Glacier and finally on our wild route up the Neverest Buttress. It had looked so improbable when Robert showed it to me on the photo in New York, but his dream had been realized.

Soon we were driving across the great plain of Tingri which had looked so beautiful on that snowbound moonlit evening seven months earlier, on the way home from Shisha Pangma. This time there was no snow to be seen, except on the high crest of the Himalaya to our south. Spring had arrived, spreading a soft green haze over the earth and everywhere there were clusters of purple iris.

The American couple asked the driver to stop at the official Everest photo spot, where I had stopped at sunset seven months earlier. The great Pyramid did not look as dramatic as it had done on that November evening, when it had glowed with such brooding redness above the frozen plain; but that did not matter, for the more tranquil light of this spring morning matched my own mood. This time, leaving for home at the end of another expedition, there was no bitterness and I had few regrets – just a rare warmth of contentment.

Epilogue

ON 2 AUGUST, 1988, I was admitted to the Royal United Hospital, Bath, to have three and a half black shrivelled toes amputated from my left foot. As I was wheeled into the operating theatre, floating on a glorious drug-induced cloud, one of the nurses rushed up and asked, 'I know this isn't the right moment, but would you mind doing an autograph for my boyfriend – he's a climber.'

Her boyfriend probably would have preferred a new karabiner, but of course I leaned over, smiling benignly and scribbled a groggy signature. I was famous and this was what was expected of me.

It started when Paul and I returned to Kathmandu. After Robert telexed from Lhasa, Wendy cunningly held the news from the press until 2 June – the thirty-fifth anniversary of Coronation Day. Then our hotel telephone began to ring incessantly with calls from the London press, and when I flew home a week later a fast car was waiting at Heathrow airport to whisk me off to the television studios. There was a lull while I rested and wrote this book and had my operation. Then in September, as soon as I could hobble on my feet again, I started the long round of lectures, magazine articles and more interviews. It has been fun, but there have been moments when I have longed to talk about something other than Everest.

Now it is December and I have been back in England for six months. Nearly every week I get a letter or telephone call from one of the others. Paul has just been out to Nepal again to do some guiding and to see Pasang. In 1990 he is returning to Everest with an expedition to the North Face. Meanwhile, this Christmas he is flying to South America to attempt Aconcagua with Robert, whose fingers have recovered completely. He did lose half a big toe, but that hardly affected him, and he returned very quickly to full-time work. One day he will probably return to climb those remaining eighty-three metres to the summit, but in the meantime he has the satisfaction of having inspired and led one of the most ambitious and harmonious expeditions ever to climb Everest.

When I last saw Joe at Shekar, he could hardly wait to get back to Connecticut. I have now seen the photos of him reunited with Ellen and his daughter Claire and no one could look happier. However, he soon had to ration time with his family as he started to pick up the threads of his commercial business, as well as working flat out on processing and cataloguing all the thousands of expedition photographs, eventually sending everyone a duplicate set of the three hundred and fifty best slides. My set was brought over to London by Wendy, who spent a few days here last month in a whirl of theatres, galleries, pubs and restaurants. I was also very busy, but we managed to meet briefly over a bottle of champagne and reminisce about our days in the snowstorm at Lhatse. Then she returned to New York to start fund-raising for an expedition to the Mekong River.

Ed will not be able to go on any expeditions for a while. He has lost parts of three toes on his left foot and the end joints of eight fingers. He was left-handed, but all five fingers of that hand were affected, so now he has to use the thumb and forefinger of his right hand to sign letters. He writes frequently and in the most recent letter he reported that he had just been out rock climbing, the day before returning to hospital for his fifth operation. There is never a word of complaint and I think all of us have been moved by Ed's courage and humour during what must have been, in spite of Randa's love and support, a period of deep private suffering.

Mimi suffered no injuries, but she found it difficult to

return to life in New York with the shock of plunging
suddenly into a one hundred and twenty-hour week in one of
the world's busiest hospitals, but recently she escaped for
two weeks' holiday in New Zealand with Robert.

My return was easier. I was spoilt and cosseted by friends
and family and Rosie seemed pleased to see me once the
initial media hype had died down. Nevertheless, it took me
at least three months to regain my strength and during the
first few weeks I often lay awake at night, troubled by
memories of the descent, particularly my struggle back over
the South Summit. It was as though the fear, which had been
suppressed at the time, now had to be exorcised in retrospec-
tive nightmares.

Now the nightmares are over and it is the colours and
shapes of the Kama valley, the exhilaration of the climbing,
the fun and the friendship which I mainly remember, as I
travel around telling the story of our climb. Last week I gave
three lectures in Ireland. The audiences were wonderful, the
Guinness tasted better than ever, and the pub we visited one
evening fulfilled almost perfectly that brief vision I had had
on the Hillary Step. Earlier that day we had climbed on the
sea cliffs of the Dingle peninsula. My truncated left foot was
a little sore and clumsy on the small holds, but I managed
reasonably well and I am sure that I will improve. It was a
beautiful day of grey mists and wind-blown grass, with
fulmars wheeling above the dark green swell of the Atlantic,
and I felt very lucky to be there, at the end of a very special
year, enjoying life with a new intensity after that extraordinary journey on Everest.

London, 18 December 1988

Appendix I
The Expedition Sponsors

Everest-88 would never have happened without the backing of our many sponsors, and we would like to take this opportunity to thank the institutions who endorsed our efforts and those companies and individuals whose generous support made it possible to realize the dream of a new route up the Kangshung Face of Everest.

Endorsed Support
American Alpine Club; American Geographical Society; Explorers' Club; Mount Everest Foundation; National Geographic Society; United Nations.

Financial Support, Equipment and Services
We are particularly happy that three of our major sponsors were also sponsors of the 1953 Everest expedition:

Eastman Kodak	Kodachrome, Ektachrome and Tmax professional films, papers and processing chemicals
Burroughs Wellcome	Actifed decongestant, Neosporin and Cortisporin
Rolex Watch USA	Explorer II Oyster Perpetual chronometers

We also acknowledge gratefully the invaluable financial assistance and support of:

American Express/Asia	Travel arrangements from South-East Asia and logistical support in Beijing
Dow Consumer Products	Ziplock storage bags

Kiehl's Pharmacy — Skincare products, cosmetics and sunscreens

Lindblad Travel Inc. — Travel arrangements to, from and within China

Petroconsultants — Finance

Weaver Coat Company — The Weaver sleeping bag/jacket

Equipment Donated by

Dollond & Aitchison — Prescription sunglasses

Duggal Color Projects — Developing, duping and printing of all expedition images

Fairydown of New Zealand — Tents and clothing

Jones Optical — Sunglasses

Mountain Equipment — Trousers, down gear and windsuit

Nike — Trekking boots, socks

Stevens Press — Promotional materials

Omni International Distributors — Stubai crampons, ice axes, ice hammers, ice screws, karabiners, wired nuts and camping tools

Ultra Technologies — Kodak batteries

Wild Country — Mittens and Alpinist harness

Equipment Supplied at Cost by

Berghaus — Trekking boots

Bibler Tents — Mountain dome tents

Bolder Designs — Fleece clothing, high-altitude down sleeping bags and climbing suits

Brenco Enterprises Inc. — One Sport mountaineering boots

Cascade Designs — Therma-Rest pads

Chouinard Equipment — Forty Below lithium headlamps

Dana Designs — Rucksacks and duffel bags

Denver Drum & Barrel — Plastic packing drums

High Adventure Sports — Snow pickets

Karrimor — Rucksacks

Kenko International — Asolo AFS 101 plastic mountaineering boots

Lowe Alpine Systems — Rivory-Joanny climbing rope

Patagonia — Capillene expedition underwear

Peak 1/Coleman Co. — Base Camp dining tent

Seranac — Neoprene and Gore-Tex gloves

Uniroyal Plastics Company — Ensolite pads

Food and Medical Supplies Donated by

Alpine Aire	Freeze-dried fruit, vegetables, soups and ready-cooked meals
Bayer (NZ)	Adalat
Common Bros. Inc.	Medical supplies
Johnson & Johnson Pharmaceutical Division	First-aid supplies
Negroni	Milano salami and Parma ham
Roche (NZ)	Multivitamins, Hypnovol sleeping tablets
Unipro	Carboplex and other energy supplements
Weepak	Dried and freeze-dried food

Administrative Assistance and Travel Arrangements by
Atlas Trekking, Kathmandu; Chinese Mountaineering Association; CAAC (China Airline); Holiday Inn, Lhasa; Lindblad Travel Inc.; Ogilvy & Mather, London; The Ogilvy Group, New York; Shangri-La Hotel, Beijing; Tibetan Guest House, Kathmandu.

For his Invaluable Help and Guidance
   William Phillips (The Ogilvy Group)

And finally, the many other individuals who gave so much time, enthusiasm, hard work and encouragement before, during and after the expedition.
Harihar Acharya (Atlas Trekking); Hillary Allman (American Express TRS); Neal Anderson (Dow Consumer Products); Michael Baulk (Ogilvy & Mather); Dan & Eva Baum; Todd Bibler (Bibler Tents); Roger Billum; John and Carol Bell (Lindblad Travel); Marilyn Bird; Garrett Bowden; Chris Bonington; Lizzie Britt; John Bruno; Annette Carmichael (BBC); Bryan Carson (Burroughs Wellcome); Dr Charles Clarke; Karen Collins (Burroughs Wellcome); John Connelly (Brenco Enterprises); John Cranford (Kenco International); Maria Cranor (Choninard Equipment); Douglas Crow; Malcolm Daly (Lowe Alpine Systems); The Davis family; Rick Depew (Dow Consumer Products); Dr Nas Eftekhar; David Ellis; Ken Fontecilla (Weepak); Bill Forrest; Lisa Freed; Karen Frishman (Patagonia); Kevin Furnary (Bolder Designs); Jean Marie Gilbert; Dr Stefan Goldberg; Bill Graves (National Geographic Society); Rosie Grieves-Cook; Tina Hatcher (Burroughs Wellcome); Paul Hardin (The Coleman company);

Sheila Harrison (Alpine Club); Andrew Harvard; Randa Hessel
(Everest-88 packing department); Dr Philip Horniblow; Daryl
Hughes (Anderson Hughes Partners); Janet Jory; Rob Ingraham;
Jean-Pierre Javoques (Petroconsultants); Bohong Jin; Harish and
Geeta Kapadia; Steve and Perry Kaminsky (Denver Barrel &
Drum); Brian Keefe; Judy Kinsky (Ultra Technologies); Dennis
Korn (Alpine Aire); Dan Larson; Jerry Lloyd (Cascade Designs);
Chris Lonsdale; George Lowe (Everest Kangshung Face 1981 and
1983); Jim Lynch (Uniroyal Plastics Company); Aanya McMeckin;
Reinhold Messner; Fred Meyer (Stubai); Aaron and Jamie Morse
(Kiehl's Pharmacy); Ann Moscicki (Eastman Kodak); Emma
Myant; Dr Alexander Neill; Kate Phillips (Alpine Sports); Tas
Pinther; Adrian Pritchard (Pro-Service Forwarding); Roland Puton
(Rolex Watches USA); Geoff Ready; Lynn Rice (Lowe Alpine
Systems); Paul Richards (Mountain Equipment); Carol Rodgers
(Lindblad Travel); Jeannie Rodgers (Lindblad Travel); Dr Fero
Sadeghian; Steve Sanford; Victor Saunders; the Schaeffer family;
Marc Shafir; Dr Marc Sklar; Barbara Strong; Vicky Surman
(Ogilvy & Mather); Pamela Steele (Holiday Inn, Lhasa); William
Sullivan (Rolex Watches USA); David Swanson; Geoff Tabin
(Everest Kangshung Face 1981 and 1983); Mel Terlisner (Uniroyal
Plastics Company); John Lee Truman; John and Phebe Tyson;
Maggie Urmston (Ferntower Secretarial Services); the Venables
family; Suzanne Vlamis and family; Michael Ward; Peter Warren
(Ogilvy & Mather); Bradford Washburn (The Boston Museum of
Science); David Weaver (Weaver Coat Company); Kelly Weir;
Mike Westmacott (Alpine Club); John Williams (Unipro); Paul
Williams (Mountain Equipment); Ali-j Wilson (Ogilvy & Mather);
Roger Withers (Wild Country); Terry Wittner; John Yates (High
Adventure Sports).

Appendix II
Expedition Members

EVEREST-88 EXPEDITION TEAM

Honorary leader:
Lord Hunt of Llanfair Waterdine, KG, CBE, DSO

Climbing team:

Robert Anderson (expedition leader)	30	New Zealand	Creative Director of Anderson Hughes & Partners
Paul Teare	28	Canada	Carpenter & mountain guide
Stephen Venables	34	UK	Writer & lecturer
Ed Webster	32	USA	Writer & mountain guide

Base Camp & Advance Base support team:

Joseph Blackburn (expedition photographer)	42	USA	Photographer
Kasang Tsering (assistant cook)	22	Tibet	Farmer
Pasang Norbu (sirdar & cook)	48	Nepal	Lodge owner & trekking guide
Miriam Zieman (expedition doctor)	25	USA	Doctor

Support team:

Mads Anderson (treasurer)	62	USA	President of Central Bank of North Denver

Wendy Davis (fund-raising & publicity)	28	USA	Photographic and press agent
Robert Dorival (food organizer)		USA	Nutritionist
Miklos Pinther (cartographer)	50	USA	UN chief cartographer
Norbu Tenzing (travel arrangements)	24	India/USA	Lindblad Tours
Sandy Wylie (treasurer)	30	New Zealand	Stockbroker – Inter-Suisse (NZ) Ltd.

Appendix III
Expedition Diary

1 January	Expedition meeting in Colorado.
5–8 January	Venables meets Anderson and most of support team in New York. Rolex press conference.
12 February	Venables flies to Bombay.
20 February	Teare and Webster fly to Kathmandu. Anderson and support team fly to Beijing for American Express banquet. They meet Mr Yang (liaison officer) and Mr Shi (interpreter).
23 February	Venables meets Teare and Webster in Kathmandu.
1 March	Pasang, Teare, Venables and Webster drive to Chinese frontier.
3 March	Complete team meets in Shekar, Tibet.
6 March	Drive to Kharta
7–20 March	Walk with yaks to Lhatse, averaging approximately 3 miles per day.
10–24 March	Stuck at 'Pre-Base Camp', Lhatse. Frequent snowfall.
14 March	Five support team members descend to Kharta.
16 March	First climb to Langma La.
24 March	Porters finally cross Langma La.
26–27 March	Delayed by storm in Kama Chu.
29 March	Arrive at Base Camp.
30 March	Anderson and Webster do recce to Advance Base (5,450 metres).
31 March	Teare and Venables escort twenty porters with supplies to Advance Base.

| 1 April | Pasang conducts pujah ceremony at Base Camp. Zieman conducts Passover. |
| 2 April | Climbing team, Blackburn and Zieman to Advance Base. |

FIRST PHASE

3 April	Anderson and Venables lead to foot of Scottish Gully. Teare and Webster in support.
4 April	Anderson and Teare lead to top of Scottish Gully and start big traverse. Venables and Webster in support.
5 April	Venables and Webster continue traverse beyond the Terrace.
6 April	Anderson and Teare fix another 200 metres.
7 April	Venables and Webster reach Cauliflower Ridge and fix Webster's Wall.
8 April	Anderson, Teare and Venables fix Fourth Cauliflower Tower. Progress halted by Crevasse.
10 April	Everyone descends to Base Camp to rest.
13 April	Return to Advance Base.

SECOND PHASE

14 April	Four climbers carry loads to Camp 1 (c.6,450 metres), where Anderson and Webster sleep.
15 April	Anderson and Webster recce Crevasse. Teare and Venables carry loads to Camp 1.
16 April	Anderson and Webster climb far wall of Crevasse. Teare and Venables carry loads to Camp 1.
17 April	During bad weather, Anderson and Webster fix Tyrolean bridge across Crevasse, fix 100 metres up the Hump, then descend to Advance Base.
19 April	Teare and Venables carry loads, to sleep at Camp 1.
20 April	Teare and Venables fix the Jumble in bad weather, then sleep second night at Camp 1. Anderson and Webster carry loads to Camp 1.
21 April	Teare and Venables descend to Advance Base and everyone returns to Base Camp in bad weather.
22–27 April	Everyone at Base Camp. Weather mainly bad.

25 April	Fine day. Blackburn, Venables and Webster walk up to Khartse Glacier and cross 'Blackburn La'.
27 April	Weather improves again. Anderson and Teare return to Advance Base.
28 April	Blackburn, Venables and Webster return to Advance Base.

THIRD PHASE

29 April	Four climbers carry loads to Camp 1, where Anderson and Teare sleep.
30 April	Venables and Webster carry loads to Camp 1 and stay there. Anderson and Teare recce towards Camp 2 and return to Camp 1.
1 May	Four climbers break trail and carry communal equipment to Camp 2 cache under Flying Wing (c.7,450 metres).
2 May	Rest day at Camp 1. Weather starts to deteriorate.
3 May	Snowfall. Four climbers descend to Advance Base to join Blackburn and Zieman.
4 May	Weather improves after twenty-four hours continuous snowfall. Teare and Webster descend to Base Camp.
5 May	Twelve climbers of Asian Friendship Expedition reach summit of Everest by North Col and South Col routes. Teare and Webster return to Advance Base. In afternoon all four climbers set out for Camp 1. Teare and Webster return. Anderson and Venables continue in steady snowfall to Camp 1.
6 May	Bad weather. Anderson and Venables return to Advance Base.
7 May	Weather improves again.

FOURTH PHASE

8 May	Four climbers to Camp 1.
9 May	Four climbers carry personal gear, breaking new trail to Camp 2, in steady snowfall.
10 May	Weather fine again. Four climbers lift Camp 2, carrying all gear up final section of East Face route to South Col (7,986 metres).

11 May	High winds at South Col. Teare, ill with suspected oedema, descends in seven hours to Advance Base. Wind drops in afternoon. Anderson, Venables and Webster start summit at 11 p.m.
12 May	Venables reaches summit at 3.40 p.m., Nepalese time. At about the same time Webster reaches South Summit and turns back. At about 5 p.m. Anderson turns back from South Summit. He and Webster shelter in Japanese tent at c.8,300 metres. Venables bivouacs at c.8,600 metres.
13 May	Three climbers reunite and descend to Camp 3 on South Col.
14 May	Descend to Flying Wing late in afternoon, after ninety-three hours above 8,000 metres.
15 May	Abortive late afternoon attempt to descend from Flying Wing. Climb back up for another night at c.7,450 metres.
16 May	Webster starts descent at 10 a.m. Anderson and Venables soon follow. Fixed ropes reached at dusk. Venables and Webster continue down through the night. Anderson spends another night in the open just above Camp 1. At Advance Base, Teare and Zieman decide to wait one more night, then abandon hope.
17 May	Venables and Webster reach Advance Base at 3.45 a.m. Anderson arrives in the evening. Zieman starts intensive care on frostbite injuries.
19 May	Everyone descends to Base Camp..
20 May	American trekking party, first outsiders for three months, appear at Base Camp. Doctors inspect frostbite injuries.
22 May	Blackburn and Teare make stretchers. Porters arrive.
23–26 May	Walk-out to Kharta, to rejoin Messrs Shi and Yang.
29 May	Drive back to Shekar.
30 May	Anderson, Blackburn, Webster and Zieman drive to Lhasa and telex news of success to Wendy Davis in New York. Pasang, Teare and Venables drive to Nepalese frontier.
31 May	Pasang, Teare and Venables return to Kathmandu.

2 June	News of success released to press on thirty-fifth anniversary of Coronation Day.
8 June	Venables returns to London.
14 June	Rest of team now returned to USA. Press conference at Explorers' Club, New York, with telephone link to London.

Appendix IV

Climbing at Extreme Altitude without Supplementary Oxygen

I am not qualified to attempt an explanation of the complex physiological problems of attempting the world's highest peaks. As far as I can gather the physiologists themselves still do not understand the subject fully and there seems to be little way of telling who will perform well at altitude. Some degree of physical fitness is probably essential and people with low blood pressure and low pulses tend to do better. But really it is the mental approach that counts: one has to want very much to succeed.

On the Kangshung Face all four of us were well suited to high-altitude climbing, because above all we believed that we were capable of it. That confidence stemmed largely from a knowledge of what had been done before, from the first tentative climbs above 7,000 metres to the recent success on the highest peaks, but it was also tempered by knowledge of the disasters, some of which are also listed here. This historical survey is not exhaustive, but it does chart some of the main events that have gradually increased our knowledge of what is possible. I have included some comparatively low climbs, where they have been important breakthroughs, but by 'extreme altitude' I really mean 'the big five' – Lhotse, Makalu, Kangchenjunga, K2 and Everest.

1905 GURLA MANDHATA, 7,718 metres
In the course of his first remarkable journey to the Himalaya, DR THOMAS LONGSTAFF explored the approaches to Trisul, in the

Garhwal Himalaya, then travelled north to Tibet, where he reached
a height of about 7,300 metres on Gurla Mandhata.

1907 TRISUL, 7,128 metres
LONGSTAFF, ALEXIS and HENRY BROCHEREL and SUBADAR KARBIR
made the first ascent of this peak, which remained the highest
summit climbed for the next nineteen years. The climb was made
in a single 1,800-metres ten-hour push from the Trisul Glacier.
Most of the previous month had been spent above 4,500 metres and
two nights had been spent above 6,000 metres.

1909 CHOGOLISA, 7,654 metres
After attempting K2, the DUKE OF ABRUZZI with three guides
reached a new altitude record of 7,500 metres, attempting
Chogolisa.

1922 EVEREST, 8,848 metres
Although the route to the North Col had been reconnoitred the
previous year, when this first full attempt started there was still
doubt about whether man could survive above 7,500 metres without supplementary oxygen. Although oxygen equipment was
taken, most of the party had little faith in it. The first attempt was
made by GEORGE MALLORY, COL. H. T. MORSHEAD, MAJOR E. F.
NORTON and DR T. HOWARD SOMERVELL without oxygen. On the
night of May 20th they camped at a record height of about 7,650
metres. The following day three of the party continued into the
unknown, heading for the Shoulder of the North-East Ridge,
moving very slowly, taking up to five breaths per step, finally
being forced to turn back from about 8,200 metres. They descended to the North Col that afternoon, dangerously exhausted, slip-
ping and stumbling and at one point saved from death by Mallory's
rapid ice axe belay.

The second attempt was made by the expedition's controversial
oxygen apostle, GEORGE FINCH, a highly experienced alpinist who
was accompanied by two complete climbing novices, GHURKA
TEJBIR and GEOFFREY BRUCE. They sat out a storm for a day and
two nights at about 7,650 metres, discovering in the process that a
few whiffs of oxygen dramatically improved their condition. Finch
was perhaps correct in attributing their survival to oxygen and it
was certainly oxygen which helped their incredible feat of continuing after that terrible storm, making faster progress than the

oxygenless first party. Tejbir had to turn back early in the day, but Finch and Bruce explored the traverse towards the Great Couloir, reaching a tantilizing altitude record of about 8,320 metres, before they too were forced to turn back, when Finch realized that Bruce had reached his limit. They descended all the way to the East Rongbuk Glacier, 2,000 metres below, the same day.

1924 EVEREST

With the exclusion of Finch from the second climbing expedition, oxygen equipment was likely to be neglected. Although Irvine worked hard to improve and lighten the apparatus for his and Mallory's fateful attempt, there was not the methodical planning that would probably have been the case if Finch had been there. However, Mallory clearly realized that supplementary oxygen would improve his chances, and he and Irvine were carrying the primitive apparatus when they disappeared on the North-East Ridge.

Four days before Mallory and Irvine disappeared, NORTON and SOMERVELL made the first attempt without oxygen. Somervell gave up on the Yellow Band at about 8,540 metres, but Norton continued to the dangerous snow-smothered slabs on the far bank of the Great Couloir, before wisely turning back from a spot which was later measured by theodolite and reckoned to be 28,126 feet – 8,575 metres – an altitude record for oxygenless climbing which would not be broken until the Messner-Habeler ascent fifty-six years later.

Norton's determined attempt has remained one of the great inspirations to high-altitude climbers, but for sheer stamina few people, if any, have equalled the record of NOEL ODELL, who worked selflessly in support of both the summit attempts, making the final fruitless search for Mallory and Irvine. During those first two weeks of June 1924, completely eschewing oxygen equipment, he spent eleven nights above 7,000 metres and twice climbed to 8,200 metres. His performance was particularly interesting because he had been one of the slowest men in the team to acclimatize.

1933 EVEREST

Hugh Ruttledge, the leader, superintended the development of an improved lightened oxygen set, but in the event most of his team had little faith in oxygen and it was never used high on the mountain. As in the past, porters were used to establish the top camp, but this year Camp 6 was even higher. JACK LONGLAND escorted porters back down, leaving PERCY WYN HARRIS and LAWRENCE WAGER to spend the night of 29 May at 8,350 metres. The next day they made their summit attempt, reaching Norton's 1924 high-point. They descended that day to Camp 5. Meanwhile FRANK SMYTHE and ERIC SHIPTON had moved up to Camp 6. Like Finch in 1922, they were pinned down by a storm for two nights, but at a higher altitude and with no oxygen to combat rapid deterioration. Nevertheless, Shipton managed to struggle up for two hours on 1 June before turning back. Smythe had the strength to continue to the Norton highpoint. Once he had returned to Camp 6, Shipton descended, but Smythe spent a third night out at 8,350 metres, sleeping soundly through another storm, before descending alone to the North Col.

Mallory may have pushed on rashly on his final climb. We shall never know; but all the other remarkable attempts of 1922, 1924 and 1933 were characterized by an admirable willingness to turn back when it became obvious that continuing would probably spell disaster. Nevertheless, struggling under the enormous stress of altitude and striving for a very special prize, men *did* abandon some of the accepted precepts of traditional mountaineering. Finch let Tejbir descend alone to Camp 5. Norton left Somervell on the Yellow Band. Smythe and Shipton split up and both had narrow escapes on their separate descents. Recently, in the 1980s, there has been much criticism of the modern ethic of 'every man for himself', but it could be argued that it has precedents going back to the 1920s.

1936 NANDA DEVI, 7,817 metres

H. W. TILMAN, turned down from that year's Everest expedition on spurious grounds of health (as Finch had been in 1921 and John Hunt in 1935), led the successful expedition to Nanda Devi, reaching the summit with NOEL ODELL. No oxygen was used and Nanda Devi remained the highest summit climbed for the next sixteen years.

1939 K2, 8,611 metres

FRITZ WIESSNER and Sherpa PASANG LAMA, climbing without oxy-gen beyond Houston's and Petzoldt's highpoint of the previous year, reached about 8,365 metres on the Abruzzi Spur of K2, late in the afternoon. Wiessner wanted to press on through the night but

was forced to turn back by Pasang Lama. Even so, it took most of
the night to descend to Camp 9 on the Shoulder and Pasang lost his
crampons, making a repeat attempt from the top camp impossible.
During the subsequent descent of the mountain they found several
camps stripped of equipment, including vital sleeping bags, due to
some catastrophic misunderstanding. The ensuing drama, in which
Dudley Wolfe and three Sherpas ultimately died, and the con-
troversy over what exactly happened, foreshadowed the even more
disastrous summer on K2 in 1986.

1950 ANNAPURNA, 8,091 metres
The first 8,000-metre peak to be climbed. After a long reconnaissance, the French expedition just completed a rushed ascent before
the Monsoon arrived. MAURICE HERZOG and LOUIS LACHENAL
reached the summit without oxygen. On the descent both they and
their support climbers, Terray and Rébuffat, were stretched to the
limit, harassed by storms, avalanches, frostbite and snowblindness.
Herzog and Lachenal lost nearly all their fingers and toes.

1952 EVEREST
On 28 May, during the first Swiss attempt on the South Col route,
RAYMOND LAMBERT and TENZING NORGAY reached a point they
reckoned to be just over 8,600 metres, after a camp at 8,400 metres
without sleeping bags. Their oxygen equipment was only func-
tioning while they were resting, so they were effectively climbing
without supplementary oxygen. It took them 5½ hours to climb
just 200 metres.

1953 EVEREST
On 29 May EDMUND HILLARY and TENZING NORGAY made what
was almost certainly the first ascent of Everest. For the first time
there was a comprehensive policy of using supplementary oxygen,
made possible by meticulous logistics.

1953 NANGA PARBAT, 8,125 metres
Overshadowed inevitably by the ascent of Everest, the first ascent
of Nanga Parbat was achieved by an astonishing solo push with no
oxygen. It took HERMANN BUHL sixteen hours to make the 1,200-
metres height gain and 4 km distance from Camp 5 to the summit,
which he reached just before dark. On the way back, he
bivouacked at about 8,000 metres, standing up on a tiny ledge,

with neither down clothing nor even his pullover, which he had cached lower down. Luckily it was a completely still night. He reached his companions at Camp 5 late the following evening. Buhl was possibly helped by the stimulant pills he took, Pervitine. Nevertheless it was a remarkable feat by a man who, like Odell in 1924, was very slow to acclimatize.

1953 K2
CHARLES HOUSTON, who had led the 1938 attempt, returned to lead the third American expedition. He and eight companions reached Camp 8 on the Shoulder, close to 8,000 metres, on the evening of 2 August. They were then pinned down by storm for four days with no oxygen. Nevertheless they seriously hoped to continue upwards when things improved temporarily on the 7th. Then ART GILKEY developed phlebitis in his leg, whereupon any hope of the summit was abandoned. The renewed storm and avalanche conditions delayed departure and it was not until the 10th that the party set off down, heroically determined, even after a week's deterioration at nearly 8,000 metres, to try and save Gilkey. However, he was swept away to his death during the descent, allowing the others to continue unencumbered and reach base on the 14th.

1954 K2
Oxygen was used by the Italian expedition which finally made the first ascent in 1954, but both ACHILLE CAMPAGNONI and LINO LACEDELLI ran out on the summit. They were too bemused to think of taking the heavy empty cylinders off their backs.

1957 BROAD PEAK, 8,047 metres
The first ascent established no new altitude records, but it did establish that an unsupported four-man team, HERMANN BUHL, KURT DIEMBERGER, MARCUS SCHMUCK and FRITZ WINTERSTEL-LER, could climb an 8,000-metre peak with neither oxygen, nor paid load-carriers.

1975 GASHERBRUM I, 8,068 metres
PETER HABELER and REINHOLD MESSNER, with the advantages, eighteen years on, of lighter equipment, went a step further – a hard new route climbed in just three days up and down, in pure alpine-style, with no pre-placed caches or camps.

1975 EVEREST

DOUGAL HASTON and DOUG SCOTT establish a new bivouac altitude record of 8,760 metres by the South Summit, after completing
the South-West Face. Their oxygen ran out at 8.30 p.m., but they
managed to survive the night in cold post-Monsoon conditions
without frostbite.

1978 EVEREST

HABELER and MESSNER, inspired by the feats of pre-war British
Everesters, finally confirmed that Everest could be climbed without supplementary oxygen. Messner had already survived, and
helped a Sherpa to survive, a gruelling storm on the South Col. He
returned two weeks later with Habeler and Sherpas in support
(they were attached to a large Austrian expedition). From the col
Habeler and Messner climbed unaided and unroped, taking just 9½
hours to cover the 850 metres to the summit. This fast rate of
almost 100 metres per hour had been predicted theoretically possible by Dr Alexander Kellas at the beginning of the century. The
ascent was a very important psychological breakthrough. Particularly impressive was Messner's ability to take cine film by the
Hillary Step and Habeler's ability, prompted by fear of brain damage, to descend in just one hour to the South Col.

1978 K2

Four months later, the Americans finally gained their long-sought
prize of K2. Of the four men who summited, three – LOU REI-
CHARDT, RICK RIDGEWAY and JOHN ROSKELLEY – used no
oxygen.

This success took some of the edge off the recent Everest climb
and contradicted the claim of physiologist, Dr Griffith Pugh, that
'probably only exceptional men can go above 27,000 feet (8,230 m)
without supplementary oxygen'. Writing to *Mountain* magazine
(No. 64), Ridgeway replied that 'I have never considered myself
anything close to an "exceptional man", much less a super athlete. I
can only run a few miles, and twenty press-ups pretty much wipe
me out . . . How then did we do it? . . . When you want to top out
as much as we did, you can make your body do some extraordinary
things, even if you're not an exceptional man. I kinda think that's
the secret.'

In the same issue of *Mountain*, the distinguished Everest veteran,
NORMAN DYHRENFURTH, made some sobering comments on

oxygenless climbing at extreme altitude, prompted by the disastrous Makalu attempt of 1961, during which PETER MULGREW
developed a pulmonary infarct at 8,350 metres, was only just
evacuated by his team mates (one of whom, DR MICHAEL WARD,
also nearly died) and subsequently had both frostbitten legs
amputated below the knee. This disaster, wrote Dyhrenfurth,
'points up one very important basic fact: any attempt on one of the
big five [Everest, K2, Kangchenjunga, Makalu and Lhotse] without oxygen is and will always be dangerous, even for well
acclimatized, very fit Himalayan climbers. It is, in this author's
personal opinion, a rather senseless risk which ought not to be
taken, in spite of the admirable feat of the oxygenless Messner-
Habeler ascent of Everest.'

1978 EVEREST
In the post-Monsoon season the Herrligkoffer-Mazeaud international circus put sixteen people on the summit by the South Col
route. Three people repeated the Messner/Habeler feat, HANS ENGL
did not use oxygen, but was assisted by an oxygenated companion
breaking trail. Sherpas MINGMA and ANG DORJE also reached the
summit without oxygen.

1979 KANGCHENJUNGA, 8,595 metres
In 1979 Messner made a semi-alpine-style ascent of the Abruzzi
Spur of K2, without oxygen. However, the third ever ascent of
Kangchenjunga, by a small team on a hard new route, with no
oxygen, was perhaps more significant. GEORGES BETTEMBOURG,
PETER BOARDMAN, DOUG SCOTT and JOE TASKER fixed 1,000
metres of rope up the West Face of the North Col (6,890 m). From
there it took several abortive attempts, including one destroyed
tent in a storm at 8,000 metres, before Boardman, Scott and Tasker
completed the route up the North Ridge and North Face to the
summit. (Boardman and Scott had previously climbed Everest
with oxygen, but Tasker had never before been above 7,066
metres.)

1980 EVEREST
MESSNER returned, with just his girlfriend/doctor to tend Advance
Base at about 6,500 metres, while he spent four days soloing up and
down the North Ridge/North Face, finally completing the exit
from the Great Couloir which had eluded Norton fifty-six years

earlier. This climb seems to have been more draining than the 1978 ascent: at his top camp at about 8,200 metres Messner, usually so professional, was too exhausted to photograph himself. However, he managed to photograph himself on the summit the next day. After another night at the top camp he ditched all his survival equipment and descended in a day to Advance Base.

1980 MAKALU, 8,470 metres

A four-man American team, led by JOHN ROSKELLEY and climbing without oxygen, repeated the stupendous French route up the West Pillar, originally tamed in 1971 by 'une grande équipe'. On the final ridge Roskelley, outclassing his slower companions, ordered them down so that he could push on fast to the summit, snatching success late in the day.

1983 EVEREST

In May LARRY NEILSEN climbed the normal route without oxygen, but with three other Americans using oxygen to break trail from the South Col. By the time they left the summit, however, all had run out of oxygen.

On the morning of 8 October, CARLOS BUHLER, KIM MOMB and LOUIS REICHARDT, completing the first ascent of the Kangshung Face with oxygen, arrived on the summit ridge to meet a Japanese team. They passed the six Japanese climbers and one Sherpa, making the first Japanese oxygenless ascent, by the normal route. By the time the Americans had returned from the summit to the Hillary Step, the Japanese were still on their way up, 'staggering like zombies'. The Americans persuaded one of them to turn back, along with the Sherpa PASANG TEMBA, who slipped and fell to his death. The other five Japanese reached the summit very late in the afternoon. All bivouacked at various places on the descent. HIROSHI JOSHINA and HIRONUBO AMURO were caught out highest without bivouac gear right up at the Hillary Step (8,800 m). In the morning they both fell to their deaths.

1983 KANGCHENJUNGA

PIERRE BEGHIN soloed the 1955 route on Kangchenjunga, unsupported with no oxygen.

1984 MAKALU
JEAN AFANASSIEFF, DOUG SCOTT and STEPHEN SUSTAD spent four committing days without oxygen above 8,000 metres in the great Eastern Cwm, coming within about 100 metres of the summit on the Headwall, when dubious weather and Afanassieff's fears of possible oedema forced them to abandon their ambitious traverse plan and start immediately on an exhausting retreat. In all they spend eight days on the immense South-East Ridge.

1984 EVEREST
The first Australian ascent of Everest was by a five-man team on a bold new route up the North Face. Their film support team gave some help in preparing the route. GEOFF BARTRAM dropped out of the final summit push. LINCOLN HALL turned back soon after Camp 4 at $c.8,150$ m. ANDY HENDERSON had to stop at dusk with frozen hands, only 50 metres short of the summit, while GREG MORTIMER and TIM MCCARTNEY-SNAPE made the very top in near darkness. All the team descended safely over the next two days, concluding a brilliant climb with no oxygen.

1986 K2
During a disastrous summer on K2, when several expeditions climbed on four different routes, thirteen climbers died. Most of the accidents happened high on the mountain, when people were descending, exhausted, from oxygenless ascents. Perhaps the outstanding success was the hard new route up the South Face, climbed in pure alpine style by JERZY KUKUCZKA and TADEUSZ PIOTROWSKI, but it was nullified by Piotrowski's fatal fall on the descent of the Abruzzi Spur. This and all the other accidents reinforced the lesson that getting up the highest peaks without oxygen will always be possible, but getting *down* is going to be the big problem. This is particularly true on K2, where the easiest route – the Abruzzi – is very steep and complex. In 1986 this problem seems to have been exacerbated by a tendency to rely subconsciously on other parties' tents, stoves and fixed ropes on the route.

1986 EVEREST
ERHARD LORETAN and JEAN TROILLET perfected the technique they had already used on Dhaulagiri's East Face to make a remarkable 'flash' ascent of Everest's North Face, taking one step further the

well tried principle that for a safe success one should spend as little time as possible at extreme altitude. Acclimatization in the Rongbuk area up to about 6,500 metres took two months. The route choice was canny – reasonably consolidated old avalanche snow up the Japanese and Hornbein couloirs – the quickest most direct line to the top. Neither tents not sleeping bags were carried and they mainly rested during the warmth of the day (they were climbing at the tail end of the Monsoon). The total ascent time was forty and a half hours. The controlled slide back down to the Rongbuk took just four and a half.

1987 EVEREST

ANG RITA, working for a South Korean expedition, made his fourth ascent without oxygen and the first winter ascent without oxygen, defying the common supposition that an oxygenless ascent would be impossible in winter due to lowered atmospheric pressure. However, it may be that the exceptionally fine weather of December 1987 produced atypical conditions. Ang Rita's mastery was confirmed by his ability to hold on the rope his Korean companion (who had oxygen) when he slipped on the descent. That night the pair were caught out by darkness just below the South Summit and survived an unprepared winter bivouac at about 8,600 metres. Both escaped with only mild frostbite.

1988 EVEREST

In May ROBERT ANDERSON, PAUL TEARE, STEPHEN VENABLES and ED WEBSTER make a new route up the Kangshung Face to the South Col without oxygen. Teare was forced by illness to turn back from the South Col. Anderson and Webster reached the South Summit without oxygen and Venables the main summit, taking a dangerously slow sixteen and a half hours from the South Col. The team made more dangerous delays on the four-day descent, but were sustained by caches of cooking gas. Messner offered qualified praise. 'You have done a very hard thing . . . but you were lucky.'

In August the crux of the notorious North-East Ridge, the Pinnacles, was finally climbed by the fourth British expedition to attempt the route. Although they were unable to continue to the summit, HARRY TAYLOR and RUSSELL BRICE climbed all the remaining unknown ground to the Shoulder. They used some oxygen for sleeping, but climbed entirely without oxygen during two days of very precarious climbing between 8,000 and 8,400 metres.

In September the French upstaged the previous spring's Asian

Friendship Expedition with a multi-media show on the Khumbu/ South Col route. Logistics were grandiose, enabling full media coverage of a massed ascent. The highlights were Boivin's fantastic parapente jump from the summit and a new speed record by MARC BATARD. He had already made a semi-solo ascent of Makalu's West Pillar the previous year and he had the example of BENOIT CHAMOU's twenty-three hour ascent of K2 in 1986. Batard now climbed the normal route up Everest, all the way from the Khumbu Base Camp, in just twenty-two and a half hours, with no supplementary oxygen. His strength and speed were particularly remarkable for having already climbed all the way to 8,750 metres during an abortive attempt ten days earlier. He halved the Loretan/ Troillet speed record, but on a trade route, with camps placed, ropes fixed and trails broken by a massive expedition.

In October LYDIA BRADEY (New Zealand) claimed the first female ascent of Everest without oxygen, by the South Col route. However, due to lack of proof (she was alone), her ascent was not unanimously accepted.

Four Czech climbers died on the descent to the South Col after making the first alpine-style ascent of the South-West Face (the 1975 route).

Index